HIGH RISK

BEN TIMBERLAKE

High Risk

A True Story of the SAS, Drugs,
and Other Bad Behaviour

HURST & COMPANY, LONDON

First published in the United Kingdom in 2021 by
C. Hurst & Co. (Publishers) Ltd.,
83 Torbay Road, London NW6 7DT
© Ben Timberlake, 2021
All rights reserved.
Printed in Great Britain by Bell and Bain Ltd, Glasgow

The right of Ben Timberlake to be identified as the author
of this publication is asserted by him in accordance with
the Copyright, Designs and Patents Act, 1988.

Distributed in the United States, Canada and Latin
America by Oxford University Press, 198 Madison Avenue,
New York, NY 10016, United States of America.

A Cataloguing-in-Publication data record for this book is
available from the British Library.

ISBN: 9781787384637

This book is printed using paper from registered
sustainable and managed sources.

www.hurstpublishers.com

'Roll the Dice' from *Ham On Rye* by Charles Bukowski.
Copyright © 1982 by Charles Bukowski.
Used by permission of HarperCollins Publishers.

CONTENTS

Roll the Dice

If you're going to try, go all the
way.
otherwise, don't even start.

if you're going to try, go all the
way.
this could mean losing girlfriends,
wives, relatives, jobs and
maybe your mind.

go all the way.
it could mean not eating for 3 or 4 days.
it could mean freezing on a
park bench.
it could mean jail,
it could mean derision,
mockery,
isolation.
isolation is the gift,
all the others are a test of your
endurance, of
how much you really want to
do it.
and you'll do it
despite rejection and the worst odds
and it will be better than
anything else
you can imagine.

CONTENTS

if you're going to try,
go all the way.
there is no other feeling like
that.
you will be alone with the gods
and the nights will flame with
fire.

do it, do it, do it.
do it.

all the way
all the way.

you will ride life straight to
perfect laughter, its
the only good fight
there is.

– Charles Bukowski

ACKNOWLEDGEMENTS

My thanks to Pidge Hutton, Bella Pollen, Sean Thomas, and Lloyd Timberlake for reading and guiding the manuscript through its many evolutions. Also to Anthony Beevor for pointers on the neuroscience of violence. To the many members of 21 and 22 SAS, whom I cannot name, for their corrections and insights. To Paul Egan and Angel Sedgwick for help with a number of chapters. To Nazha Harb for generously sharing her knowledge of the Ashura Ritual.

In memoriam: Gavin Hills, David Cornwell and AA Gill, for advice and encouragement.

My sincere thanks to my agent Ben Dunn, at Dunn Literary, for making me feel like I was his only client and for tirelessly seeing the project through.

I am indebted to Michael Dwyer and his fantastic team at Hurst, especially Alison Alexanian and Daisy Leitch, for their hard work and extreme patience.

Above all, to Kate Weinberg for showing me the way.

PREFACE

FLASHBACK, MIDDLE EAST, UNDISCLOSED LOCATION

I always knew my life would end badly. I'd been told so by count-less school-teachers, Special Forces instructors and wishful ex-girlfriends. But this? This was going to be a genuinely shitty, shameful, and scary way to die.

I could hear the religious procession on the main street just as the shouting mob surrounded me at the edge of a sandy lot which was strewn with building rubble and stank of urine. They jostled each other in a vague semi-circle: most radiated anger, a few seemed bored, others curious. But some had the jerky move-ments of the possessed. It was those guys that stooped for a bit of cinder-block, a roofing tile, a glass bottle.

I don't recall being scared. This wasn't due to some version of tough-guy bravery; it was all about the vast amounts of opium and crystal-meth circulating in my system.

A man from the religious police, his face pock-marked by acne, was out front, gabbling angrily. Occasionally he stabbed a finger in my direction. He was accusing me of selling pornogra-phy on one of the most sacred days of the Islamic calendar. Which—to be fair—I had.

I didn't want to be on drugs. I didn't even want to be in the Special Forces anymore and I felt bad about buying the drugs with money I'd earned waterboarding someone. Try telling that to a screaming mob.

I wanted to escape but didn't know how to. The moment was erupting in my head. If I could just remember how I got here I would be able to find my way out. I saw splinters of my past, jagged memories of a life before all of this.

As more people picked up rocks, I had only one thought: 'How did I get here'?

INTRODUCTION

GAME THEORY

All things are poison, and nothing is without poison, the dosage alone makes it so.

Paracelsus

You never know what is enough unless you know what is more than enough.

Blake, *Marriage of Heaven and Hell*

Flashbacks are a great narrative device. But they're a fucking nightmare when they happen in real life. At precisely the moment you're trying to think straight and figure out how to save yourself, your brain storms in with a slide show and 'your life flashes before your eyes'.

Be cool; your brain is only trying to help. Each slide is a memory that was snapped during a previous high-adrenaline event and hyper-linked by the mind for emergency use. Your memory flips through these red-flagged events to try to find a workable template for immediate action that will help you survive. I've had this happen to me many times: it's a reverse slide show of my life from my most recent peak experience to the earliest thrills.

I would love to tell you that it is a stunning montage full of stirring images of incredible valour, battlefield heroics, winning

1

one for the school team and meeting some lovely girl in the poetry section of a secondhand bookstore, but that's not what I see. Instead, I am forced to watch—*Clockwork Orange* style—a torrent of violence, drug-taking, blue-sirens and obscenity; sometimes I wonder if my brain has put a few of the girl-slides in upside down (but they're not).

In the past, when they used to hang criminals, it was so common for the condemned to get erections and ejaculate as they danced their final moments in the air, that the hangmen used to refer to it as 'Angel Lust'. I doubt they were seeing the demure maidens of paradise in their future; rather they were looking at the slide shows of their past. I know I would be.

If I'm going to answer, 'How did I get here', then it might be worth starting at the beginning of my own slide show.

All of these memories cluster around a small patch of France where the Lot and Célé Rivers meet. The very first adrenaline-soaked images from my childhood—the bunker, the cliff-jumping, the cave—all occurred within a few miles of each other. It is where I spent some of my childhood, and it's a place I keep going back to, to walk and fish and think. It's a land of oak-forested, high limestone causse, cut through with rivers beneath honey-coloured cliffs and criss-crossed with pilgrimage routes.

I don't particularly want to tell you about my childhood, but that's always the first question people ask when you're a junkie: was there some fork in the path during those early years when you took a different way?

I'd say, sure, I was about eight years old when things started to go right.

* * *

Several miles into the oak forest, by the house we used to stay in, was a Resistance bunker. In the local village, old men in the cafés around the market square told us stories of heroism and fighting that ticked all my childish notions of what war meant. 'Think it always, say it never,' they would say with Pernod-soaked pride and swear us to secrecy about the bunker's existence.

Its entrance was hidden by a large oak, and we would never have found it—it looked like a hole in an abandoned badger's sett—except for the tell-tale tangle of rusty barbed wire around it to keep out kids like ourselves. The shaft dropped into the darkness, a pebble took two to three seconds to hit the bottom. With torches we could make out the scalloped footholds carved into the shaft's walls, alternating down each side; they had a good grip at the top, but were wet and slippery, like rotted leather, further down. At the bottom, the passage twisted into a larger chamber where fat toads sat on empty ammunition cases. The place stank of raw earth and rebellion. There was another, far smaller tunnel that left the main room at a shallow angle towards the surface, but no one knew where it went, or had tried to find out. We told ourselves that this was the 'escape tunnel' in case the Nazis had discovered the main entrance, but now I suspect it was merely a ventilation shaft.

It was a squeeze, even for my eight-year-old body. My breath shone in the torchlight. The soil glistened with mineral reflection and nacreous tracks of slime. There were centipedes with carnelian bodies. It was way too tight to go backwards so I kept going forwards, digging through places where the shaft had collapsed and wriggling through. I could feel my heart pounding against the piles of loose soil underneath and through the back of my ribcage and against the tunnel that gripped me. When I had to turn my head sideways to get through a narrowing, the dirt got into my mouth and I could taste the clay. On and on I shimmied and squirmed against the weight of the earth, past tree roots and rabbit skeletons, skeins of rot and cobwebs, towards the muffled blue glow of daylight far above.

At the end, I pushed through a mulch of ancient leaves and acorn cups and lay on my back panting. The forest canopy was a daytime heaven as awe-inspiring as any night sky: the branched constellations of life; symmetry and chaos in balance; the perfection of crown-shyness between trees. It wasn't really what I saw but *how I saw* that filled me with wonder: this was ultra high definition, loaded with colour and saturated with a form of meaning that seemed far greater than myself and filled with a benevolence that was greater than love.

It was my first journey into an altered state, those exotic lands beyond ordinary consciousness. Fear was the portal; I wanted more.

* * *

At one point in the Lot Valley was a cliff-jump: a spar of rock that jutted out above the trees, the blur of rock wall and the deep river pool far below. It was a celebrated dare in the village and a rite of passage for local kids. On the weekends, teenagers would gather and goad each other on. Impossibly beautiful French girls would sun themselves on the riverbank, chewing Bazooka gum nonchalantly, and many would outleap the boys. I fell in love with any girl that could out-jump me. (I still do.)

The path to the jumping point was a worn trail up through a scree-slope held together by knotted oak roots to a breech in the cliffs, the handholds as polished as steps in an old church. This was sacred ground; I felt like an initiate in this temple of fight or flight.

When I first climbed that path, adrenaline surged in my system: the dry mouth, hammering heartbeat, heaviness in the limbs, churning stomach, and I knew that the only way to get rid of them was to jump before fear had the upper hand.

At the top: blue skies and those honeyed cliffs above a sea of oak with the river far below. Adrenaline enhances many things—taste, humour, friendship, sex, love—but few things beat the palette of colours or their resolution when danger is involved. It is not merely the details of what I was seeing but that 'way' of seeing again.

And on that edge, a swirl of feelings that would come to define me: the fear of pain and death versus the terror of not living this life fully.

I took the glorious view in, and a few deep breaths. Then I jumped.

The seconds dilated, stretched to the infinite moment, the sense of dissolving myself in the colours midair, the weightlessness of the fall, the impact of the water and the exhilaration. My landings weren't always perfect. Sometimes they were painful, but the rewards and punishments offered by the laws of physics seemed far fairer than the other rules I faced as a kid.

I have always understood that freefall into oblivion as a leap of faith. Each jump gave me a shot of deep learning that made me love my sun-soaked world even more. It was both liberating and deeply connecting. And above all—above everything else—it was fun. A form of mind-expanding joy that seemed without end. I've never mastered fear, but I have tried to befriend it. Fear was the tell-tale sign, the white rabbit. If I followed fear, I knew I would be happy.

* * *

I return to the valley regularly, and I started writing this book there, beneath those same cliffs. I had just been to Iraq and wanted to walk one of the ancient pilgrimage trails and generally get over myself.

In Paris, I had a very romantic send-off dinner at L'Européen opposite the Gare du Lyon: the largest *fruits de mer* on the menu with extra oysters (from Utah Beach in Normandy no less). As the sun set, the waiter lit the candles; my rucksack was on the chair opposite, gazing at me adoringly. I took the overnight train and was out on the trail before first light. That felt good. I would reach the cave of Pech Merle in a couple of days.

The trip to Iraq had been a decent one: I was there as security and there were enough close calls to earn my keep, but we all got back safely. I went to Babylon. I went to the shrine of Iman Husayn at Kerbala and gave thanks (and apologised for my shameful behaviour among His followers, as you'll see later on). I ate fresh fish over a campfire with the Marsh Arabs in their floating world between the Tigris and the Euphrates. In Mosul, I had to dig human flesh out of my boot treads. I crawled through ISIS tunnels to see ancient Assyrian statues still buried beneath Nineveh. Deep underground, mindful of booby traps and human bones, I remembered the Resistance tunnel. They all join up: red-flagged, fun-flagged.

I love wandering in that corner of France: the limestone trails gouged into the riverside cliff-faces. In places the paths have the same smoothness as water-worn stones from a thousand years of feet like mine. These pilgrimage routes were once rivers of souls, channelling meaning, hope and desire.

I walk, but the destinations aren't important—it's the journey and meeting fellow travellers. My rule of thumb is: 'Follow those who seek the truth; run from those who claim they've found it.' I like those who seek the sacred, but also, and perhaps more importantly, those who seek the profane. It's possible to be a pilgrim on the road of excess too. I am just as interested in crack-houses as churches, whorehouses as nunneries, casinos as mosques. After a while you start to see patterns emerge; you realise that it's the same people visiting them all.

What drives people to these places? What substances do they abuse: gold, flesh, drugs or symbols? What is the most danger-ous? The most addictive? What does each feel like? How does the pursuit of pleasure become so hellish for some, while others, who put themselves through hell, seem to achieve transcendence? How far will a person go? Can they hack it? And what does that say about them? Do deities meet us in altered states, or do we simply see ourselves anew in those places?

INTRODUCTION

As for 'purer' pilgrimages, I rock them too; I am fairly universal in my tastes: I followed St James across Cornwall, travelled along his way as St Jacques in France, and across the Pyrenees in Spain I rode a horse for a month, to his shrine at Santiago de Compestela. I have been to the grotto at Lourdes where the Virgin Mary appeared; ditto the Black Madonna in the troglodyte church at Rocamadour. In India I trekked through the heat to see Vaishno Devi in her mountaintop cave. In northern Japan I spent months traipsing through the snowy mountains to meet Buddhist saints who, a thousand years ago, had entombed themselves in caves and mummified themselves while alive in the lotus position. Many pilgrimages end in caves.

The Special Air Services regiment (SAS) adopted the poem 'The Golden Journey to Samarkand' almost as a prayer. It's a terrible poem, but it does have some killer lines. It speaks of pilgrims who 'For lust of knowing what should not be known' seek a prophet in a cave 'who can understand why men are born'.

I believe the cave bit is right, but that it exists within the chambered recesses of our minds. By pushing ourselves beyond our limits we are granted access to it. If there is a prophet or a saint they are deep within us, half man and half beast.

* * *

At the end of my trail, close to where the Célé and Lot rivers meet, is the small village of Cabrerets. Above the village in the scrub oak forest is the cave of Pech Merle, which is adorned with Palaeolithic art. If humanity could share a collective 'life flashed before our eyes' moment, these images would be the earliest slide.

I could write about my first trip there as an earliest memory. Or I could tell you about my recent visit. But the feelings would be the same: childlike awe. Descending into the cave feels spiritual. The shuffling penitents, the torches and the lighting on natural corridors and vaulted arches draped with stalactites. It is the descent into time itself that generates such a state of awe, that ego-dissolving swim in aeons past. Down there is a silence so complete that the desire for words is lost. The one sound is the slow drip of water, a drop here or there, that has carved and sculpted this subterranean world over millions of years. The only living thing is a very old oak root coming down through a crack in the ceiling from the forest far above. In the deep-time of the cave it looks as ephemeral as a lightning bolt.

Twenty-five thousand years ago, men, women and even children (tiny footprints have been found preserved in the cave) ventured into the darkness with guttering animal-fat lamps and decorated the cave walls with images of their world above: great mammoths, aurochs, reindeer and the two iconic spotted horses surrounded by hand prints.

There are human images too: a pierced man and several women. The 'pierced man' motif appears here and in other caves too: either a twisting body perforated by spears or a man in an ecstasy of dance, or both.

The hand prints are the simplest images, but the most powerful. They are in the negative, created by putting a hand against the rock and spitting red mineral paint over it or through a hollow bird-bone, the earliest aerosol. They float, waving on calcite curtains. I understand them as acts of yearning for connection with something greater, a record, 'I was here' and a greeting from the past.

The art is so old that we can say very little about it with any certainty, but I know of no other images created since then that speak to me so profoundly. They are the first sparks of our humanity, a fire in the darkness. I see them as full of love and wonder, terrifying beasts drawn beautiful, friezes of fight and flight, a stalactite-veiled passage of rites, tribal rituals and rites of passage, mad dances and altered states.

INTRODUCTION

In Palaeolithic art, among the images that fascinate me are the hybrid creatures or therianthropes: half human, half animal. There is the famous the Bird-Man of Lascaux; the *Löwenmensch* (Lion-Man) of Hohlenstein-Stadel, from 40,000 years ago, the oldest sculpture in the world. Deep under the Pyrenees, in the cave of Trois-Frères, is the 'Sorcerer', a humanoid-reindeer figure. And further back, in the labyrinth of the same cave system, amidst a wild frieze of prehistoric beasts, a Bison-Man or Minotaur. At the dawn of art, with the very earliest acts of creativity, our ancestors chose to paint these remarkable figures. They record a world where we were still part of nature—and nature was still felt to be a part of us—that civilisation has since spliced, but which I recall, as a half-remembered dream.

When I first ventured into those caves—the long, glittering passages deep in the earth—it felt like I was journeying deep into my own mind, along calcite corridors and neural pathways common to us all. The art in the depths was less a discovery than an expression of something within me—within ourselves—that I had always known but struggled to articulate.

Altered states, reached through fear, adrenaline and great drugs, return us to that juncture of mankind and nature. It is always a wild ride getting there; it has to be. The adventures in *High Risk* are simply the steps I took to return to that point, to cross the threshold to a realm of oneness that feels like a homecoming.

* * *

High Risk is also a series of postcards from the edge. It's a pilgrimage through altered states and a close look at my fellow travellers. As a pilgrim I am still very much a work in progress. I did not stumble upon any big or profound answers. In fact, along the way, I seem wilfully to have ignored omens, calls to reason, or moments of clarity. But I had lots of fun and was

9

often scared witless. It is a journey that took me through the toughest military selection on earth, to vicious urban warfare in Iraq, via recreational drugs and extreme sex to the abyss of heroin addiction. Sometimes there's a 'lust of knowing', but there's a lot of regular lust too.

At the end of this road, I believe that I am a slightly better person than at the beginning. But it's a low bar: I'm an asshole. I have been as honest as I can about my asshole-ness in the retelling to give you an accurate picture of my mind at the time. It also makes what little redemption I feel at the finish that bit sweeter; there's not much, but I am quite fond of it. At no point on this journey do I think I am better than any of my fellow travellers, nor do I seek to judge them: I admire people who push themselves; the direction is often a secondary consideration.

* * *

Some context and a couple of caveats:

With the exception of the first execution story and the final epilogue, the events in this book took place between 2003 and 2013 and are set out roughly chronologically.

I studied archaeology at university and later in my life picked up a few medical qualifications. If I didn't have such a low boredom threshold, I would have been an archaeologist; if I was bright enough, I would have become a doctor. But I'm neither. Instead, I have used what little knowledge I have of both subjects to frame my personal experiences. I am fascinated by finding common themes in uncommon places. Archaeology, along with myth and ritual, help us understand our shared heritage. Medicine, especially neurobiology, is our common wiring: both are helpful for charting and navigating what altered states are and for understanding what they mean.

Occasionally 'I can't talk about it'—in regard to the military or other jobs. This is because I signed the Official Secrets Act; but also to honour non-disclosure agreements. That's not an 'I can't talk about it because I was on a classified op deep behind enemy lines fighting for your freedom.' It is a 'I can't talk about it because I signed a bit of paper that also covers my half-assed boy-scouting.' If you want to read a book by a genuine hero, look elsewhere. I have changed names, dates and locations to ensure secrecy is maintained.

And for a similar reason—the Unofficial Secrets Act (Thieves' Honour)—I have tried to afford the same protection to my drugged-out comrades, strippers and degenerates who are the real heroes of *High Risk*.

Lastly, there are far too many books out there written by ex-Special Forces types about peak human performance, optimising your day and being your best possible self. This is the opposite. I have learned far more about myself mainlining heroin as the sun goes up than in all the times I downed kale-smoothies and did ultra-marathons. My life has been a search for some sort of balance between the two, the correct dosage. I've lost too many good men to kale. Sure, asceticism and self-discipline have their place, but so do chaos and self-abuse, excess and debauchery. Few things are as genuinely liberating as self-destruction.

Where possible, I have included as much practical information and science as necessary to help you be your worst possible self. Because it's not just good enough for me to answer 'How did I get here?'; I want to help you get there too.

1

WHAT IT FEELS LIKE TO BE EXECUTED
(*BULLET*)

Ella was eighteen and beautiful; she had dark hair, freckles, blue eyes and could silence a bar by walking into it; she could halt tank traffic. I was a kid who'd read too much Hemingway and decided he was going to be a war correspondent. The moment I left school, I headed for the nearest trouble I could find: the conflict in Yugoslavia. In short, I was a teenage war tourist. I don't know what she saw in me. Ella could have had any man for a hundred miles. It crossed my mind she only chose me to piss every one of them off.

Ella and I were on a mountain above the sea, on the Dalmatian Coast where Croatia tapers off into Herzegovina. The front lines were less than a kilometre to our east. We were sharing a picnic and watching a mortar attack on a small fishing village: puffs of smoke and dust would appear and the sound would follow two to three seconds later. Each explosion looked like a scrap of dirty crepe paper unfurling and drifting lazily on the light onshore breeze. The Serbs must have had three or four mortar tubes firing, because they landed in quick succession. On one salvo they managed to get the opening beats to Fats Domino's 'Blueberry Hill'. *Da da-da, da, da-da daaa.* To this day I can't hear that song and not think of her and what followed later when 'I found my thrill'.

This was our first proper date. I'd met Ella in Dubrovnik on the gleaming Stradun. We'd had a coffee. She had her school backpack with her. She showed me her modelling shots for some armed forces calendar, which was: her, in a camouflage top, clutching an AK-47 with another girl. Ella was very committed to her future as a model. She had an address book, which had two shades of Tippex in it: fresh and aged. On the first day of the war with the Serbs she had erased all her Serb friends. She did the same with her Muslim friends a couple of years later. I had taken this as proof of how the trauma of war had disordered her innocent mind, but even her closest girl friends said she'd been, like, a total bitch for years. The old women, in their headscarves and widow black dresses, who sat by the sandbagged fountain at the old town gate, told stories of how Ella's mother had to thrash her senseless to get her onto an evacuation boat when the shelling was at its worst—to Ella war was exciting—and then thrashed her again on her return when she found out about the calendar.

For the picnic, we had some beer cooling in a stream that flowed out of a cave nearby and a bagful of local oysters—small and very salty—that were going cheap. Ernest would have approved. There was also some paté, but it was grey Communist meat-paste and we didn't bother with it. It came in little tins that looked like the anti-personnel mines we had kept an eye out for as we climbed the path upwards. Behind us, the incline steepened: trees giving way to scree, cliff and limestone peaks of an escarpment. In an orchard below there was an old, fire-damaged farmhouse and further down olive groves, the coastal road and then the rocky Adriatic shore with small beaches and the occasional ugly-as-sin, burnt-out Eastern-bloc hotel. Someone—a soldier or vengeful neighbour—had nailed the family dog to the door of a nearby farmhouse. It looked like an oversize squirrel made of beef jerky; vertical roadkill. If you think that is a stupid description, it is not half as stupid-looking as the dog. It still had its collar on.

As the sun set over the Adriatic the escarpment behind us was lit like alabaster. Then shadows climbed the cliffs till just the tops still glowed and the other colours faded, settled and merged, and there were those brief few minutes in the Mediterranean where the light greens of the olives and the dark greens of the cypress trees are the same shade against the lavender-grey haze of dusk.

We hitchhiked back into town and slipped through a fence around an old Hapsburg villa that had been shut since the war began. In the sea-facing garden there were grand staircases that split and rejoined at different levels down to the rocky shore. Untended for years, the wisteria had run amok and swept down the moonlit marble, twisting around balustrades and lapping at the feet and hooves of statues of goddesses and mythical beasts that were caught in the flood of vine and flowers. We spent an hour in some small round pavilion perched over the shore. Afterwards I walked Ella back to her flat, kissed her and headed out of town towards the coastal road. It was late.

On a corner on the road out of town was the Bar Adolf, which was every bit as bad as its name suggests. It was a small room, the bar opposite the door. Behind the bar was a Swastika flag and on the walls half a dozen or so black-and-white framed photos of the Third Reich's greatest highlights and heroes. The clientele were local drunks and thugs from the HVO, a vicious Croatian paramilitary unit, who saw themselves as the heirs of the Ustaše movement that had slaughtered hundreds of thousands of Serbs and Bosnian Muslims during the Second World War. It was the last bar in town to shut, somewhere for 'one for the road' and a good place to get a lift heading south. That night it was crowded, about twenty people, guns everywhere. Most men were in uniform, with unit swatches I hadn't seen before, but I recognised the barman. Maybe he recognised me. I ordered a beer and went to the cigarette machine against the back wall.

There was a guy beside the cigarette machine, almost in my way, and I asked him to move. I was polite, perhaps too polite, because he tried to strike up conversation. I was tired and thirsty, and could tell he was just a bit of a dickhead; something in the posture, something in the way that he was standing there alone, the fact that he was trying to make small talk with a stranger. I didn't even bother replying in my basic Serbo-Croat. He had that familiarity with rejection that only the congenitally unpopular truly know.

I returned to the bar, where a litre bottle and a small glass waited for me. I poured out a glass, drained it—cold and good—refilled and lit a cigarette. I imagined my actions were a little over-pronounced; that paradoxical teenage state of feeling that no one cares and yet caring chronically what others think—a bit of a dickhead too.

Some guys in the corner started to give the cigarette-machine guy some grief and I looked around. I couldn't make out what they were saying, but it was a one-way discussion and getting heated. He was getting ribbed for something, and it was the only show in the bar.

I don't know who lashed out first, but the cigarette guy was alone and went down quickly. It turned into a proper kicking. I turned my back, trying to stay out of it. I stared at my beer and took another drink. Someone said something to me. I looked up at a tall soldier and shrugged. He repeated it. I shrugged again and rolled my eyes slightly—not at him, but at the situation behind me, like it was the weather or a late bus. He grabbed me and swung me against the wall and held me there. My cigarette guy was dragged up and made to stand next to me. I was about to say, 'I don't know him so leave me the—' when the tall soldier drew his pistol and stuck it in my face. There was a lot of shouting. The lights seemed unusually bright. All I could feel was his fist around my bunched-up jacket and the rough plaster of the wall against the back of my head.

I started to try to talk to him, but he simply pressed the gun into my face, mashing my lips against my teeth; I shut up.

The cigarette guy next to me was ashen and shaking, but I assumed things would calm down: the tall soldier had shown who was boss, his men were in charge, they were all heroes. Let's have salutes and beers all around, drink to whatever, and go home.

But this was not happening. The mood was getting worse. The shouting was getting louder. The tall soldier said something to the others who were holding the cigarette guy. They yanked him away from the wall and pulled him towards the door. He didn't struggle but protested in a good-natured kind of way, like he knew them. It was the way habitual victims respond the world over when bullied: 'Hey you guys, come on guys, not again'— trying to placate, josh, and plead all at once.

I looked at the tall soldier down the length of his gun and his long arm, but he was looking at the guys leaving the bar. I followed his gaze. The cigarette guy was being marched towards the door by a couple of soldiers, they had taken only a few steps when someone tripped him—it just looked like a prank, 'hey you guys'—and as he tried to rise someone stepped forward with a Kalashnikov and fired into his head. He looked like he was sneezing a great shadow. The noise was awesome, and it changed everything. I realised I only had seconds to live and a sadness of such purity and scale that I hadn't known since childhood filled my world entirely.

I looked back at the tall soldier, who was looking back at me and smiling: yellow teeth, stubble, grime and an alcohol sheen. He ground the gun into my face and mimed opening his mouth, so I opened mine, and he slid the gun deep into my throat. He flipped the safety. He was going to do it there and then.

People seemed to be shouting but not making much noise. There seemed to be a problem with the generator as the lights got very bright before dimming all around me. Everything felt very distant and claustrophobic all at once. My mouth was very dry; my insides liquid.

Cliché: time stood still.

Then time started to slide backwards. I saw that day's events before me and the slide show. It felt like drowning; the light of reason seemed far above me as I thrashed about in a tsunami of past experiences, emotion and despair. This is what I remember remembering: I saw Ella, her freckles and everything else; I heard 'Blueberry Hill' and saw Alaska—flat tundra, bears, sunshine and snow-capped volcanoes—the last place I had eaten blueberries on a fishing trip years before, the first place I had ever fired a handgun...

Then I came to my senses. A full second had yet to pass.

Alaska and blueberries were replaced by a feeling of humiliation. Despite having gone to a good English public school, I have never sucked a man off or been raped, but I imagine it's a lot like having a gun in your mouth. On a practical level, I was learning about the gag reflex: the pistol fore-sight was jammed against the back of my throat; I was gurgling, and my eyes watered furiously, as I fought the dry heaves. Then there was the primitive humiliation: the gun was power, his power, lead ejaculate, and I was sucking on it not merely for his pleasure but for a show for his comrades.

We pretend life is a glittering cavalcade, but in reality it's a troubled *danse macabre* around a dark cluster of sex and death. As the sign at the AIDS clinic says: 'Life is a sexually transmitted disease that is 100% fatal.' From your parents' ecstatic coupling to your gruesome emergence and eventual death, it's a messy merry-go-round of red-faced screaming, emotional shock and bodily fluids. Giving birth isn't personal; we all arrive the same, our experiences of nine months in the womb are shared, only naked in our biology. We all meet our maker—or face that black mirror—as uniquely as we have lived but naked of hope and naked of the future as the remaining moments are stripped away. Watching someone die up close may be one of the most essentially human things that you can ever witness. This guy, with his barrel in my mouth, had a front-row seat for my final moments.

But I saw something too, just for a glinting second. It wasn't a vision but it had the power of one, as if I was finally being shown this life—in all its magnificence—just as I was about to leave it. At the edge there was a form of knowledge that felt like freedom.

The bartender started to protest.

Thank you; hope.

But no, he was only complaining about killing me inside his bar. He made gestures about blood and plaster. He was worried about the mess. My life, my brains, my soul, the content of my character, and the uniqueness of my wit, everything that is 'me' was about to be reduced to his cleaning problem.

The tall soldier told the bartender to 'fuck off' and smiled at me again. He put his finger on the trigger and said something to me I couldn't understand. His friends started a chant like they were challenging him to down a pint in one. A few other people left the bar shaking their heads. They didn't want to see it.

The guy outside was cooling meat, once a mammal, now nothing, no more. I was about to join him in that nowhere place. But where? I wouldn't be anything, just a body. Anybody, somebody, nobody, certainly a body... my mind was floundering, vomiting up nonsense from the depths of the unconscious.

I looked into his eyes as if I might be able to catch sight of the unfolding process in that bastard's brain: a neuron firing (saying 'kill him'), an electrical impulse along nerves that would lead to his finger muscle contracting, the mechanics of the trigger, the chemical reaction in the percussion cap, the physics of the bullet meeting the biology that was me.

My mind was trying to handle an absolute by breaking it down into the physical components. It wasn't working. It couldn't understand the idea of a complete lack of being, all of me changed instantly to none of me. And the oddest thing, the most humiliating thing, was that everyone in the room knew it and understood it. Everyone was looking at me, but no one would look me straight in my watery eyes. I was totally without hope. I had everything to live for and no way out. My status as victim was absolute—as was my fate.

So I did the only thing I could. I don't know why. I concentrated on the gagging: it must have looked to all like I was crying, and I didn't want to die with everyone in the bar thinking I was blubbing. Maybe it was a matter of pride; denial certainly. My vanity somehow popped up intact from the melee of my mind. I was done with sadness and was now getting angry.

I bit down on the gun and began to work it away from the back of my throat. I tried to protect my teeth from the hard metal edges with my lips but couldn't gain a grip. So I bit down on the barrel hard, released a tiny bit and then pushed with my tongue. The chant was reaching a crescendo. A bullet through the brain is quick, but how quick is quick? Would all the lights go out immediately? Would I feel myself fall? Would I taste cordite—or perhaps blueberries? It all felt like a cartoon. These were my thoughts as I bit down and worked the barrel a few times and tried to swallow...

I didn't gag. I didn't gag, and it was so brilliant and surprising and such a total victory in my tiny, fuddled mind that I grinned at him. It caught him completely unawares, as it did me.

WHAT IT FEELS LIKE TO BE EXECUTED (*BULLET*)

He waved to his friends with his other hand for quiet and peered into my eyes theatrically for the benefit of his chums. Then he said something to them. They all cheered. He slid the gun out of my mouth, dragged me to the bar, and bought me a beer. My own beer was still there, ice cold with foam as if it had just been poured. My cigarette lay there, still lit, half-ash. Two minutes had passed. The bartender said something to me. 'I don't speak a word of your fucking language,' I told him angrily. 'An Englander,' cried the tall soldier, and everyone cheered again. I smoked the cigarette and could smell Ella's cheap perfume on my hand. I drank the beer and washed away the taste of blood and gun-oil and leant against the bar heavily because my legs had begun to shake violently. I held the beer bottle to my lips to try to cool their swelling; the cold glass, beading condensation, the label slippy at the edges. Fuck, fuck, fuck. When I went to light another cigarette I couldn't operate the lighter; my fingers felt like flippers. The tall soldier lit it for me. Other soldiers came over and bought me beers; I drank them all. The bartender was now my mate as well. I didn't tip. How quickly power shifts.

Outside they were dragging the body away; there was blood on the ground and small pieces of chewing gum that I realised were brain. Blood at night absorbs all light and looks so dark it could be a hole in the world. We went out on the piss till dawn. In every bar in town the tall soldier retold my story, and everyone laughed and bought me more drinks and sang, 'Don't worry, be happy.'

2

HOW TO BE COOL

Now, by heaven,
My blood begins my safer guides to rule,
And passion, having my best judgement collied,
Assays to lead the way

Othello

Adrenaline—$C_9H_{13}NO_3$—was my first love.

That night in the bar was my first proper date, though it was far from consensual. Just as it's hard to write any love story without cliché, it's hard to write about adrenaline without slipping into them too: I got goosebumps, a chill ran down my spine, my blood ran cold, my stomach churned, it took my breath away, time stood still... Like love, adrenaline generates clichés because it produces similar feelings and sensations in all of us. In this chapter, we are going to take big fistfuls of these clichés and throw them at the page to illustrate the looping physical and cognitive cycles that adrenaline speeds within us.

First, we will examine the physical effects of adrenaline, then we'll have a look inside the brain, and then we're going to take lots of drugs and panic. Finally, just to ram the message home, we'll meet some cartoon animals. Sound good?

By the way, if you think I am talking to you like you're fucking stupid: I am. Several times a year I am an instructor on a hostile-environments course: I teach journalists, diplomats and other clever folk how to survive in war zones, riots and natural disasters. All of these people are far smarter than me—you probably are too—but they will all be made dumber by the effects of adrenaline: the higher the risk, the lower the IQ. There is nothing big or clever to surviving high-risk situations: it is about making common sense decisions in extraordinary circumstances. Adrenaline turns us all to morons and being aware of that—as all junkies know—is the first step towards recovery.

Adrenaline is a spectacular drug. It sends us on a journey into the cave, wreaking a metamorphosis upon body and mind that turns us from humans to hybrid-monsters to animals. It warps reason, numbs coordination; it turns legs to jelly and fingers to rubber; it skews vision and hearing, impairs memory, and makes you want to throw up or shit yourself. More importantly—and here's the really fun hook—it makes you incredibly high.

We speak of an 'adrenaline rush', but adrenaline itself is merely one hormone in a cascade of drugs that are similar to cocaine, cannabis and heroin. The most important thing you need to know about adrenaline is this: at precisely the moment you want to think and act clearly, it spikes your drink. If you can remember that thought—and hold it rationally when the shit hits the fan—then you can follow that thread of reason out of the labyrinth of your mind, slay the Minotaur and rescue lots of Athenian schoolkids. This is all about fighting monsters while on drugs.

In any life-threatening situation you are subject to the fight-or-flight response, also known as the Acute Stress Response, or Hyperarousal. In extremis you are in the grip of very ancient forces which predate our humanity and were formed when we were thumb-sized mammals being chased by dinosaurs.

BANG!

Rationally, at a conscious level, you may have heard the gunshot, but the instinctual, implicit part of your brain is off already, and is way ahead. Nobody thinks 'I should flinch,' nor do you tell yourself to scream; these are pure animal reactions from our deep past that bypass the neocortex, or the thinking part of the brain. We are now in survival mode, and it isn't the time for higher thoughts, for pondering abstracts like how things were or how things ought to be. At best, the clever bit of you hangs on for the ride, slightly separated from your other selves. Our language reflects this, and here come more clichés: beside myself, scared out of my wits, losing my mind. From this moment on—until we wrestle back control over the fight-or-flight mechanism—our animal instinct has the upper hand.

Your brain first processes the signal—*gunshot*—in the amygdala. After this, the hypothalamus triggers a hormonal cascade. Cortisol and adrenaline are released, creating waves of physical and cognitive reactions that start a triumphant and terrifying transformation.

You gasp and start to breathe faster, drawing more air into the lungs and oxygenating the blood. Adrenaline binds with liver cells to boost production of glucose; cortisol turns fatty acids into additional energy. There is a release of blood-clotting agents into the bloodstream in anticipation of injury. Your heart begins to thump rapidly, pushing this oxygen-rich, energy-laden blood around your system, but especially to your muscles, juicing them up for violent action or escape. Your brain hasn't decided whether to fight or flee, so it's getting ready for either.

As blood is sent to critical areas, your skin temperature drops; this is the 'chill' of fear. Cliché time: our 'blood ran cold'. In response, your body hairs stand up to insulate your skin, giving you goosebumps. Amongst males, there is also an inhibition of your ability to get an erection, as your body decides, literally, to not give a fuck.

Salivation tends to decrease. This may explain why some people lick their lips when they're uncomfortable (preparing for a fight, or when lying). That's my own personal 'tell' when I'm going into fight-or-flight mode. I get a taste in my mouth like sucking on a copper penny. That's the taste of trouble to me. It is good to get to know your own 'tell'. It's a cheat. Recognising it, or any of the signs of adrenaline, at a conscious level, helps you dial them down and bring yourself back to reason. You're not tweaking, just peaking.

At the same time as the body is doping itself up, other systems are shutting down: stomach and upper-intestinal actions aren't key to fight-or-flight, and are using huge amounts of precious blood. The only way to shut off the digestive system is to get rid of any food it might contain. Sometimes the person may vomit or defecate or merely experience 'butterflies in the stomach'. There is also a general relaxation of the body's sphincter muscles. Some experts also believe it is a very ancient way of getting rid of excess weight in preparation for flight. I have seen soldiers vomit before going out on patrol and have smelled plenty of farts in the Humvee as it passes out the main gate. I haven't pissed or shat myself yet, but this is just luck, and probably a matter of time. A survey of US troops in the Second World War found that a quarter of all soldiers admitted to pissing themselves, and an eighth had shat themselves. The proportion for frontline troops was probably higher.

As your pulse rate continues to climb, you will be entering a critical phase. At about 115 beats per minute (bpm), fine motor skills begin to deteriorate; it becomes difficult to write or work complex pieces of kit, like satellite phones and radios, or to attend casualties requiring complicated life-saving procedures. From experience, I find it very hard to recall correct drug dosages or oxygen-flow rates. 140bpm is often regarded as the optimal level for survival performance and reaction time. At 150bpm, your brain and body can no longer thread a needle, but it's at peak ability for gross motor skills: running, punching and kicking.

Very rapidly, you are being transfigured into something else. The very feelings of this primitive takeover can be a source of horrible internal anxiety, only adding to the external terror of gunshot, gun, gunman.

Next, the body shuts down the hearing. Or, in my near-execution experience, it tried to. I remember that I was deaf some moments and could hear the shouting and chanting clearly the next. It was like a wa-wa sound at the end of a record. Over the years I've realised my body does this more than many people I know. I first became aware of this in military training and would often remove my ear-protection during complicated live-fire exercises so as to hear the shouts of those around me (and my hearing suffered as a result). In Iraq, during the fighting in al-Anbar, soldiers would blame the dust; there can be a magical silence following a sandstorm, like a hushed morning after heavy snowfall, when all sound is absorbed. I once saw a soldier in a firefight think his weapon was jammed because he couldn't hear the shots as he fired. The choices your body makes under extreme duress are often beyond the realms of rational thought.

The face we make when we're frightened is universal—from Chelsea fans to Khoisan Hunters—but whether we try to repress it is cultural. Americans are happy to scream away, while the Japanese try to maintain their reserve. Over 150 years ago, Charles Darwin proposed that the fear-face might have evolutionary advantages, but it was only very recently proved that people making frightened faces have a wider range of vision, make faster eye movements and have a better sense of smell, as more air passes through their nostrils. Conversely, making a disgusted face—scrunched nose and squint—blocks foul odours, and we see less of what offends us.

Making a war-face uses many of the same muscles as a frightened face, with the same sensory benefits, yet it channels these primitive, dark emotions towards a positive ending. It's also fun. If you don't know what a 'war-face' is, watch *Full Metal Jacket* ...

... Are you back? We're looking at looking now. Your vision does two clever things: first, it goes into tunnel mode, binning all peripheral information, so that you can focus all your attention on what is directly in front of you. Second, the pupils dilate, to take in all the available light so that you can see every detail. Colours are intensified; there can be extraordinary clarity of detail; a small, mundane scene is transformed into a sacred still-life. During house-to-house fighting in Iraq, I stumbled across a small room with two chairs and, between them, a low round table; on it was a vase of plastic roses in a shaft of dust-whorled sunlight. In that moment, the scene looked like a Vermeer; I can remember every detail.

Not only is the brain trying to think rationally, but it is also struggling to make sense of the animal feelings that fight-or-flight situations create. If this is your first time, the feelings can be terrifying: wild heartbeat, sweating, our 'fur' standing up on our skin, the cold flush of blood, the warm flush of urine. It is an animal metamorphosis. But these changes are going on not only across our body but inside our heads too. Our brain is witness to bewildering physiological changes as it too is being transformed.

The brain is on drugs. And drugs induce an altered state of consciousness. The passing second slows, shudders, elongates into a continuous *now*. Simultaneously, fireworks of memory explode in fast-forward: slides from your life so far.

It feels like a collapse in time itself. And in many ways that is exactly what is happening. Your brain lacks a single 'timer'.

Instead, time is experienced across the higher, rational, executive parts of the brain. Animals have no need for the Rolex of the neocortex. In humans during fight-or-flight situations, this part of the brain is sidelined, as instinct and emotion take over.

As this is happening, your memory fires up and begins to work both ways: record and play.

It begins to record events in the highest definition it can afford. These are often referred to as flash-bulb memories. From an evolutionary perspective, it is very important to learn about a mortal encounter so you can survive the next time. So your brain, specifically the anterior insula, takes everything in. Your brain is designed for this moment: it can take in and store vast amounts of sensory data when it is flooded with these strong chemicals (and sometimes it takes in too much, which can lead to PTSD).

But the sheer effort of ultra-high-definition recording of every sensation will often create a sense of temporal dislocation: time slows or even stops. You are not actually operating in slo-mo but the short-term memory is bunching up and giving you a sense that you are. It can be terrifying, surreal and even comic.

Tachypsychia—meaning 'rapid mind', from *tachos* (swiftness) and *psyche* (spirit/soul/mind)—is a neurological condition that alters the mind's perception of time. It is almost always reported that time slows for the witness: the adrenaline-soaked events in the Bar Adolf took less time than a cigarette takes to burn down, but felt as long as a Shakespeare tragedy. In some rare cases events speed up so much they appear blurred. Tachypsychia is classed as a type of dyschronation—or time-distortion—hallucination.

Tachypsychia isn't a medically recognised word, but that hasn't stopped it being used a great deal in military, law enforcement and the emergency services. Martial artists are obsessed by tachypsychia, but pronounce it as two separate words: 'tacky psyche'. This takes us to the root of the problem with fight-or-flight research: scientists need to get into more bar-fights, and ninjas need to hit the books harder.

Simultaneously, just as your brain hits 'record', it also flips open its memory library and presses 'play', and the slide show of your life begins to flash. At its best, this is a simple case of 'I smell smoke + smoke is associated with fire + I burnt myself as a child = run away'. At its worst, it can be like your mind typed random words into a search engine and your brain vomited up useless gibberish just when you prayed for clarity.

* * *

So there you are: gunshot, an animal metamorphosis, slow-motion special effects and then a slide-show trip down memory lane. Think you can handle it? Of course you can. Because your body is just about to mainline the finest drugs on the planet into your system.

Just as the hormonal cascade of adrenaline and cortisol in your body transformed it into a fighting and flighting beast, so too this batch of the Big 5 neurotransmitters will reshape your mind into survival mode, into an altered state of consciousness. This cocktail is the true heroic dose.

Serotonin: I've put this first in our list, although its effects are felt at the end of the fight-or-flight response. I did this to clear up a misunderstanding: that adrenaline creates the high. This notion feeds into the stereotype of 'adrenaline junkies'. The after-glow of danger is actually a serotonin high; it can go for days. Serotonin is the neurotransmitter of optimism. It helps us persevere and keep a grip on the situation. A common anti-anxiety medication like Prozac works by stopping the re-uptake of serotonin in our system and spinning its effects for longer.

Endocannabinoids (endogenous means 'within the body', and 'cannabinoids' are like cannabis) are our bodies' own version of tetrahydrocannabinol, the main psychoactive component in cannabis. Endocannabinoids, or more specifically anandamide (from Sanskrit *ananda*: joy, bliss, delight), are released during high-intensity activities. Anandamide also helps damp down feelings of fear and promote lateral thinking. Post-coital bliss? That's anandamide. Runner's high? Ditto. Its tasting notes might read: cleansing, loving, with a cheeky hint of cosmic insight. If you want to get all gnostic, then I believe anandamide is the closest neurotransmitter to the divine spark.

Endorphins—my favourites—(*endo* again, and *orphin* meaning 'like morphine') are your body's own golden pharmacy of pain relief. Endorphins bind with opioid receptors in our brain and stop the cells from sending out any painful messages. There are forty different types of endorphins, some of which are 100 times more powerful than medical-grade morphine. Endorphins reduce stress by suppressing shame and self-criticism. The brain is muting irrelevant signals and diverting all its processing power to survival. It can make you feel superhuman—like all good drugs should.

Oxytocin has been nicknamed the 'love drug' or the 'cuddle hormone', because it is one of the key chemical signals between mother and infant. It is released during physical contact, and can help people bond. Professional fighters produce lots of it, and this may be one of the many reasons there is such a deep bond amongst combat soldiers and a family feel to the best Jiujitsu and boxing clubs.

But the 'love hormone' moniker is slightly misleading. It's an us-or-them hormone, and can just as easily create distrust and suspicion as it can create bonds. In a fight-or-flight scenario, oxytocin makes us bond with people we consider safe and avoid people we think of as threats. Oxytocin gives salience to social situations, creating a greater contrast between the wheat and the chaff, and it links social cues to the dopamine-driven reward pathway.

Dopamine. Last on our list but the most important. You might think this is a book about Special Forces, combat or heroin—and it is—but it's really about dopamine and a pilgrimage down the reward pathway within our brains.

Dopamine has been likened to a hit of cocaine but that's the wrong way of looking at it: cocaine causes the brain to release dopamine and then—like Prozac with serotonin—blocks the re-uptake. Cocaine hacks your own supplies in small amounts, enough to make nightclubs look sexy or boring people to think they're interesting. (Personally, I can't get over how fascinating I am on cocaine.) But the amount of dopamine released in extreme, near-death situations feels like mainlining creation.

Dopamine is pure desire. It cuts through the battlefield or lights up the escape route. Dopamine is the spinning roulette ball, the unopened present, the undressed first date, the anticipation of victory, the magic of the unknown, the thrill of the chase.

Dopamine connects the dots, like cat's eyes on the road of excess; like a laser-marker it makes our target fluoresce with meaning and potency. It creates a tunnel of attention that we must go down.

Your body produces this awesome pharmaceutical arsenal, but it takes some practice before their performance-enhancing abilities come to the fore. Most people who have never been in a genuinely terrifying situation tend to overdose on their first hit. That's completely understandable.

* * *

Many of these systems rely on each other; they feed off and feed-back to the next system. Stimuli produce a variety of neurological and physiological responses, which can produce terrifying emotions, which in turn produce yet more responses, twisting off, curling back, reforming and increasing in strength. And you're facing this tsunami on a cocktail of drugs that would get you prison time almost anywhere in the world. What little is left of our rational self is carried forth on a violent tide of atavistic emotions and fractal sensations, threatening to drown us in panic.

* * *

Without a basic understanding of neuroscience, it is easy to see all this as a battle between our human and animal selves to be masters of our fate. To lose to your animal half is to give in to your primal nature. This is how the ancient Greeks saw it. The word 'panic' comes from the Greek god Pan.

Pan was a therianthrope, one of the half-human, half-beast creatures painted on the cave wall. These hybrids have been with us since our earliest days. They followed us out of the caves, through the forests and across the steppe. They were liminal creatures in the boundaries of darkness by the campfire, a glimpse at dusk in the clearings, peripheral movement when we ploughed the first fields, something beyond the city walls. What form they took depended on your geography and the animals that were totemic to your culture. In the far north, there were werewolves and were-bears; skin-walkers took the form of bison or wolf on the American plains; mermaids lived by the sea. But perhaps nowhere was richer for hybrids in Western history than Greece: there were the harpies and sirens of the air, nymphs in the rivers. Men-horse could be either centaurs or satyrs; on Crete, where bulls were venerated, the dreaded Minotaur lived in his Labyrinth. But chief of all of these was the Goat-God Pan.

Pan was the god of the wild forests and mountains, a companion of nymphs and protector of shepherds. He was half human and half goat. He also taught the shepherds to play the Pan-pipes and how to masturbate. Catching sight of Pan or hearing his shout caused his victims to Pan-ic: to lose all sense of reason, to be overwhelmed by irrational forces, overcome by their nature and driven towards temporary madness or even death.

What can you do in the face of such elemental terror?

Do nothing.

Doing sweet fuck-all is often the best survival tactic. And doing nothing comes naturally too. Remember that we are using bits of neural architecture that evolved while we were shrews—or their very scared equivalent—and we had no chance of outfighting or outrunning our predators. It's really the fight-freeze-flight response. If you can, get out of immediate danger—drop to a knee or get down behind some hard cover—but then take a moment to chill.

Do nothing.

Then breathe.

In a fight-or-flight situation your breathing rate is the only automatic response you can switch to 'manual'. Breathing is the wedge between our rational and animal selves.

Take a few breaths—in through the nose, hold, out through the mouth. Repeat. Do nothing. Open your eyes, move your head, take it all in, then decide your next move. Navy Seals refer to this as 'Relax, look around, make a call'. Breathing oxygenates the blood and clears the head. It is a balm to the senses, an antidote to panic. It is free medicine; remember to take it.

It's not just the few short breaths themselves; it's the command 'Breathe'. It is the voice of reason. Once you can control your breath, the other operating systems start switching back to rational control and not auto-pilot. The rational 'you' doesn't even have to take over full control: let your inner beast out a bit. The key to any good relationship is communication: brain scans of people who are very good at high-risk environments show heightened levels of communication among brain systems. It's not just the acceleration that allows you to attack effectively, it's the braking too; combined, it's you setting the pace. And in that sweet spot, all those wild drugs we mentioned begin to work in your favour.

HOW TO BE COOL

You're in the beginning of a flow state.
You are cool.

* * *

To be cool is to be somewhere between the chill of reason and the heat of passion. Cool is relaxing into the fight, accepting blows, dialling back the static of pain and watching the patterns emerge, waiting for the right moment. It is an act of faith in your better self. To be cool is to sever the puppet-strings of passion, to master your feelings and marshal your thoughts as a benevolent despot, ruling over a riotous mind.

The word makes its first appearance in English in *Beowulf* when describing emotions coming in 'waves', first 'boiling' and then 'cooling'.

In *A Midsummer Night's Dream*—a play entirely devoted to the liminal space between humans and nature and the powers of transformation, presided over by Pan (or Puck) himself—Shakespeare speaks of cool:

> *Lovers and madmen have such seething brains,*
> *Such shaping fantasies, that apprehend*
> *More than cool reason ever comprehends.*

Cool has been part of our language ever since. 'Cool under fire' was Second World War terminology, and used in official dispatches and medal commendations in Korea. Most of my cool screen heroes from that period had also seen action in the Second World War: Paul Newman, Lee Marvin and Steve McQueen. (McQueen was too young to fight in the war but served as a marine and rescued comrades from the frozen seas in the Arctic, which is somehow doubly cool.) Paul Newman epitomised sangfroid (cool-blood) in his fight against The Man and flight from the prison system in *Cool Hand Luke*.

Norman Mailer, who had fought against the Japanese in the Philippines, described the desire to be cool as a 'decision to encourage the psychopath in oneself.'

But being genuinely cool requires its opposite: the heat of the moment. To be nobly aloof demands a baseline of outrageous circumstances. It's hard to be cool when life itself is a tepid, peaceful affair. Composure in the heat of battle is an extraordinary thing to witness; composure in a nightclub is just posturing.

By the time I was growing up, the contemporary cool, disengaged look was typified by the Heroin Chic of fashion models. All those dark eyes and that feigned insouciance was a grungy rebellion against the well-lit, glitzy perfection of the 1980s. These models were so aloof from worldly affairs they were comatose. This reached its apogee in the 2000s with photoshoots where the models pretended to be dead. The skinny girls were way past cool and genuinely devoid of metabolic warmth. This is what happens when you leave important concepts to geriatric French homosexuals. And that's not a bad thing. We've had peace in the West for almost seventy years, and we can be forgiven if our thermostats are a little skewed. It's a small price to pay, unless you take your cues from fashion and buy lots of expensive clothes.

* * *

All of this is a lot to take in. It's hard to remember even on a good day, but I want you to be able to remember it when you're having the worst day of your life, when the effects of adrenaline have looted your library of memories and upended your clever plans.

Everyone who works in high-risk environments has developed systems for cheating. Fighter pilots have those cute little window patches on their trousers for their flight-plans. Deep-sea divers use the buddy-buddy system and give each other the thumbs up. Astronauts say 'check' back to Houston every move they make. Check-lists, kit-lists, standard operating procedures, actions-on, mnemonics, aide-mémoires, acronyms, aphorisms, markers, bezels and visual-reminders are all simple cheats employed to counteract the mind-bending, memory-dissolving effects of adrenaline. KISS—'keep it simple stupid'—is the Boy-Scouts' other motto. But sometimes making something fucking stupid helps it stick in the mind. Nothing sticks in my mind like the bizarre. I hope it works for you too.

Within the brain, there are several brains. The Neocortex, or the 'new' brain, is roughly 2.5 million years old. This is your Monkey Brain. The Neocortex is also called the 'thinking brain'. You've used this brain to chip flint spearheads and talk about strategies for hunting mammoth with your friends. This is the brain that covered the glittering cave walls with the finest art.

Monkey Brain is wrapped around the Mammalian Brain (also known as the Limbic system), which was formed about 250 million years ago, and includes the amygdala and the hippocampus. We are going to call this your Shrew Brain. You used this brain for about 247.5 million years when thinking about acorns, fighting over acorns, running away and hiding (having grabbed a handful of acorns).

The Mammalian Brain is, in turn, wrapped around an even earlier structure known as the Reptilian Brain—that's your Brain Stem and Cerebellum—which dates back 400 million years. This is your Lizard Brain. Lizard does the basics.

In a dire emergency, all your brains want you to survive, but they don't often agree how best to achieve that.

For the last sixty years, the three-brain, or Triune, theory has dominated neuroscience, but in the last decade it has been facing retirement. I still find it very useful. It is a rough schematic that neatly sits over Freud's tripartite view of the mind: superego, ego and id. It also works well with head-thinking, heart-feeling and gut-instinct.

Just because the gun was invented doesn't mean we can't use a knife up close, and that's how I'm proposing we use this theory. The three-brain theory provides a neat shorthand; it's good enough for the extreme places that we'll visit in this book: war, drugs, terrorism and kinky sex. Just don't air this theory at a neuroscience conference. It would be like bringing a knife to a gunfight. Are we cool?

Here comes a cartoon. Let's paint it ridiculous to make sure it sticks:

I am back in France and driving along a stretch of road not far from where our story began. Except it's not me in the car. It's my three brains...

Picture the Monkey, Shrew and Lizard in a classic car racing across southern France. A 1969 Dodge Charger in duck-egg blue with a nitrous system? And a convertible? Of course, for the sun is shining and it's an achingly stunning route—because life is beautiful. I see our three friends speeding along the limestone causse on a twisting road through scrub oak. The crickets are singing 'La Marseillaise' as the car roars past. The roof is down and the dashboard is crammed with mustard-yellow French maps and a red Michelin Guide reflected against the windshield below a sun-bleached, pale-blue summer sky.

Meet Monkey: Monkey is us, the bit of you reading this book. Maybe it's the bit of you wondering what possessed you to buy it. That's cool. Monkey is critical like that: reasoning, analytical. Monkey is *Homo sapiens*, wise enough to be sapient, vain enough to give itself the title. Monkey can do all manner of shit none of the other animals on this planet can do: plan for the future, imagine abstract scenarios, create art, plot murder, crack jokes, apply reason, solve complex problems, assess risks and delay gratification. Monkey sits on a golden throne of identity, with a sceptre of purpose. Monkey is possessor of the divine spark, the Promethean fire. Monkey is prone to losing it. Monkey is in the driver's seat.

Beside him, in the middle, is Shrew. If you were asking 'what possessed you' it was probably Shrew. He does that. Shrew robs Monkey of reason; he makes impulsive choices. Shrew is all

emotion: wild desire, fear, rage, arousal and anxiety, love, attachment, social interactions, emotional longing. Motivation.
Intuition. Instinct. Shrew actually does a lot of the driving. He
can handle the basic stuff, the long, easy stretches of straight
road, while Monkey daydreams and checks the map. But for the
complicated bits in town, or when parking, Monkey takes over.

Lizard's job is the mechanics and reflexes. In charge of regu-
lating the basic systems: digestion, sweating, shivering. He is
the engineer, in charge of monitoring hundreds of dials: digestion, temperature, electrolytic balance, blood sugars. Being the
engineer, he says things like, 'The Engines cannae tay-keet any
maw cap'n'.

Monkey wants to sip espressos and look at frescoes. Shrew
notices the waitress in that roadside café has a great derrière. I
am ashamed that Shrew objectified that young French lady.
Such antiquated thoughts have absolutely no place in a civilised
world. What can I say? Shrew is a beast. Lizard keeps an eye on
the fuel gauge.

All is swell until our three friends round a corner on a peril-
ous stretch of mountain road and there's a geopolitically
unlikely, but narratively significant, terrorist ambush. That's
not all! There's an earthquake and a landslide; boulders are
bouncing everywhere, and out of the sulphurous cracks in the
earth appear swarms of zombie-Nazis from Second World War
bunkers. Next come human waves of wildly unforgiving ex-
girlfriends, bartenders you owe money, and that nice kid you
used to bully for his maths homework.

It's a fight-or-flight situation. Shrew launches a motoring
coup-d'état and snatches the wheel. Lizard fires up the nitro-
system and hits the accelerator. Lizard also cracks open the glove
compartment, which contains an endless Pandora's Box of drugs
similar to cocaine, methamphetamine and several dozen types of
opiates. All three freak the fuck out. Monkey may try to restore

order rationally—'hey you guys'—or pull a full-blown whitey; Shrew drives faster and tries to ram anything in sight; Lizard gets the bong out. The higher they get, the more they snort and the faster they drive—and the worse their road rage gets. Acceleration and anger make everyone take a heroic dose, which sends our three companions even higher.

This is panic.

But that's not what we do. Fuck no. We are cool.

Monkey breathes. Shrew's training kicks in. Lizard realises the engines can take much, much more. They don't fight over the wheel but drive together. They ride the rush of the drugs— somewhere between Asterix's potion and Popeye's spinach— down a glittering dopamine highway, a Goldilocks Zone between human reason and animal savagery. Everything they see is in technicolour slow-motion: hyper-aware of their surroundings but neither overthinking it or being too emotionally drawn in. The slow-motion is their friend. Time ... is ... on ... their ... side.

Our three friends look at each other and laugh. Yeah. Oh Yeah. Fuck yeah.

Cool is like that. It's the biggest positive there is. It's *all* right. It is an ephemeral element with a momentary half-life, but *it is there*. It seems to contain and confirm the architecture of the universe. Sometimes you have to smash a lot of protons to find the God Particle. It feels like the punchline of the cosmic joke.

And in the midst of all the chaos, the gunfire, the glinting brass bullet casings, the smoke of burning rubber and muttered Nazi-zombie curses, Monkey realises—with all the glory of his monkey-mind—that it is moments such as these which make life worth living.

3

SELECTION

Man is troubled not by events, but by the meaning he gives them.

Epictetus

The Brecon Beacons are a range of mountains in South Wales. Ancient red sandstone rises up to a series of escarpments: Pen-y-Fan and her sister summits of Cribyn and Corn Du on a serrated edge. To the north, cliffs and scree drop a thousand feet down into gentle valleys, scalloped by the last Ice Age. To the south the mountains keep their height for longer: they hang in springy moor, sag into bog and mire, then buckle into deep v-sided valleys, wooded gorges and waterfalls.

I could see none of this, because it was 5 am, dark and raining. We sat on our backpacks—or Bergens—in untidy rows, weapons in our hands or lying across our boots as we fiddled with kit, making last-minute adjustments. Men, rain, mud, trucks, on a bit of forest track somewhere near the base of the mountain. The rain came in squalls. My constant memory of that time is the sound of rain against the side of my waterproof hood, like volleys of birdshot. There was a growl of diesel engines and indiscriminate shouting. The scene was lit by the vehicle lights of army trucks that disgorged more and more recruits who lugged equipment across the beams, throwing towering shadows like cartoon monsters across the conifers and bracken.

This was Special Air Service Selection.

When the SAS was born during the Second World War, its founders tore up the rule book and created a new type of unit comprised of the toughest, brightest and most ruthless men.

But these founders also insisted that recruits held to five precepts:

Humour.

Humility.

Self-discipline.

Classlessness.

The unrelenting pursuit of excellence.

To pick men, they devised one of the toughest military ordeals in the world, imaginatively named: SAS Selection.

At the front, an officer from the Training Wing asks recruits why they are here. None of their answers seemed good enough, which sends him into another rant.

'SAS Selection has to be tougher than natural selection. Or we'd be like you lot. And then who would we be?'

I looked around. No one seemed to know what he was talking about.

To my immediate left was a fucking giant who sat on his Bergen like it was a knapsack, gripping his rifle like a child's baton. His name was Sebastian. He had a rapt expression on his face, but then he always did.

I had got to know the names of a few of the other recruits from the pre-course briefing days and basic fitness tests. Some of the cynics had said there wasn't any point in making friends early on, because the failure rate was so high. Of the 400 who attended the first day maybe a dozen would be given a beret nine months later. I was certain I wouldn't get that far; I was just there for the ride. As for friends? I'm a friendly kinda guy, but most of the people around me were uniforms rammed full of muscle and eyes crammed with belief—not really my crowd.

To my right was Rob. He was impossibly good-looking, covered in tattoos, rarely without a cigarette in the corner of his mouth, yet he also always—like, without fail—had his shit together: his kit administered just right, webbing snug; not fussy, just a man with a good hold of himself. The only other thing I could say for certain about Rob was that he was very clearly a terrible deviant. You could just tell.

The officer started off again.

'Death is nature's way of saying you've failed SAS Selection.'

'Get *Her*,' Rob muttered. *Rob* isn't his real name. I asked him to come up with a name, so: his name is Robert Paulson.

The officer scanned the rows of recruits and, for the first time of many in my short military career, I thought: don't pick me. 'Why was I there?' I didn't have a good answer for him. I didn't even have a decent answer for myself. I was in my late 20s when I decided to give this a shot; I'd spent the last decade studying archaeology, which I parlayed into a job doing forensics on criminal investigations, which led to undercover journalism and finally back to war zones, making documentaries. That's the type of narrative I'd tell an employer. Between you and me: I had hit life like a monkey at a salad bar and was looking for fun and misadventure.

If the officer had held a gun to my head—which I was half expecting—then my best-boy-scout answer might have involved wanting to learn new skills. I'd been working with a friend, 'Tim', in Iraq who'd just done twenty years in the Regiment, and I admired him for being able to fix cars, bandage wounds, navigate and speak several languages. I wanted some of that. In Iraq, Tim had told me about 21 SAS, and gave me a number to call.

'Just remember two things,' he said. 'Firstly, hate all officers. Secondly, remember that you will always be a civilian twat.'

I gave him a salute.

'And don't ever salute anyone again or I'll punch you.' I almost managed all three.

But, if I were to be brutally honest, I badly wanted to give up smoking and had figured some task-based replacement was the ideal approach. Or at least that's what it said in an article in a magazine I'd read at a Sexually Transmitted Disease clinic, and I tend to be especially vulnerable to redemptive and ambitious ideas when waiting for test results. Like most big decisions in my life, I hadn't really thought it through. When I mentioned the SAS to friends they laughed their asses off, which only riled me further. So I never spoke of my plans to anyone, and—left to my own devices—started to ask myself one of those dumb-fuck questions only a spectator way up in the bleachers can ask: *come on, how tough can it be?* I'd always wanted to run an ultra-marathon, though not so much that I'd bothered to run a marathon or even a half-marathon or anything more than four very flat miles along the river in London. But if the army was willing to pick up the cost of my training and even pay me as well: why not?

As for any experience of the military: zilch. My only firsthand dealings had been death squads in Yugoslavia, and that had hardly been a recruitment drive. Back home, my knowledge of the British Army was a few dinners at St. James's Palace where chinless officers droned on about natural leadership and recounted historical anecdotes about bits of regimental furniture but couldn't recall the names of their men who were serving them food. These were formal occasions, and I hadn't known which was the correct fork to use to drive into my leg to stop myself from falling asleep.

In the abstract, the military was everything I loathed: authority, uniformity, team spirit, flag-waving, silly music. And if the

Special Forces were the condensed version of all of the above then of course I was going to fail. But—until that point—I'd treat it like keep-fit with costumes, quit the smokes and possibly even learn something. That was the plan. But as the military will tell you, 'no plan survives first contact with the enemy'—the enemy, in my case, being the twats who say such things in the first place, and I was surrounded by them.

The officer read out from a list with our names and our march numbers. Rob, Sebastian and myself were somewhere near the end. Sebastian put his basha up against a low fence and we got under it while Rob brewed up some tea. We sat with our backs to the fence and admired the scene before us, slowly blueing in the pall of predawn. It felt like we were submerged at extreme depth, in the abyss; maybe it was the sheer weight of the summits above us, the compacting pressure of expectation or the weather, which was more water than air. Men with strong jaws and head-torches eyed the dark hills like Angler Fish.

Looking around, it was easy to see who was going to pass: mountainous freaks, tough-as-nails brawlers or men who beamed charm and certainty like sepia cut-outs from the days of empire. They were impressive. Some people seemed to have 'it'. Most didn't. They were like extras. I felt like an extra, a walk-on in someone else's tale of derring-do. But I was cool with that. The tea was hot and sweet, with the babyish taste of powdered milk. I enjoyed the moment, because I knew it was fleeting. I also appreciated the gestures: the buddy-buddy systems and practical manners which fitted together like a robust dovetail joint rather than the marquetry of etiquette that I was used to from English officer-types. These recruits would never just make tea for themselves or take only one cigarette out of their pack (those cigarettes *did* look sweeeeet). Such moments buffered the shock of the military: the surreal scene of grown men in black make-up; the crayon-like smell of greasepaint, the spotlights from the truck headlights on a muddy stage where some camp man screamed out his rehearsed lines; the make-believe of military exercise; the 'theatre' of war.

'It's like a movie set,' I said to no one in particular.

Rob stubbed out his cigarette: 'Every day it's the Oscars, mate.'

Rob and Sebastian showed me how to pack my Bergen so that I knew where everything was—even in the dark—and how to wear webbing so it didn't flap and rattle, and even how to carry my rifle convincingly (not like a wizard's staff). The pack weighed 45lbs, my rifle 7lbs and belt-kit with water and food another 5lbs.

The instructions for the marches were fairly chew-gum-and-walk. Recruits were given a map, a compass, a set of coordinates to memorise and then told to navigate there within a given time. We were lined up and set off at two-minute intervals, individually.

When my time came I went up to the Directing Staff or DS, confirmed my number, was given the coordinates and asked to identify it on the map: it was a fairly mundane piece of high ground on a flat wedge beyond the saddle of a ridge. Once the DS confirmed this, I set off.

For a while, I felt like I had a chance.

For all of about 300 metres—150 of which was on a flat farm track.

After that, the path pitched upwards into sedge and disappeared. There was a drystone wall, possibly a forest, but it was all peripheral. My view was of my boots and the ground: coarse, short grass, reddish dirt, copper bracken and tussocks of whatever-the-fuck, which all stretched up wordlessly into slopes, corries, scree, rain and cloud. Looking up, I could see the tiny, staggering figures of the other recruits climbing the ridge, some keeping their spacing, others catching up or falling back and bunching up. Pen-y-Fan's summit is 886m of purest Welsh mountain, but seen from its base, weighed down with over 55lbs of Bergen, webbing and weapon, it has the astonishing scale of a Himalayan peak.

The path was full of dead sedge and grass, muddy, slimy, slippery and steep, like trying to climb a tapeworm through a sheep's arse. Then it tapered out. After another 100m the metamorphosis hit me—not some Jedi moment or Highlander quickening towards Valhalla, but the reverse: a creeping realisation of sheer puck-fuckery, as I became a pack-mule, rasping, breathing to bleating, hee-hawing, eye-straining, neck muscles bulging. My legs wobbled and I stumbled and went down on all fours as I used my hands to clamber up. Some small part of me was still conscious enough to marvel at just how incredibly shameful crawling is: being a baby again, or a bad doggy, and—perhaps sensing this—my Bergen tried to take me doggy-style. I was soaked from rain, sweat, snot too. And I was angry; proper kiddy tantrum, not-fair angry. That choking rage of impotency when faced with the utter simplicity of a hill that couldn't be bargained with. The straps on my Bergen cut into my shoulders and I could feel my pulse against them. The pain went from dull, to whining, to screeching like the wind. One step, another step, breathe.

After an hour, I made it to the top of the ridge, and realised I was lost.

Here was the 'other' bit of SAS Selection: navigation. The shoulder of the hill flattened out into a plateau of featureless moor. The only thing I had to do was follow a bearing, which is a relatively simple task, but, drunk on the effects of adrenaline, this became a walk-along-the-white-line-in-the-middle-of-the-road sobriety test. It was hard to flip the switch, to go from a lowly beast of burden to high *Homo sapiens* with compass and map. I reached for my army water bottle and drained it as I surveyed the howling wastes. The wind across the bottle made a plaintive note like a solitary pan-pipe. I told myself: *Man up! This is what it's all about. Me, alone, a man against the elements. I would strike out on my own course!*

I didn't believe a word of my own bullshit either. And luckily, in the spinning mists, I saw someone else far ahead. So I followed him.

SAS Selection involves marching and running in order to beat the clock: march up hills, jog along flats and run downhill. Along that stretch of moor, I jogged, or rather, I developed this swinging waddle which propelled my legs forward and my rifle from side to side while also stopping my Bergen from trying to rape me. And a rhythm came to me, sloshing through the peat-mud, sheep tracks, sheep shit, stream beds and around peat hag and rock crag. You do this alone. There was no one there shouting instructions, encouragement or abuse. It's just you and your self.

At the checkpoint (CP) there was a low, olive-green tent in the lee of a grass-tufted cairn, outside a DS with his hands in his pockets. At his feet was a recruit on one knee, rifle resting across his forward foot and using both hands with map and compass. To the uninitiated it might have looked like a lazy benediction, or an extreme Welsh dogging site. But the scene was standard: we had been taught to drop to one knee when stationary because it made us half the target. *Stay low, move fast.* And the rifle on one foot was a way of ensuring it was always within reach.

I ran in close to the tent and dropped to a knee, waiting to be called forward. Beside the tent were a few recruits who had given up due to injury or some other failing. One sat on his Bergen with his boots off, nursing blisters; two others were in their sleeping bags trying to keep warm, alone with their thoughts. I buttoned up my pockets and tucked a few things in, wiped my nose, rehearsed my lines, trying to look the part; *Every day it's the Oscars, mate.* The DS waved me in. I gave my name and number. He gave me a fresh set of coordinates. I showed him on the map, and he seemed happy: 'Well, fuck off then.' So I did. And, leaving that first check point, I felt pretty fine about the world.

SELECTION

I passed that march. Not first, but not last either. As I sat there waiting by the truck I put on some warm kit and had a protein drink. I thought ... nothing, and it was refreshing. I liked the simplicity of the challenge. I had pushed myself more physically than I had ever done before. There was a cleanness, a neatness to that.

* * *

On those bleak and ancient mountains, I began a relationship with pain. It was as real as any other person on the course. I had met pain before in life—an ouchy here, some heartbreak there—but only in passing. It was to be avoided or escaped. I'd never had to spend any time with it.

There were no hip straps on the Bergen; my shoulders took all the weight. The straps cut into my trapezius muscles. It shook my ribcage on the trot, crunched vertebrae. It rubbed the skin of my back raw. Then the pain joined all the other laments of sinew and lungs, burning legs and blisters, wet and cold, to become a stuttering snapshot of my nervous system: a walking, talking, moaning, whining thing of itself.

So I did what I normally do when faced with any relationship: I tried to ignore it. Then I tried to suppress it. Neither worked.

Pain danced between brain structures: it could howl with pure animal keening and I would try to reason with it and console it; or it would speak clearly and with perfect logic, 'This is madness, let's go home now.' Pain was clever like that: mutable, chimerical, passive-aggressive, a fucking bitch; it was me. And I would switch between being horse and rider, mutt and master, shrew and monkey, until I was chasing my tail. Trying to pull myself together was like captaining Noah's Ark in a storm.

* * *

On the next few marches the navigation was far trickier. No easy Check Points, and no one to follow either.

What makes SAS Selection so revolutionary is that you do it alone. Almost all other Special Forces in the world do their tests as teams. The SAS is a cult of individuals. It demands all the insane levels of fitness, endurance and aggression, but it also wants you to be able to think for yourself, by yourself. The ability to navigate is a rite of passage. It is more than a skill; it is a metaphor. The map is a sacred text; you are never allowed to mark a map, but you must be able to recite eight-figure coordinates like Psalms.

The map was a 1:50,000 Ordnance Survey folded down into a relevant square for the march that neatly fitted into a waterproof map-case and into the right cargo pocket of my issue trousers. The compass was military: divided into 6400 Mils as opposed to 360 Degrees. I had treated myself to a pair of Danner Goretex boots, two sets of socks, one pair very thin and the other thick, to slow the blisters.

Speed = distance over time.

A simple equation from which all manner of personal chaos could erupt.

On nearly all routes it was not enough to follow a compass bearing straight to the next checkpoint. If I had, it might have taken me down into valleys, across bad ground or over other features that would lose me valuable time. So instead, I had to hold the bearing loosely and skirt the obstacles, trying to neither lose nor gain too much altitude. These were the factors I had to bear in mind as I ran along.

All of this would require careful thought on a fine day, when features on the map are visible as landmarks to the eye, but such days are rare on Selection. Much of it is done in hill-fog or at night. Measuring distance was a bitch. In the clag, wind, rain and exhaustion it was very hard to know how far I had come along a given bearing, and thus where I might be. The DS showed us tricks to measure distance: a pocketful of pebbles to count paces or a piece of paracord with plastic worry-beads to thumb progress. And in my head I drew up tables for S equals D over T, counting paces in different conditions, with columns for gradients up and down, and level, across broken ground and sheep trails, bogs and forest with further calculations for weight, day, night, fog.

I measured time on a military watch and began to understand it as the perfect tool it was. The rotating bezel on the wristwatch was invented by early airmen and divers who had to mark time against fear. It allowed pilots flying on a cold night by the stars to count off minutes along a course and reserves of fuel, and to calculate the point of no return, or frogmen to count down to zero oxygen at depth. A rotating bezel is a personal marker on time, a true point amidst the adrenaline, fatigue and pain that cloud memory. Time warps in the Hills. Legitimate time is undermined by your bastard senses: pain-time, uphill-time, nighttime; it plodded when I did, almost froze on some ascents, and haemorrhaged when I took a wrong turn.

At each CP I'd repeat the same drill: name and number; absorb an eight-figure grid reference which I'd point to on the map; then take a compass bearing and rotate the watch bezel to match the minute-hand. Then off. I loved the bezel's ratcheting sound of perfect functionality. To this day I mark time between when I last had to use it (Syria, three months ago). To me, it is the sound of time lived well.

* * *

We had to do the marches solo—that was the rule—but sometimes nature threw us together and the company was welcome. In this case it may have saved me. I'd fallen in step with Rob above the Talybont Reservoir in the early evening gloom after a long day of rain and hail. It was on a bald slab of hill between two forestry blocks. The light was dropping fast as another storm came in and the sky looked sick with a jaundiced light. We picked up our pace as the rain scythed in, impacting on the grit in muddy eruptions, as we made for the treeline.

We tabbed through the dark forest, down a bit of track that had turned into a violent, muddy creek which, in the head-torch glare, looked like strong cold tea. The wind roared through the woods, shaking the treetops with an occasional crack of snapping branches. There were a couple of recruits here and there lying prone with medics in attendance; one guy was hunched over, sobbing, clutching a photo of his girlfriend, which was cinematic but impractical. Instead, in the half-light forest murk, each scene lit by head-torches along the stream, it looked like a botched wildlife migration caught on film.

Hypothermia is a bewitching condition that robs the sufferer of the rationality to self-diagnose; in the driving rain and wind-chill it almost feels like a kind of warmth, a narcotic coddling of the senses.

Its symptoms are the *umbles*: mumbles, grumbles, fumbles, stumbles and tumbles. That could describe any number of recruits on a warm day at home; or most of us after a night out in Hereford. I had already seen a few cases on the Hills, but you could never be sure of a diagnosis until it was almost too late. Slowly, though, I had come to recognise the telltale signs of irrationality, slurred speech and lack of coordination. I also noticed that sufferers tended to show a maudlin whimsy, akin to the sentimentality of drunks, when hypothermia set it. It took a number of people to collapse in front of me before I realised this was a neurological element of the condition and not just a pre-existing character defect.

I felt good—too good, and maybe that was the tell. At the same time, it felt like someone was walking through the corridors of my mind and switching off the lights—thunk, thunk, thunk—down east wing and west, towards my core. (That's probably a bit grandiose—on a great day my mind is a one-room shack.) I was piss-wet through and quite chatty—which isn't much like me. Rob could tell I wasn't right.

'Let's take a break,' he suggested. We found an old conifer which kept some of the rain off, and I sat down. The shivers came in squalls. He got my warm kit out of my Bergen, made me strip down and handed me dry and insulating clothes. He then pulled two cigarettes out of his pack. I thought I deserved one of them. I hugged myself warm, rocking back and forth, gathering my thoughts. Only when my senses returned did I realise how far gone I'd been. A cigarette has never tasted so good.

* * *

One morning, up in the mountains, the wind hit so hard that it drove the water uphill and everyone lost their balance. Part of it was the strength of the gale, but it was also the sheer disorientation of seeing water move up, like nature itself had lost the plot.

And on that march, we all fell over each other, again and again, and some of us found it funny and others had a sense-of-humour failure. Either way, it was surreal: trying to get up through that final notch of valley where the stream fell from the earth in a waterfall that shot upwards in a rooster tail of spray and was carried away across a vast saddle of blasted peat that led to a track-junction somewhere. It looked like the moor had been set on fire, and I couldn't see the ground for the cloud that streamed past my feet. Men staggered about, and only the peat hags stood resolute as rocks in a milk-white torrent, a vaporous slipstream.

The weather picked some men off and not others. I could feel the wind, cold and exhaustion get inside us. It was one thing to acknowledge how I had felt to myself or to another recruit, but it was dangerous to feed the feelings with too much attention. Those that did saw their emotions bloom into a chorus of doubt, despair and narcissistic rage, robbing them of all reason. This was different from the resigned self-pity of hypothermia; there was more energy, more drama. The very men I had been so sure were going to pass—our stars—were the most vulnerable. They drowned, flailing in inch-deep puddles of their own emotion; hysterics and histrionics in a peaty *Sturm und Drang* before an audience of bored Welsh sheep.

The language of the Hills reflected this. If a march got to you, it was fine to say it was 'a bit emotional' or 'a bit dramatic', even 'intense'. But you could never say the weather was 'bad' on Selection, in case Pikey Lee was listening. It would send him into a rage, and that was far more terrifying than anything the Fan had to offer. That Pikey Lee existed at all was scary enough.

Here is a brief history of Pikey Lee: He is from a settled element of the traditionally itinerant, Irish community. His surname means 'wanderer' in Gaelic. Age twelve, his step-dad took him out of school to rob houses and poach deer. At fourteen, he started to fight for a Traveller's boxing club, and was so lethal that in a few years he was running the door security of the club during big nights. He has more words for criminality, villainy and violence than the Eskimos have for snow. At sixteen, he became a groundsman for an Oxford professor and read his way through the man's library. At eighteen, he met his fiancée, Jessica, who was the country's highest-earning stripper. She paid for him to go back to college, where he finished with a master's degree. Then she hung up her clear heels and told him it was his turn to earn. Jessica was the only thing on earth that Pikey Lee was terrified of. Apart from wasps.

Early on in Selection, during a quiet moment, when we were cleaning weapons, I asked him why he got so angry about 'bad weather'.

'It's the pathetic fallacy, you twat.'

I looked at him blankly. He stopped cleaning his weapon and stared back. He was smiling, which only set me more on edge.

'Poets putting emotions into nature?' I said. He looked at me like he was about to flip again. 'Wandering lonely as a cloud? Wordsworth?' I mumbled. Why was I having this conversation?

'What a jumped-up, whiny cunt,' he half shouted.

'Yeah,' I said, because what else do you do with an armed Pikey raging about long-dead, flower-snorting poets but agree with him? Or was he talking about me? In which case ... my answer would probably still be the same.

It wasn't that Lee hated the Pathetic Fallacy. He hated the ego that it involved. Lee taught me the value of humility. The secret of the Hills? They just *are*.

This is what he told me: 'You have to be big-headed to take the elements personally: the mountain isn't trying to kill you, the fog isn't bad, the wind isn't in your face, the rain isn't getting you wet and time is definitely not against you. To imagine so is to collaborate in your own failure.'

His head was perfectly round, with a buzz-cut. He looked like a very happy—but slightly psychotic—emoticon. Especially if that emoticon had been stealing apples as a child—which is in no way a racially stereotypical activity for emoticons—and had accidentally eaten a wasp.

'The Hills don't give a fuck about who you are. Or your feelings. That's *your* baggage. You're already carrying all this kit, why carry more? Take ego out of it.'

Humility to Lee wasn't an optional trait but a perfectly functional survival mechanism. Staying humble was staying low—one

knee on the ground—to avoid making himself a target to whatever outer gods or inner demons might have him in their sights.
If you took yourself too seriously you were likely to star in a
drama of your own creation—which is called a tragedy. Those
with a bit of humility saw the comedy. To Lee it was a choice.

I suspect Lee could have chosen any number of phrases other
than 'pathetic fallacy' to make his point, but it was his way of
putting me in my place. Which I needed. He was enjoying it.

'You didn't think you'd hear big words in the military, did
you?' he said.

I'd heard the odd, polished phrase—but then they polish
everything, don't they?

'I bet you had plenty of practice with lots of little words first,'
I told him.

* * *

I did OK on those early marches, but they were a struggle. One
morning, when I was last in the line-up and watching the sky
brighten to the east, I fell in conversation with an old regular. I
can't remember what we chatted about; he had a classic VW
Campervan, which I admired, and there was something of the
well-built surfer about him. When my number was called, he nodded up at the Fan and said six words that changed everything:

'Lad, just try to enjoy it.'

And that became my main effort: to have fun.

* * *

I fell in love with the Hills. The silence up there is profound, a
foundation for all the other senses, the bars upon which all the

other notation sits: clean mineral air, wind over the ridge, through the splintered maw of impossibly old rocks, rattling through the stalks of last season's flowers, dripping heather, ticking micro-percolations of peat, the babble of waters meeting in a nearby tannin-stained brook ... before: heartbeat darkly slapping your skin from within, gasping breaths upwards against the Bergen's downward weight, boots sloshing through mulch, the metronome swing of the rifle in both hands, squeak of straining straps, and smock thrumming like a pennant in a gale.

I felt free up there. The rocks, heather and heavens that draw some people up like a spiritual reverse of gravity, the narrative of the march, the easy metaphors that come with path, course, bearing; the quenching heights. I came back from each march with fewer problems than I'd started with. And the ones that did return with me seemed a little more manageable.

I came to appreciate the colours: the smudges of umber bracken, brown ink of peat, the pale apple-green grass in the depths of winter. The colours were more vivid for being hard-won, and I came to understand that this was the sweet spot—the charging rush of fight or flight—but also being calmly and rationally aware of the moment, as it dilated with wonder. This was adrenaline and life flashing before my eyes, but on 'record' rather than 'play'.

* * *

At the top of a mountain is a great place to talk about Peak Experiences. Abraham Maslow was one of the great psychological thinkers of the twentieth century. In the 1940s, he made a study of high achievers, trying to tease out why some people could achieve greatness, while others fell short. The highest states of human existence were self-actualisation, which he put on the top of his famous Hierarchy of Needs, and self-transcendence. Self-actualisation is the zone where a human realises, activates and acts upon their full potential. Maslow noted that all the people who reached the top were intrinsically motivated, and the steps towards this highest form of personal development were a series of Peak Experiences. He described them as those 'rare, exciting, oceanic, deeply moving, exhilarating, elevating experiences that generate an advanced form of perceiving reality'. And the characteristics of this reality include: 'truth, goodness, beauty, wholeness, aliveness, uniqueness, perfection, completion, justice, simplicity, richness, effortlessness, playfulness, self-sufficiency'.

He went on to add that a peak experience 'Is felt to be a highly valuable—even uniquely valuable experience, so great an experience that even an attempt to justify it takes away from its dignity and worth. As a matter of fact, so many people find this so great and high an experience that it justifies not only itself, but even living itself.'

At the same time as Maslow's study, a child named Mihaly Csikszentmihalyi was languishing in an Italian prison camp:

> I realised how few of the grown-ups that I knew were able to with-stand the tragedies the war visited upon them, how few of them had anything resembling a normal, contented, satisfied, happy life once their job, their home, and their security was destroyed by the war. So I became interested in understanding what contributed to a life that was worth living.

Whereas Maslow had interviewed the great and the good, Csikszentmihalyi set about talking to an astonishing array of ordinary people to work out what gave them happiness and ful-filment. He interviewed dozens of athletes, composers, surfers, artists, chefs, Navajo shepherds, elderly Korean women and Italian farmers. All of these people, from opposite sides of the world, described similar experiences to Maslow's peak experi-ences. They spoke of an inspired state of concentration and engagement, where 'everything comes together'. So many of his interviewees used the word 'flow' to describe the effortlessness, and the sense of being swept up by something greater, that he named these experiences 'flow states'. He listed nine ingredients for a flow-state: a balance of challenge and skill; a sense of action and awareness merging; definite targets; unambiguous feedback; concentration on the task; sense of control; loss of self-consciousness; time transformation; and, finally, autotelic experience. The key three precursors are definite target, feedback and the challenge/skill balance.

On the Hills I had a definite target: next checkpoint at a given time. I had feedback from my body, my watch and the environment. But it was only when my body and mind developed with the training that my skills began to match the challenge. Flow occurs when high skills meet tough challenges, at a sweet spot between arousal and control. And that was when the flow kicked in.

At its most basic form, flow feels like a Runner's High: that floating sensation past the pain threshold, when it's just runner and trail, and life glides past without notice or care. At a neurological level, flow begins when higher parts of the brain turn off and cruise on automatic. It is a beautiful moment: when Monkey throws the keys to Shrew and says, 'You drive'; conscious planning and reason give way to instinct and intuition. This is pretty easy to achieve for simple tasks, like when running hard along a road—left foot, right foot is a fairly easy process to switch to automatic—but it requires more practice and training for more complicated tasks, when more variables are to hand. That's the paradox of flow-states: the harder the task, the deeper the flow-state feels when it is finally achieved.

The flow on the Hills was deep. Way better than a Runner's High; better than most drug-highs too. The paradox of my experience was that everything that should have made my march harder eventually did the opposite. It felt like drawing a compound hunting bow: the effort wasn't linear; it started off hard, and the peak draw weight was a bitch, but on the other side was an easy stretch towards a point of effortlessness. On the Hills, all the obstacles brought me closer to a critical mass, where flow was easier to dip into: the heft of the pack gave me weightlessness, racing the clock gave me a sense of timelessness and the exhaustion quelled my mind. It was the very *extremeness* of what I was doing that gave me a deep spiritual peace. I was in love with the task but also aware of that love in the moment. It took months of painful training to reach a flow-state; the take-off point—the switch—happened when my ability began to match the challenge of the Hills. I got to know my skills so well that they became second-nature (Shrew-nature). I could automatise them too and enjoy the ride.

This all sounds mystical and druggy. Flow-states involve vast amounts of anandamide, endorphins, serotonin and dopamine. These performance-enhancing drugs flood your system when you are approaching mastery over a fight-or-flight situation. Flow feels like The Force; it's a bit trippy. I couldn't work out whether I was clutching a light-sabre or a bong. I felt an intimate and profound connection with the mountain, the rocks, the trees and the people who lived there in the past. It's not just flow; it's a rush. It felt generous, endless and benign. It felt like water flowing uphill.

* * *

My relationship with Pain developed. I no longer tried to ignore it or argue with it. Pain just wanted to be acknowledged. Like a lot of things that feel they need to be heard, Pain had very little to actually say, but about a thousand ways of saying it. Unlike any other relationship, Pain didn't expect a reply. All I had to do was listen, bear witness and neither resort to reason nor get emotional. The moment I heard its voice I'd follow it, embrace it and go through it. If I managed this, Pain gave me a free pass to do all sorts of wild things to my body. Pain was unsparing, and a bit twisted like that. Let's be honest—who are we kidding—it was only ever a matter of time: bestiality had broken out on Noah's Ark. I made all the other animals watch.

* * *

The SAS is the only Special Forces unit in the world that insists on a sense of humour. At first, I was sceptical. Funny how? Military humour is about as wacky as military art. 99.99% of situations in the average military day are repetitive, whereas situational comedy is only occasionally funny first time around. Military jokes are about rain, bad footwear or useless weaponry. I'd heard all of them from the other recruits within minutes of being issued my waterproofs, boots and basic-training rifle. The jokes are as standard-issue and well-worn as the kit, as predictable as a set of orders—catch-phrase humour with the safety-catch on. It's permitted, portioned, Pathé plucky; it's a brew-up, a knees-up or a sing-song; it is to genuine laughter what army rations are to home cooking or a forces sweetheart is to true love. Maybe better than nothing if you're waist high in water at the Evacuation of Dunkirk. Definitely worse than nothing if you're waist high in a Welsh Bog. (I bet it was fucking annoying at Dunkirk too.)

The SAS wants more. They demand wit.

Good humour can be described as socially warm and competent. Good for me, good for you; great to share. It is a character strength that helps buffer stress, lifts spirits and gains intimacy. Along with hope, gratitude and spirituality, it sits with a package of positive attributes labelled 'transcendence'.

Humour is also the difference between thinking and feeling, and one is a whole lot more operationally effective than the other. Walpole said: 'The world is a comedy to those that think;

a tragedy to those that feel.' *Wit* is the Old English word denoting the seat of knowledge. It shares its roots with the Sanskrit *veda* 'to know' and Latin *videre* 'to see'.

The phrase I heard the most during Selection was 'This is a thinking man's game'. There is no greater test for thinking on your feet than a battle of wits. Your ability to crack jokes says a lot about who you are. This is a matter of biology. Think back to Monkey-Shrew-Lizard stacked on top of each other. Laughter is almost exclusive to humans, occurring only in a few other primates. Humour is one of the supreme achievements of our species, a glittering crown on Monkey at the top of the totem-pole. And it is the first to go: to *lose your humour* or have a *sense of humour failure* are bywords for being overwhelmed by events. Maintaining a sense of humour through Selection was about keeping a cool head, reining in your emotions, marshalling your thoughts and retaining your crown.

At a basic level, humour is another test of navigation, but through a human landscape. It requires sophisticated social mapping, an ability to see patterns, connect dots, chart-shifting pack dynamics, circle or summit taboos and spot pitfalls. Using not just one map but simultaneous, multiple frames of reference to recognise incongruity—to see situations and people as they are and as they could be—and the path of humour between the two. You could even say it is about distance and timing: knowing when not to go too far, but getting in first with the quip.

One level up, humour is a lot like fighting. The SAS aren't just chasing chuckles. Wit involves a lot of dual-use cognitive processes that can be weaponised: rapid lateral thinking, targeting ambiguity, improvisation, adaptive thinking; the audacity to seize the moment, take power over the audience and deliver the knockout punchline. *Improvise, adapt and overcome.*

If you can tell a killer joke, imagine all the fun you will have with a gun?

SELECTION

The study of humour is still in its infancy, largely because scientists have long taken themselves far too seriously—almost as seriously as militaries. E.B. White once said, 'Humor can be dissected as a frog can, but the thing dies in the process and the innards are discouraging to any but the pure scientific mind.'

Researchers at Stanford University did just that, but with dead fish. Subjects were shown emotionally negative images: car accidents, corpses and dentists, etc., and then asked to make spontaneous jokes about the upsetting imagery with either positive or negative humour.

For example: in one photo, a bloodied man is gutting a fish at a processing plant. A positive joke was 'He always wanted to work with animals.' A negative, disparaging joke was 'Ideal workplace for people with body odour.'

Afterwards, the subjects were given an emotional test. Those who had made a quip showed more emotional resilience than those who didn't. And those who made a positive joke were more likely to feel better about themselves than those who had made a negative joke. The researchers believe that positive humour can affect a real reappraisal in the mind, whereas negative humour merely creates the illusion of distance from the image and not a new mental scenario. It is this ability to rapidly and constantly reframe that is so useful to Special Forces thinking.

Another follow-up study at Stanford also found that positive humour can change cognitive processing: bolstering creativity and improving cognitive flexibility. Being witty not only increases your emotional resilience to bad shit; it boosts your ability to think outside the box and gives you greater neuroplasticity to adapt to new challenges. Funny that.

SAS humour is almost exclusively positive. It is dark but uplifting. Often it is incredibly offensive. But that's the point of the SAS: they are airborne forces—death from above. They freefall through the burnt blues at the edge of space into darkened valleys far below and kill. It's the oldest story: a man goes on a journey and a stranger comes to town; high noon at midnight. That's not merely the ultimate offence; that's divine comedy.

The lads took the piss out of each other often; it was a form of sparring, a test of mettle. Being able to take a joke was hugely important and—generously—I was singled out for more practice than most. It was also a means of peer pressure-testing each other for any unwanted ego. I was surprised just how short-fused our resident psychopaths were when teased. Many of them were very funny with mimicry and mockery, but they were trying to leverage pack-popularity at another's expense. We could smell their weakness. When their turn came, it was quick.

It was brutal and bonding but positive. Acceptance is earning a nickname; mine was *Trousersnake*—not original, I know.

Above all, it was fun. And the SAS wants you to be funny because, after all, they are the good guys. It wasn't unusual to have to run up to a CP and deliver a joke, or to be honest when the DS asked what was the worst thing a girl had ever said to me in bed:

'Are you in yet?'

(I was).

Oh come on, I never said it was a python.

* * *

The Relentless Pursuit of Excellence had always struck me as a self-help koan. Excellence and I had never been close; one of those words that spell-check is for. But one day I'd stumbled across it through sheer laziness. Nothing makes me happier than doing nothing, the more, the better—to oblivion and beyond—and I had fallen in love with my sleeping bag. In army-speak it was called a 'maggot', but mine was such a lustrous green that it looked more like a caterpillar. It was a cocoon. That was my prize. At the end of every march I would climb into it and read

SELECTION

my book. The faster I tabbed, the more down time, it was as simple as that. Being able to visualise the goal only increased my drive; the resolve lightened my load.

I began to finish first. And got to do *nothing* more.

* * *

The Hills phase culminates in a test week, a series of daily marches over the Brecon Beacons, each one a little longer and more complicated than the last; and every time the weight in the Bergen gets greater. The last march is hideously long, the weight of the pack leg-buckling and the navigation incredibly tricky. I could show you the route on a map but it would barely represent the journey itself which felt like a pilgrimage into another realm. I'll leave you with some synonyms of endurance: tolerance, bearing, sufferance, fortitude, patience, stoicism, guts, grit, doggedness, resolution, stickability, determination and spunk. Feel free to add plenty of nouns: contours, peat, hail, rain and rocks.

I passed. I didn't feel like I had won, simply that others had failed. Nor did I feel particularly tough or any of those other clever words. I was just myself and happy with that *It's a good day to be me* feeling. There were very few people left to share my thoughts with.

4

FULL-AUTO SATORI

If you know the Way broadly, you will see it in all things.

Miyamoto Musashi

The next stage of SAS training is so secret that no one has ever been allowed to describe it in detail. This is one of those parts of the book I warned you about: I can't talk about it.

But please believe me when I tell you this: all those closely guarded secrets—the tactics, weapons and kit—are the least interesting parts of the process. What is far more fascinating— and maybe useful to you—is the neuroscience of Special Forces training and that sublime moment when we take everything we've covered so far—fight-or-flight, flow states, peak experiences, altered states, fistfuls of delicious neurotransmitters—and use them to transform ourselves into something better.

In order to understand Special Forces training better, let's have a look at what it isn't:

Any other form of learning involves brain changes. Brains are designed to restructure themselves to develop. The more funda- mental a lesson is to our survival the easier and faster the information will be absorbed. We are rewriting parts of the neural circuitry to perform basic missions; we are burning simple programs or habits. The fiery ink of this script is dopamine—the stuff of desire. The more dopamine, the more accelerated the learning.

The antithesis of desire is boredom. Regular militaries are masters of boredom: classroom, drill-square, power-point, dull and endless repetition. Take weapons training: a basic recruit will do countless rifle drills—stripping, cleaning, assembling, bayonet practice and marching—before being allowed to fire a few bullets at distant targets on a bare, featureless range. It takes an eternity to etch a new pattern into a bored mind, but that's OK, because mundane classroom-based, drill-square repetition is very cheap. Most traditional militaries love spending money on hardware (guns and tanks) but hate spending it on software within their men.

This has been very effective in the past for traditional warfare—march, shoot, reload. It's great for producing large volumes of men who can do simple tasks. But this form of learning can't be upscaled to burn the many and complicated programs required for a Special Forces soldier to operate. 'Skills fade', that entropy of good habits, will have its way. A different form of learning is necessary.

Special Forces training is about creating fight-or-flight levels of excitement that induce an accelerated deep-learning. It uses metamorphic flow-state to create a paradigm shift. The more authentic (AKA near-death or simulated near-death) the training, the more the brain takes in the information, because nothing accelerates learning better than when existence is at stake. The training we went through allowed us to leap-frog conventional learning and acquire these new skills far faster than ordinary methods.

The opposite of etching a pattern onto a bored mind in a classroom is hyper-real scenarios with lots of explosions, kill-houses, and insane expenditure of ammunition. Nothing gets the dopamine flowing like going full-auto.

The more realistic the training scenarios, the more fear is generated. Death is a great motivator. Fear is key because it provokes desire, the ultimate desire: the desire to survive. Desire is dopamine. Dopamine is the key to neuroplasticity. Realism is the forge that makes the brain more malleable, burning programs is the same as forging habits.

The realism to heat this forge is eye-wateringly expensive. The average cost of basic soldier training is $50,000. The cost of training a Special Forces soldier to Navy Seal, Delta or SAS level is $5 million.

* * *

Let's put this theory into practice and see how it feels to undergo this transformation. In order to squeeze this section past the censors but still keep it vaguely military we're going to look at a basic infantry tactic—Fire and Movement. It is as simple as it sounds: shooting lots and running fast. Anytime your comrades are shooting, you are moving and vice-versa. It can be used to attack and also to withdraw. The bullets keep the enemy's heads down while you get closer to them or as you run away. Think of it as the 'stick and move' of boxing. Fire and movement is as old as gunpowder. Hell, it's probably older than that, dating back to the bows and arrows era when rival bands of hunters encountered each other on a trail, deep in the woods.

And 'deep in the woods' is where we will set this scenario:

Another fine morning in Valhalla. We stood in the dappled half-light of the forest in a wide semi-circle. In the middle was an instructor, who radiated menace and mirth equally. He was a black man, and like every Geordie, insisted on wearing a T-shirt irrespective of the conditions.

'You will patrol in four-to-six-man teams going down that trail.' He stabbed his finger down a path. On the right side was open forest, on the left was an endless thorn thicket wrapped in vines. It didn't take a military genius to see what was going to happen.

Yours truly and five others patrolled down the track. Even though I knew what was about to happen, I could feel the adrenaline thermometer begin to climb.

I'm not going to bore you with the details, but a target popped up on our right and we all emptied our magazines (blanks) and then teamed up to retreat in bounds away from it—to our left— and into the thorn bushes. All military exercises have a narrative arc, and this prickly clusterfuck had been placed in our way to see what we'd do. We went to shit.

This was a very long way from fighting terrorists. We were battling spiky trees. And we were losing. To start with: the thorns hurt, though not massively. Each one sent a righteous signal of pain that added to the sensory overload. Then there was all the noise of gunfire, which yawed in the peaks and troughs of adrenaline. There were plenty of explosions and smoke grenades and instructors screaming voice-of-god commandments from the 'burning bush'. My weapon had chosen that precise moment to malfunction—but of course, the weapon was fine; it was simply my brain jamming. Lastly, there was lots of shouting from comrades to synchronise the complicated, interlocking partnerships of fire-and-movement.

On the whole, I was more special needs than Special Forces. Just between you and me? These skills had never been on my wish list—I had never really foreseen them as part of my life's rich story—and I couldn't have given a fuck which was the correct tactic. It all looked like folk-dancing in a forest fire. But I was surrounded by people who cared deeply about the craft. I'd come to like—even respect—a few of them, and it's easy to get carried along by pack-enthusiasm.

Why was I so bad at it? The few recruits who were very good all had lots of previous military experience, but that didn't explain it. It wasn't a special military bush. To me, it was a hideously interconnected thicket of brambles, neural circuitry, personal doubts, thorns, misfiring neurones and fused weaponry. There was a way, but I couldn't see it, and that was a source of frustration. To the instructors, I was a source of amusement: I made very tough army men cry ... with laughter.

What it boiled down to was aggression and brains, which is very different from the endurance and brains of the Hills. Most men can be made into raging savages; that's the easy bit. The question here was whether the recruit could control the process. Could he go into full-fight beast mode and still retain the fine motor skills to send rounds down with incredible accuracy and also coordinate with teammates. Also, how fast was the switching: on and—just as importantly—off again.

Much of this depends on where the aggression came from. Some men simply didn't have any at all, and were binned. Others juiced themselves up on some hidden reserves of personal anger and tore through the obstacles with ease, but then they just kept charging, or were so blinded by the red mist that they had lost any sense of situational awareness. The latter is a term that only the military could come up with: 'awareness' comes from the Saxon word for consciousness. The military wants its soldiers to be conscious of their surroundings: to absorb information accurately, assess it rationally, and respond appropriately. This doesn't sound like a big ask until you've been around people completely losing their shit.

Back then, I had thought anger would be the fuel of choice: most of the bar or street fights I'd been in, or around, had been rage-driven. But that was amateur thinking. Anger is an unstable fuel, hard to store safely; it burns too quickly, bleaches the senses and is too corrosive in the long-term. Above all, no one wants to be in its company for long.

This was professional violence. The instructors were looking for aggression, as a thing in itself, wielded as a tool. Anger was emotion. Pure aggression wasn't personal; it was just business.

We did that drill endlessly, but I was still popping fuses. I tried to match the speed of the drills—or go even faster, trying to get ahead to allow myself some time to think—yet it was always the same: disintegrating fine motor skills and fumbled magazine changes; forgetting entire elements of the drill; and either seeing everything speeded up too fast to react to, or so treacle slow that I was making long-distance calls to my limbs.

My moment of clarity came during pistol drills: quick-draw from a concealed carry position, a pancake holster over rear right hip, either to shoot or smash someone's face in, or both. Basic Gun-Fu. And I was a mess at that too, until a friend said the magic words: 'Slow is smooth and smooth is fast'. It unlocked the mental spasm. Taking my time allowed everything to come together. Previously, I had felt like the kid in a Far Side cartoon desperately straining to push open the front door of Midvale School for the Gifted. The door marked 'Pull'. Afterwards, I could relax into the fight. Which was good timing, because we moved up to live-fire drills.

* * *

When I started basic weapons training, my mind had resembled the thorn-bush: an unholy thicket of abstract drills, weapon designs, hand signals, military jargon and penis jokes. Dopamine hacked a pathway through this neural jungle and gave the desire to go down it; adrenaline gave me the strength to do so. It was less about the physics of going through the bush than about the belief that I could do so. Neural pathway and real trackway converged. It takes a mind to create a path and repetition to maintain it. As the nature writer Robert Macfarlane wrote, 'Paths are the habits of a landscape'. The way had opened before me.

It was the most counterintuitive head-fucky wormhole imaginable: slowing down was speeding up. To stay cool I had to embrace the chaos. Pain was the guide. Adversity was my friend, hardship the path. I didn't have to be superman, I just had to be myself—in a flow-state.

Reaching a flow-state on the Hills was one thing, but achieving it in something as fiendishly complicated as a live-fire weapons drill was another level of complexity again. I had to learn fast to get my skills to match the challenge of the weapons: the split-second timing, the interlocked teamwork. That type of learning required vast amounts of fight-or-flight neurochemistry to make my mind malleable, and lots of repetition to hammer out new habits. Luckily for me, my mind wasn't just neuroplastic; in all the excitement, it was neuro-jelly. Once I had got into the groove, the flow was sweet.

* * *

Dr Arne Dietrich suggested a neurobiological explanation for flow-states with his theory of Transient Hypofrontality. Transient means temporary, hypo means 'less than' and frontally refers to our Prefrontal Cortex. Dietrich's theory is that in physical activities the brain down-regulates the Prefrontal Cortex to put its resources towards accomplishing the goal or task. This is very similar to the separation of Monkey and Shrew systems in a fight-or-flight response: in Transient Hyperfrontality there are time distortions (our old friend tachypsyche), disinhibition from social constraints, reduction in ability to feel pain and increased feelings of floating, peacefulness, effortlessness and living in the here and now.

The difference between pulling a full-blown whitey in a fight-or-flight response and surfing the flow comes through training. In the beginning I was fusing out—not insane panic, but way too much emotion to accomplish the task at hand. The training helped condition me to the bangs and shouts and let me dial them out. Eventually I had some editing skills to my senses: I could ignore the pain, befriend the slo-mo, and focus all my attention and desire on murdering the target and coordinating with my colleagues. Each repetition of a given drill etched the program or habit deeper. We began to flow together. Flow is all the best bits of fight or flight without being carried off by the fear. Flow is being cool.

The key to learning is dopamine and the reward pathway. The reward pathway is a piece of neural architecture conjoining Shrew and Monkey, a sliver of synaptic connections like a leash between the two. The greater the reward—survival, a sandy-coloured beret, a beautiful girl—the greater the amount of dopamine and the deeper the lesson is learned. Dopamine is the neurotransmitter of desire. It focuses the mind on goals, creating a tunnel of attention, and gives us the emotional urgency to head down it. But here is the kicker: each time dopamine is used it subtly rewires the synaptic connections. It hacks a path through the neural jungle at the expense of other possible routes. Where these paths take you decides whether these are good habits or bad habits—dopamine doesn't care either way. Employed wisely, it is a force for good, but the leash works both ways, as anyone who has fallen madly in love can testify. Our brains are not hard-wired; rather they are a teeming world of synaptic colonies vying and allying with each other for connections. Neurons that fire together wire together. Dopamine tips the balance in favour of one circuit over another.

Dopamine's role in training is two-fold: it focuses our attention on the goal and it reduces background noise in neural networks. This allows us to recognise new patterns. When a new pattern is learned the dopamine pump in the mid-brain paints the shape of this pattern, a configuration of circuitry within the brain. The pattern is not learned as a series of points but as a whole or, to borrow a term from cognitive psychology, as a 'chunk'. Every time that pattern is repeated there is an additional hit of dopamine which strengthens the neural configuration along that particular route—each repetition will be faster than the last. This is the core of all learning but in high-risk situations, where motivation is the desire to survive, that learning becomes vastly accelerated. What started as an intention rapidly turned into a behaviour, then a practice, a habit, second nature, until it was who I was.

This ability to bundle and automate packets of training is hugely important in flow-states, as, during Transient Hypofrontality, when the PFC goes increasingly offline—Monkey powers down and Shrew powers up—we begin to lose decision-making ability and memory recall. Not what you want in wannabe ninjas, but training can override this. With enough repetition and desire, I began to lay down some chunks: magazine changes, grenades, fire and movement. I knew my way around different weapons systems. I could sense what my colleagues were doing around me. I could feel what was coming next ... and I didn't fear it.

Some of my colleagues referred to this as 'muscle memory', but what we were really doing was forming habits. Fight or flight, flow-states: in essence a witches' cauldron of neuroplasticity designed to carve habits deep. So deep they can survive anything the enemy or the environment can throw at you. Dopamine is the key to habits. We were training instinctual parts of the brain beneath consciousness. If Selection was about taming the Shrew, this stage was about training the Shrew. Acquiring chunks is about training your inner beast, consequently it takes roughly the same amount of time as teaching a dog to fetch or—in our case—a Shrew to shoot.

On top of the basic chunks—the raw moves—we learned SOPs, or Standard Operating Procedures. These were habits-to-handrail, or quick-reference 'recipes for disaster' that covered most of the 'what ifs' of creating mayhem. The recruits who really thrived were those who could get a good flow going but switch back to higher critical thinking if necessary and dance between these two states.

At the same time as dopamine worked its magic, my body was pumping itself with the other good stuff: oxytocin, serotonin, anandamide and endorphins. I felt like I was high on their effects but sharpened rather than dulled by them. Flow was Asterix's Potion with endless refills: the more problems thrown at me, the bigger the cocktail I was served. Pain, complexity, risk, danger, they all added to the flow. I drunk deeply. Sometimes flow almost felt like it was sentient, like it was trying to help me.

In the midst of all that gunfire I did feel an inner peace. Well, why not? Only amateurs have to feel murderous to murder. After a while, I began to feel quite Zen squeezing the trigger. I suspect it has always been thus: it was only a few whiny survivors who said the Beserkers had 'Rage'. It could have been quite dreamy hacking a swathe through a bunch of bleating monks.

* * *

As Miyamoto Musashi wrote, 'If you know the Way broadly, you will see it in all things.' Musashi was a wandering samurai, or Ronin, who killed sixty men in duels and then retired to a cave to write the 'Book of Five Rings' and 'The Path of Aloneness'. He also became a sublime painter and poet. I'm not comparing myself to an ancient warrior—I was just a heavily armed try-hard with a passion for caves—but I fell in love with that sentence. Please remember those words; they will explain how I got to a very dark place later in this book.

The moment the training took hold of me was a gentle revelation that was so accelerated and so deep that it had me converted before I noticed it. I got it. Or rather, it got me. That was the looking-glass nature of flow, and of the fast-track nature of the reward pathway. It was utterly transformative, on the other side I couldn't understand how I'd never seen it before.

What did 'the Way' mean back then? It was a path through that horrible spiky bush. The thorns no longer hurt. I could hear my comrades clearly over the din of gunfire. Mag changes were smooth. Brass casings glinted in mid-air. I could move quickly through the slow-motion. What I'm trying to tell you—despite all the rules of secrecy surrounding SAS training—is that I looked fucking awesome.

The relentless pursuit of excellence is about cutting a trail through the most unforgiving jungle of your mind and treading that path daily. The hidden joy of it was the feedback loop: the more relentlessly I pursued excellence—and the more motivated the repetition—the easier it became. Once I had that virtuous circle spinning, the less effort I had to put in to keep it at speed. Past the suck, on the other side of the pain, at the eye of the shit-storm was a calm, self-perpetuating eddy that held me close.

This attitude spread to other elements of my boy-scouting. I enjoyed their interlocking nature, like a gyroscope had been set spinning in my mind. My perspective narrowed. I grew more alert to problems that could be fixed, and hardened to those that couldn't. The goal of finishing telescoped before me, and peripheralised anything that didn't serve my cause. There was a self-guiding nature to good habits—a feeling of a well-trodden path, the groove of it, a glorious tunnel of attention.

* * *

Let's take a pause from training and look at the final precepts: classlessness and self-discipline. The SAS has to be classless because it is functional. It operates as a ruthless meritocracy that is designed to do one thing: win. It is an elite based on natural order. It is open to everyone, and has no regard for race, creed, gender, background or personal choices. I mean zero: a glittering, perfect indifference.

It's 'Who Dares Wins', and they start with the 'Who'. SAS Selection asks 'Who are you', again and again, increasing the pressure with every answer, stripping recruits down to their bare selves. Most of us, even on a good day, are a small bit of self carried by a web of associations—the ties that bind—and Selection cuts those puppet strings one by one: family, school, team and tribe; lies, conceits, received wisdoms and unexamined traditions. Who are you?

Class makes you think you're better than your fellow man. At the heart of snobbery is a compensatory narcissism. The joke is on the believer. There was a gap between their imagined order and the natural order. Selection targeted that ambiguity. Ditto for any other notions about race or nation.

Did I laugh? No, it was painful to watch. When that realisation came—that the engine of their self-belief was a pack of lies—it was like a kick in the nuts; they folded. One guy from an entitled background had fallen for all the 'natural leadership' schtick that his parents and school had taught him, and was genuinely shocked when the others didn't respect his super-power. Another man was a working-class hero to himself: he thought his hard-knock life made him tougher. It didn't. Ditto for another who was always 'keeping it real'. A fourth thought his Kung-fu black-belt made him a big man, and the less said about that the better. These were all decent men; I'd be happy to have a drink with them tonight. They probably have far fewer flaws than I do, but the flaws they did have were making them miss the mark. The SAS just wants to know if your vision of yourself matches your capabilities. It wasn't personal; it was as practical as aligning a scope with a rifle.

Many recruits fervently believed that the SAS had the power to change them into something they weren't already. But all of those questing for a metamorphosis were doomed to fail. It's a winged dagger, not a wand. A similar trap waited for those who sought to test themselves: the very desire revealed something lacking. Both groups mystified and intensified the process until they choked out on meaning.

SAS Selection isn't about whether you are tough enough. It is about whether you are true to your word. Did word equal action. Did who you were match what you were? And were those words written through you like in a stick of rock candy. To find out, they break you. Can you put yourself back together again and keep going? Is your default setting negative or positive?

But it is you who has to do it. That requires vast reserves of self-discipline. It's not like other militaries, where they break you in order to remake you as some perfect soldier. The SAS is arrogant but not that arrogant. Instead they hold to a radical belief in their fellow man: the perfect soldier already exists as an ordinary man capable of doing extraordinary things. Selection is trying to work out which man to give the gun to. The SAS is simply the collective noun for such men.

* * *

Sebastian was as close to a 'perfect soldier' as anyone I have ever met, and yet he lacked self. He was also very kind and helpful towards me, although much more so when the DS were around. Sebastian was the golden boy, the polished product of public school and military. He saw the world in code. He was a subscriber to the system—'Lawful Evil'. He eroticised authority. He had a plan for everything. Psychologists will tell you it's due to severe potty-training and, perhaps this was true in his case, for he looked down on chaos the way some people viewed germs. Through some event, agency or person in his past, Sebastian had come to believe that he was only truly good if he was tidy; or was only excellent if he followed all the rules. Sebastian thrived on rules, and often mistook them for morality. Perhaps it had been a huge success at school and in his previous regiment, but there was also a sense that something was lacking beneath that charm. Rules and codes are useful, the scaffolding and supports that we can grow and train character on, but at some point you've got to let that character stand on its own. Sebastian was all scaffolding, all façade. He reminded me of Hervey Cleckley's words in *The Mask of Sanity*: 'something that suggests a subtly constructed reflex machine'.

Rob Paulson hated him.

Rob was pure chaos. I viewed Rob as a germ too, but more like gonorrhoea: a liability, a badge of dishonour but lots of fun too. Rob was a walking ASBO, a menace to sobriety.

Over the months, I had gotten to know Rob better. Or rather, I had come to understand that there was a lot to know about Rob, and that it was going to take time and, even then, many questions might remain unanswered. He was a largely closed system, but his eyes would flicker open dreamily if pain was mentioned. He drew energy from it. He ate pressure too. I once saw him touch himself after he threw a grenade and waited for the explosion. I don't know if he did that because he didn't think anyone was watching, or because he knew that I was watching; you could never tell with Rob. I knew that he supported Arsenal Football Club (from the tattoos), and that he thought the new army rations were better than the food he'd had in many prisons, but I didn't know which prisons or what he'd served time for— yet. Rob had other tattoos: a 'Fortune Favours the Brave', and a full sleeve from Thailand.

I don't have any tattoos, mottos or a football club. I would like to pretend that this rugged individuality is innate, but it came from a long childhood where I was last to be picked for any sports team, and this sullen hatred from the sidelines had grown to include all flags, colours and teams. I had experimented with various ideologies, bands and brands as a teenager, but after numerous posters the Blu Tack gave up. (That's a metaphor.) I still harboured a deep urge to get a tattoo, but had never come across the right symbols or the wrong girl, and doubted I ever would.

Sebastian had an 'Honi Soit Qui Mal y Pense' tattoo. It's the motto of several regiments, the Royal Family and the Order of the Garter. In Old French that means 'Shame on him who thinks bad of it', but in Modern French it is used ironically to imply hidden agendas. Its origins come from a chivalric snore-fest myth involving Edward III putting on a lady's garter—his son's betrothed—at a dance because she'd had a medieval wardrobe malfunction. The whole thing is double-barbed to imply you'd be an unpatriotic rotter if you think this story is a completely unlikely clusterfuck.

Rob looked thoughtful. 'I would have done the same,' he said.

I waited. After Pikey Lee's bollocking on the Pathetic Fallacy, I was fully prepared to believe that Rob might be hiding a secret passion for Plantagenet history.

'Well, it's the type of story you'd make up the next day, isn't it, with a really bad hangover, if you'd been caught finger-banging your daughter-in-law on the dancefloor?'

Rob had his own mask of sanity. He used it around authority. He was a human mimicking a robot. There was absolutely nothing you could fault in his acting—it was Oscar-winning. You could get the most snarling, anal, drill-bashing sergeant or a team of clinical psychologists with clipboards and Rob would score perfectly. Yet there would be something so unsettling in the performance that everyone would be left in no doubt that the whole charade depended on Rob's mood, which was constantly being fought over in his head, like a dildo at a clown orgy. He freaked Sebastian out.

Rob hadn't read Cleckley's book. But he had watched *Blade Runner* far too many times. He knew the script by heart, and would only speak to Sebastian to ask him Voight-Kampff test questions—designed to unmask robots—from the film. Rob always picked the most inopportune moments he could find: crawling through the mud into assault positions. In the near pitch-black, in the middle of Sebastian's carefully planned ambush, when everyone should be silent, Rob called out along the treeline: 'Sebastian, describe the good things that come into your mind about your mum.'

The last time I saw Sebastian, he was in the back of an army truck that was trundling off through the trees. He hadn't even bothered to say goodbye. I asked a DS what had happened. The man shrugged. 'Something he didn't have a plan for.'

* * *

Whether the Regiment is very British or a rejection of Britishness depends on your view of the country. It was founded by a Scotsman and perfected by an Irishman, and some of its early members were criminals, homosexuals—and even French. It has learnt more from its enemies than from its allies, and can appear wildly piratical in the way it steals tactics and adapts weapons systems. It doesn't do parades, forgets to salute and uses first name terms across the ranks. (There is a tradition that a trooper can call the PM by their first name.) It rejects hierarchies of class, race and gender in exchange for a ruthless meritocracy. It is a secretive elite that is open to anybody. Oh, and it wins.

* * *

After the five precepts, there is one last, unofficial one: 'The man is the Regiment and the Regiment is the man'. It is one of the most incredible acts of trust in the individual by any organisation I know. The Regiment operates outside of normal warfare, far beyond the front lines, often without support or communication. They are masters of chaos; they need dynamic rules. The super-secret playbook for an SAS trooper walking down an unknown street in a war-torn scrap of the Middle East? Precisely what he is doing. He is the embodiment of the rules, its values incarnate. He is the Regiment 'walking like a man'.

And that is kinda the point of it all. When they finally handed out the berets they gave them to the people who breathed these values.

What I loved most about the whole process was this: being tough simply wasn't good enough. Sure, all people who passed could rock the hard look, but more importantly, the qualities were really modesty, courage, social intelligence, self-control, open-mindedness, love of learning and humour. These weren't hazy abstracts but innate essentials that were the very keys to surviving and thriving in the job. You either had these qualities or you didn't. Some weren't aware of these qualities and had to dig a bit deeper than others to find it. The winged dagger didn't bestow any coolness; all of them were pretty cool to begin with.

It was called Selection, but that gives the impression of them picking you. That's only a small part of it. The main bit was really you picking you. It should be called self-selection; it was a form of self-actualisation, but with awesome weaponry.

Robert Paulson got a beret; so did Pikey Lee. For the lucky lads it didn't feel like an achievement; it felt like a homecoming. Like any true pilgrimage, it came full circle: arriving at the beginning and 'knowing the place for the first time'.

And for some reason, they gave me one too.

5

IRAQ—BATTLE FOR RAMADI

Picture this: It was dusk across an unearthly, flat land. What little colour had gone; everything was monochrome that wasn't in shadow. There was the barest hint of sunset in the western sky. To the east there was a faint glow from Baghdad. A vast runway and helicopter landing pads trailed off to the horizon like exercises in perspective. I walked along an endless blast wall that disappeared into the darkness, my boots scrunching across alluvial gravel from the Tigris and the Euphrates. The first stars were out. Behind me there were small huddles of tents ringed with HESCOs (large, stackable cages filled with rubble) and sandbags. It was bitterly cold.

I stopped and braced myself against the blast-wall. The smooth concrete was ice to the touch and stood mute against a glittering sky like some alien monolith cast down upon this barren land. I felt like a penitent, hands and head pressed against the wall, muttering.

I couldn't pee. It was too painful.

I had a cigarette instead. I lit it with my eyes shut and then smoked it in my cupped hand to protect my spreading night-vision. By a tent there was a wood pallet spilling plastic water bottles onto the ground. Sand bunched up around the bottles, giving them the appearance of beach litter. I reached inside the pockets of my fatigues for some antibiotics.

An air-controller came out and popped infrared cyalume sticks. That meant my helicopter was close. The dull pop was the same sound that my antibiotic pills made as I freed them from their plastic strip. I washed them down with the military bottled water that always tasted of fluoride and dust. The water was warmer than the rapidly falling air temperature.

The helicopter would take me to Ramadi, to the most dangerous city on earth and the heart of the Sunni insurgency in Iraq. It was six months after getting my beret. I had managed to pull some strings and get an embed with US forces in the city. Let me be very clear: I wasn't wearing any uniform, and rarely carried a weapon.

The Americans were fighting for control of the city from al-Qaeda in Iraq. Weeks before I arrived the insurgents had declared Ramadi the capital of the Islamic State of Iraq. If the US didn't win back Ramadi, they would lose the province of al Anbar and possibly the war. The Americans brought their best men to the task, ripped up the rule book and tried to fight a very clever counter-insurgency that sought to win over the local Iraqis. It was a hugely risky gamble.

The man who helped with my trip, whom I had gone to meet, Capt Travis L. Patriquin, one of the new gurus of counter-insurgency, had been killed the day before I arrived. His colleague, Major Megan McClung, who had also been killed, had given me a place with the Marines fighting out of Camp Corregidor in Ramadi. I asked for the most dangerous Combat Outposts (COPs) in the city. I wanted to see it up close.

I dropped my pack against a low wall and sat down on my flak-jacket. Three or four other guys came out of the shadows and did the same. They looked SF: no badges, not much uniform, good hardware, unshaven. Each had that familiar, easygoing vibe of looking after themselves but not really caring what they looked like. Lean, functional, laid-back; the older guy could have been a college professor who liked running ultra-marathons.

In the dark I can't tell you who spoke, but we talked about the stars: we discussed desert navigation and astrolabes and competed to name obscure constellations. Almost a third of the stars in heaven have Arabic names in the international system. Much of this comes from the Golden Age in Islamic Sciences, from the ninth to thirteenth centuries across the Arab world, but especially from al-Andalus and the House of Wisdom in Baghdad. When Baghdad was sacked by the Mongols in 1258 they threw the books into the Tigris and the river ran black with the ink.

I showed them Mizar (or al-Maraqq, meaning 'The Loins', because it is in the tail-end of the Great Bear) and Alcor, which are also known as the Horse and Rider. Mizar is the second star from the end and Alcor—the Rider—is a fainter star that sits just to the north. In previous centuries it was a test of eyesight to be able to see the Rider. Everyone in our group passed.

They had two off-schedule rides going to al-Anbar and a spare spot for me.

The air-controller called out two names and in the gloom two massive shadows broke away from the darkness and ambled towards us. They looked like grizzly bears on their hind legs, but they just turned out to be two very large Navy Seals.

Then the sound of the helicopters. We all crouched down beside some HESCOs to avoid the rotor wash as two Black Hawks came down. At night, each was a roaring abstraction, a clattering, reality-mauling shadow rather than a machine, largely invisible except for the faint green glow of the NVGs the pilots wore. The air-con walked us out in a line, loaded us up; smells of exhaust, hot metal, rotor oil, stale sweat and farts on canvas seating. As the engines roared up he checked our belts—four-way spider buckles on the chest—and tightened them, and there was something in his routine care, the pressure on my chest, the adrenaline and the smell of grease that reminded me of a fairground worker doing checks on the passengers of a rollercoaster before it starts.

The engines bellowed with a noise that became part of us, and we were lifted up and swung into the night.

Steadily we climbed till the individual dots of light on the runway became lines and the shape of the airfield could be made out. Then I could see the perimeter lights and the headlamps of Humvees and trucks out on the road, the shape of neighbourhoods and then Baghdad in the distance. The capital was a patchwork of light and dark; some city blocks and suburbs had electricity and others didn't. Soon we had left Baghdad and were racing into the vast darkness of the western desert following the course of the Euphrates. It was hard to gauge our height until I saw a pair of bright lights from a Humvee patrol. We were low, very low; almost street level. I could make out the outline of a small walled family compound. Before we careened past I tried to imagine the scene inside...

I looked up and saw the crowded heaven, bright in the way only the desert sky can be. As the pilot banked to left and right I was pushed down into my seat by the Gs and in their grip I lost all sense of what was up and down. I looked out of the window, but it was too dark to make out the horizon. The pilot banked again and we shot out across the river itself. Far, far ahead was the glow of a massive base. The second Black Hawk surged forward till we were neck and neck.

Down to my right tracer fire drifted lazily in the distance. Lights danced everywhere I looked: the tracer fire, perimeter flares over a distant base; in the reflecting waters below I could make out individual constellations and once or twice shooting stars. Following the course of the river, the pilots both banked hard left again. They were showing off.

I noticed everyone seemed to be nodding—as if they agreed with just how cool everything was. No, they weren't nodding, they were head-banging to some shared beat. The marine leaned over and offered me another set of the Blackhawk's radio headphones. I put them on; they were hot-wired to a music system. Even over the roar of the turbine and the blades, the music—that music—the drumming of Disturbed's 'Down with the Sickness' was in perfect sync with the helicopter's blades. For many soldiers it was the anthem of that war.

* * *

There were no connecting helicopters into Camp Corregidor that night, so I got a few hours sleep in the transit tent of a large base. In the morning I was invited to a memorial service, so did my best to shave and look smart.

I arrived late. There were about 150 men—most of them spotty teens—standing in a large tent with a too-low mesh ceiling waiting for the memorial service to begin. It was for three combat engineers who'd died in a massive IED explosion just outside the main gate. Their photos were on a screen by the small podium. There was an occasional murmur as the wind flapped the heavy tent fabric, and a screech-crackle and feedback in the speakers while they set the PA system up: '1–2, 1–2, testing'—the shorthand not for a rock session but for a dirge. It smelled of canvas, the detergent in their uniforms and nervous body odour. I caught a few stares and returned them; I was someone unrecognised—an outsider—in this intimate moment. They looked elsewhere, craned their necks, searching for what or whom I don't know, and when they thought I wasn't looking would glance sideways at me with wet, trembling eyes. Even though they stood in rows they seemed to jostle each other like bullocks in an abattoir yard. They were all still in shock and desperately wanted someone to come and talk to them. They were just kids; they needed an explanation and a hug. Instead they were about to get a US military standard memorial service, an emotional assault course, which breaks most people.

The service started slowly, with a few nice words from the chaplain, then there was some amateur video of the guys goofing around, scrapping and wrestling in the dust somewhere on the main base. It was followed by a reading of Shakespeare's Crispin Day speech—we few, we happy few, we *band of brothers*—and that got the first sobs. I was thinking about Agincourt and they were thinking about a Spielberg Second World War mini-series. Then they played Lynyrd Skynyrd's 'Free Bird', and quite a few people bawled. I was fine until an officer next to me said—in a 'gee, what a swell guy' voice—that one of the kids had left his Xbox in his will to his unit. I walked out.

Sure, big-up the dead—'Cheerful to the death' and all that— but all I could think was that these kids were writing wills about their toys. I wasn't sad specifically for these dead kids I didn't know; I was angry at the live politicians who had put them there.

I had a cigarette and calmed down. Then I wandered over to a solitary toilet just as a bugle started playing Taps back in the tent.

The shitter was a stand-alone, festival-type portable toilet. It was made from that same tough plastic with a slight sheen they use for the playground: Fisher-Price, mauve/green, a splash of violent blue detergent in the bowl, a few flecks of fatty, too-white shit. The walls were covered in graffiti, mostly jokes and laments (the larger four-to-six-person toilets had a whiter, cleaner surface that was better for genuine art).

There were lots of silly doodles of Osama bin Laden peering out from odd places, the odder the funnier. Osama had replaced the big-nose *Kilroy Was Here* of previous wars, peering over a wall.

Writing was invented in Iraq. The first act of graffiti was by God (Daniel 5:25) when He wrote 'Mene, mene tekel upharsim' (counted, counted, weighed, divided) on the walls of Belshazzar's palace during a piss-up in Babylon, late one night, 3,000 years ago. The graffiti US soldiers left was much funnier: it ranged from the happy '24 days till I go home' to the sublime 'Chuck Norris' tears can cure cancer, too bad he doesn't cry' or 'God is love but Satan does that thing you like with his tongue'. But most of it was like this: 'Fuck the President', or 'I just wanted money for college'. I used to take photos of the really good ones. It was the most honest commentary I ever saw on the Iraq War.

I'd never had an STD before and never listened when guys spoke of 'pissing razor blades'.

I coaxed my injured dick out of my pants and braced myself for the ensuing torment. As I did so I made vows to the almighty that I wouldn't do something so stupid again—but half-hearted, bargaining vows that involved lots of small print: no more women with Celtic-inspired tattoos or dream-catchers above their beds.

God wasn't listening: It *is* like pissing razor blades; *and* hot lava *and* acid. It's not even a pain you can man-up for, but an under-the-radar, smack-in-the-nose hurt that makes your eyes water and your snot run in a shameful, childish way because you did something naughty and now your wee-wee hurts so bad you want to cut it off with a combat knife.

Someone knocked on the door and I told them to wait. I tried different poses, bracing myself against the walls of the shit-house like the Vitruvian Man. Some wag had written 'Reenlistment Papers' with an arrow pointing to the toilet-paper. I tried to read more but my eyes streamed. I tried to pee harder but it was useless, just a dribble of fire from my cock as tears ran down my face.

There was hammering on the door which shook the dust from the vent in the ceiling and I started swearing as I did up my flies and undid the black plastic latch on the door. I stepped out onto the gravel squaring up with this huge soldier; behind him there was a very long line of his peers from the memorial service that had just finished. He was massive but base-fit, gym-heavy; he didn't look fast with it.

I stared at him angrily, ready for a fight until I noticed he'd been crying too. My own face was streaked with tears and dust.

'It's tough, man,' he said and gave me a great big hug. It was a proper American hug. My nose came up to the name tag on his chest. He smelled of laundry and biro ink.

'They were heroes,' he said as we slapped each other on the back.

But then he turned to the next soldier and said, 'This guy needs a buddy.' So I hugged him too. And the next. At first, I wanted to get away, I felt fraudulent. But then I kinda got into it. I stood there and dished out hugs to everyone in the queue.

* * *

Camp Corregidor was on the outskirts of Ramadi, east of the city. It straddled the main Baghdad road: MSR Michigan. Before the war it was an agricultural college, a series of low buildings set amidst date palm groves. All the classrooms and dorms had been heavily sandbagged and protected; mortar attacks and small-arms fire were very common.

To the east it was mostly fields and the odd workshop. To the west, the city: suburbs and then downtown, the government buildings and the main mosque. A featureless grey sky hung low over the city. There were the occasional observation blimps, bristling with long-lens and night-vision CCTV, that gave the place an Orwellian, steampunk vibe.

If you haven't been to an urban battlefield before—if you have no military or war experience—then the closest thing I can think of is that it's a bit like a vast, city-wide building site.

There is that same smell of pulverised masonry, hot steel, and the grease and diesel exhaust of the heavy machinery that lumbers past.

The sounds are industrial too: the monster machines, even the clack-clack of the tools—especially the Kalashnikov—the rotary-saw sound of a drone overhead and the occasional earth-shaking, arse-clenching quarry blast of some tank-flipping Improvised Explosive Device.

Small teams of men go out to their various jobs—it's largely blue-collar work, but for a few officers waving plans and schematics—and everyone smokes and bitches in their down time.

Except the work is not construction but destruction: to kill, maim, deplete, deprive, reduce the other side before they do the same to you. That is the day-to-day, night-by-night, 24hr grind of war.

I got embedded with the 15th Marine Expeditionary Unit (15th MEU) that was fighting in eastern Ramadi, the Sina'a area north of the main road and a vicious area to the south called the Malaab around the football stadium.

My first unit was 4th Platoon, Echo Company, 2/4 Marines. They ran ECP8 in the Sina'a, a defensive checkpoint split between two buildings across the road from each other. ECP8 was probably the hardest hit outpost during the Battle of Ramadi. They had been getting attacked several times a day and night for weeks and, just before I had arrived, had lost a much-loved corporal.

I rode out up there in a Humvee one night—a three-vehicle patrol—driving out of Corregidor to the northwest, past OP South House, and on to ECP8. There was random gunfire throughout the city. We drove without headlights and I watched the street scroll past in my NVGs: there were deep craters in the road from IEDs, wrecked and burnt-out vehicles; every other house was a ruin, a tumble and a tangle of cement blocks and reinforcing rods, electricity wires and broken pipes. It had been raining and the roads were thick with mud; the dust in Iraq had a way of turning to cookie dough after a downpour, and in the

NVGs it looked like we were a convoy in snow. When we got to ECP8, we opened our doors. There was gunfire, someone shouted 'Run!' and we ran for a breech in the sandbagged position. It was a local house, commandeered and fortified by the Marines.

4th Platoon was run by Second Lieutenant Seth Nicholson and Staff Sergeant Brent Miller. I was introduced to the platoon by the new corporal, whom everyone called Panda. None of them wanted me there, which was completely understandable. No squad wants an outsider around at the best of times, and these guys were having the worst of times. I was intruding on their tribe, and on their grief. I spent the evening helping them clean squad weapons and keeping my mouth shut.

At midnight I went across the street and climbed up a makeshift siege ladder to the roof, which defended the other side of the checkpoint. There were a few Marines up there, but I decided to leave them be, and instead lay on my back on a pallet with my NVGs on, smoking cigarettes. I'd hoped to bag a few meteors from the Geminid shower, but I was a few days too early. I still wasn't back to smoking full-time. I just did it on nights out or around the military. In the midst of all the fighting it seemed a little churlish to think about the longer-term risks of lung-cancer. I blamed that degenerate Robert Paulson for me smoking again, taking advantage of me when I was weak with hypothermia, or something like that.

There was gunfire all over the city: the snappier sounds of US 5.56mm and the heavier Iraqi 7.62mm. Back in training, on the ranges, there were guys who could identify different gunfire like birdsong. In the echoing clusterfuck of urban battlefield I could barely make out even the basics.

One of the Marines asked if he could bum a smoke. He was on the squad M-240, which was mounted on a bipod on sandbags, on the corner of the roof, and so I got up to give him a few. His name was Bruce, but everyone called him Weed, and we got chatting about nothing much. His arcs were over a few ruined buildings and some scrub ground towards the market place. Together we watched three men in the distance approach through the broken ground: Weed through his night-scope and me through a thermal imaging scope. At 200m they dropped down and started crawling. I could make out the silhouette of a weapon against the white outline of body heat. At less than 100m they stopped and one began digging—or that's what Weed said he was doing. In the thermal scope the man looked like he was doing mime in space or swimming with one hand. I remember his heat-signature in colour.

'Really?' I asked Weed. Putting an IED in front of an American checkpoint is generally smart if you're an insurgent but at that range, knowing we had night-vision capability, was kinda ballsy.

I heard Weed flick the safety so I knew what was coming. The three men were killed in an instant, and I watched them tumble. They looked like pastel rainbows in the scope, and their bodies jerked as more rounds knocked their corpses around. I looked over the scope into the strobing darkness but the muzzle-flashes didn't illuminate the scene. Weed stopped shooting and we had another cigarette. It was still another two hours before the end of his time on the roof. Even though it was a cold night the bodies still glowed faintly in the scope when we climbed back down the ladder. Here is the weird thing: although I remember the vision down that scope in perfect technicolour, I have looked up the thermal scopes the US military used at the time and all their imaging was in black and white back then.

* * *

The next morning I found Panda, Weed and a few of the others in the small courtyard trying to put together a flat-pack Christmas tree they'd been sent by folks back home. Weed was drawing three more stripes on his body-armour in biro. He was almost up to 15 kills. Everyone did it—four marks and a fifth in diagonal like marking off time—but that didn't stop his friends mocking him. There was pushing, shoving and a scuffle. The Marines were high-energy and rogue: mismatched uniforms, mixed-weaponry, bandanas and knuckle-dusters, but the moment we patrolled out of the house they were the slickest unit I've ever seen.

On that first morning we walked out the door and down the main street, past bullet-riddled cars. The nearest—an Opal—had swarms of flies on the blood on the seats, even though it was too cold for flies. As neighbourhoods go, it wasn't bad: broad streets with two- or three-storey villas set back behind high walls, and large sheet-steel gates for cars. Half the buildings were destroyed; all of them had some form of damage. Dun-coloured houses, ruins and rust; a bit of blue tarpaulin that stood out in the grey morning light. Rubble had tumbled into the street like scree and the rain had washed channels through the mud and sand. There were tangles of wreckage everywhere, and every twist of electrical wire looked like it was hooked up to an IED. The sky was overcast and low. Somewhere overhead a drone whined away.

When I say 'slick', I mean that Panda's squad flowed down that street. The instant they left the sandbagged main door they switched into a collective mindset and moved as one. They did it in bounds, covering their arcs and each other, moving between points of cover like mercury. They did it silently and effectively. The only sounds were their boots on the mud.

Then the shooting started.

Everyone dropped into the nearest cover and checked each other; then we had a look around and tried to work out where it was coming from. It was from the back of a building a block over, through a gap where a house once stood. We had barely made it 300m. Panda radioed Sgt Miller, who ran over to get an eyes-on fix on the building. In his heavy Texan accent he called in a tank. We sat out a light rain of bullets from behind a blast wall that jutted out into the street. Weed moved back and forth with his M240 firing from different positions. In-between bursts he started singing his 'Haji' song, which he said always brought out the enemy into the open, 'You know, like a rain-dance.' It sounded like 'Warriors come out to play-ay...Warriors come out to play-ay'.

* * *

While we wait for the tank it's not a bad time to talk about some of the positives of violence. All of those beautiful qualities that we discussed on the Hills are here: simplicity, richness, self-sufficiency; pure concentration, total involvement; using your skills to the utmost; of being swept up in something greater. Combat is a peak experience—it might be a brutal, savage peak—but it is one of the highest in the range of human experiences. When I said Panda's squad 'flowed' down the street, I meant that literally: they were in a flow-state. All these heightened sensations were felt individually and collectively, and that is an incredibly bonding force. Peak experiences or flow-states, they all come together amidst the bullets and the mud and rubble.

But remember, these states involve a disconnection with time. It creates a paradox that stays with you: minutes float; seconds are not dots, but long threads; the moment elongates into a perpetual now. And because that moment feels like it will last for ever, part of you thinks it does.

And I know many people who have this recurring dream: that it is still going on—because how could that amped, terrifying, fully lived, colour-soaked moment ever truly stop? And in their dreams they get on a certain plane to Baghdad one night and then find the right phantom Black Hawk that takes them back to that moment, that battle, with all of their comrades, because that is reality and everything else since then has been a grey abstraction.

* * *

We felt the tank before we saw it, like an earth tremor. I watched a pebble on the road do the jitterbug as it approached. There were small rockslides in the rubble, and then it came around the corner. It was so vast, even in the wide street, that it didn't so much feel like it was coming towards us, than we were on a conveyer belt being fed towards it, like dirty fabric into a mangle.

It stopped five metres from us, and Miller used the radio to speak to the crew inside the beast. The tank's main gun swung around and lowered towards the house. A few enemy rounds optimistically dinged off the turret. Then we waited, and waited. I can't tell you if this was an elongated moment or the gunner was just "retarded".

KA-BOOM.

The muzzle blast created a shock wave that raised a dust-storm on the street from beneath all the rubble, like our small world was on fire. The shell completely fucked the house.

* * *

That patrol was fairly standard, and set the pace for the next few days: walk around the neighbourhood until someone shot at us. Rounds would pour in, almost always from a single shooter, but sometimes more. They were just hit-and-runs, never proper ambushes. The worst bit was the anticipation, the lull before the shooting started, a feeling of weightlessness combined with a tightening on the chest: breathe—inhale, hold, exhale—breathe. It didn't always kick off, but mostly it did. Doing tactical bounds in silence was ruthlessly logical, but I could never get rid of the silly feeling it gave me of not knowing if there was anyone out there pointing a gun at us. Maybe the fear compounds the goofiness, or maybe I should quit being a narcissist and focus on the threat. When the shooting began—and I knew everyone was safe behind cover—I felt relief that it had started and we knew where it was coming from.

Sometimes the enemy didn't run after a few shots. It was house-to-house fighting but not room to room. The neighbourhood was not just a grid of streets but a warren of interconnected tunnels, theirs and ours, which allowed fighters to move between buildings. One Marine in the squad would carry a sledgehammer for creating openings in walls, and another would have a crowbar or a shotgun for disabling doors.

The houses that were still standing in the Sina'a, especially those near ECP8, were largely empty; but they had been left in a hurry. Often in the house-to-house fighting we'd stagger into a still-life of a previous life: keys on a dresser, a child's homework on the table, mildewed laundry in the washing machine. The moments were both comforting and otherworldly. An oasis of calm even though the gunfire chattered outside.

On my last day with 4th Platoon they spent several hours battling it out on one street. Many of the buildings had been hit with big munitions which had collapsed the floors and roofs into concave shapes amidst all the rubble. It felt like fighting in a cross between a skateboard park and a quarry. For most of that long afternoon we were on the roof of one of the few houses that were still standing. There was a low cinder-block wall up there and another half-level above it, with a water-tank on top.

I watched the squad in action. Maybe it was the rush of combat, but it seemed like the pall of mourning had lifted from them too. Even as the rounds tore into the concrete above us they were laughing and joking. Weed got out the SMAW rocket to fire across the street and did a bunch of heroic poses before he fired it at the enemy and destroyed one of their positions. Panda and I sat with our backs against the wall watching it all unfurl. For him, and for a lot of his men, combat was the ultimate game, the most extreme contact sport this life had to offer; there was— quite simply—nothing like it. Panda and his squad were one of the best teams I have ever seen.

Amidst the gunfire we watched flocks of pigeons fly over the ruined city as the daylight faded. Iraqis love to keep pigeons; I've seen them circling in every city in the country. Sometimes they reminded me that life would always continue. Other times they looked like panicked doves of peace unable to find a home. To this day, anywhere in the world I see a flock of pigeons, it takes me back to Iraq.

That evening I got a Humvee back to Camp Corregidor.

* * *

I came to like Camp Corregidor. It was small but incredibly friendly. There were Marines, Army and Navy Seals there, but none of the petty tribalism of bigger bases. Less bullshit too: there were a lot of regulations about safety—body armour worn at all times, red filters on head torches—but very relaxed on uniform standards or minor discipline issues. There was a small chow hall run by Bangladeshi contractors, and it had some of the best military food in Iraq.

I spent a few days there and rotated out to other COPs. Most of the time I was with Marines—OP Hotel, COP Eagle's Nest, night patrols around the Stadium—but I also got to go with the Colonel to meet local tribal sheiks who were running the 'Awakening', which was the main effort of the counter-insurgency. At one meeting it was supposed to be just the Colonel, the sheikh and his neighbour for dinner, but twenty-five local sheiks came in to pledge their support. It was the moment—my tipping point—when I thought we might win this. That evening I sat outside the sheikh's house with a young intelligence captain and we played games with the sheikh's children—marbles in the dust—the kids racing around with glow-sticks we'd given them.

* * *

Iraq has a terrible way of playing tricks on you. Somewhere in the dust storms, the night missions, the helter-skelter helicopter rides, the pixellation of the night-vision goggles, you get lost in time. Sometimes all of you for just a bit; sometimes just a bit of you for always.

This was the opposite of the elongated moment of combat. It was something else, like a killer déjà vu. I'd get onto a helicopter and fly into the night and land at some small Landing Zone and taste the dust and cold. In the dark it's only possible to make out shattered mud-brick buildings and a few palm trees, and it could be anywhere or in any time. I'd scan for tangles of electrical cables, tank tracks, the outline of a Humvee—some sign of the present. Did the flight land in the twenty-first century, or did I crash in some shitty bit of the Bible? Was that a good trip or a bad trip? Where am I? When am I?

On a bad day it could be biblical everywhere. It was at once innately familiar and utterly alien. Outside Ramadi, the road sign was to 'Damascus'. All the doomed lines of our history seemed to meet here. Once, I watched three old Iraqis—bearded, sandals, frayed clothing—trying to get past a bored-twitchy US checkpoint. It looked like the Three Wise Men trying to deal with a bunch of red-neck centurions. It was a month before Christmas. It was on the route that three Magi, coming from Iran, would have used 2,000 years ago.

One night we drove in Strykers out to Cemetery Hill on the eastern edge of the city. Armoured vehicles unnerved me. I preferred to be on foot. I didn't like surrendering control. I climbed into one doubled up in my body armour and helmet with a bunch of other guys, then the heavy doors slammed shut like a submarine's hatch and the Stryker moved off. The submarine-like design is no accident: the blast pressure from an IED is the equivalent to being hundreds of feet below the sea. In daylight it is hard to make out speed or direction through the scratched, opaque ports, and at night it is impossible. I had no way of judging how fast or where we were going so I sat there, like a kidnap-victim in a car-boot, trying to figure it out. For the entire journey I kept clenching my arse, thinking every bump was a pressure plate on the mother-of-all-IEDs. The vehicle stopped and we were spat out in some new time and place.

We debussed from the Stryker into a piss-wet night. We couldn't see beyond each other with the NVGs, and the young officer had trouble getting his bearings. I could hear in his voice that he was starting to flap. The guys on the hill weren't on the radio, possibly asleep, and we didn't want them waking up with us coming through the wrong arc. Eventually we got the 'go' and trudged up a mud-chute, but it was like trying to climb a frozen waterfall in sneakers. It probably wasn't even that big, but if felt epic in the dark and the rain, with all sense of scale lost.

We staggered to the top to be met by a sergeant who showed us the positions. You could barely make anything out, even when your eyes had adjusted fully. We sat in a trench with a few sandbags and a firing position. It was the First World War all over again; maybe it was Bastogne or Khe Sanh. We were around a small dimple—one of several—at the top of the hill. It was hard to tell whether they were pocks in the landscape or shellscrapes or craters. Everyone wore ponchos and most of us tucked under a small basha that flapped in the wind like a wet flag.

I smoked a cigarette with Henderson, or rather with his large, lantern-jawed silhouette. To this day I can't tell you what he looked like in daylight. He had a soft Southern accent and a bashfulness that you sometimes get in well-raised giants. He loved history, devoured *National Geographic*. When he found out I studied archaeology he showed me a jawbone he'd found. Others brought out their collections. We had a show'n'tell by flashlight.

'Is it human?' he asked.

It was: half a jaw, quite heavy, and looked like it had been in the ground a long time.

'I think it's male,' I said. 'Or possibly...'

'A large lady, like with a big mouth?' Henderson said.

'I guess'.

'MacGregor,' he shouted. 'We got your mama here.'

Tell is the Arabic word for a colossal pile of rubbish. (*Tepe* in Farsi or *Høyuk* in Turkish.) It is an artificial hill formed of repeated occupations of a single site. Each generation of a town builds on the remains of the previous, and over hundreds of years the town slowly raises itself above the surrounding landscape. Most important ancient sites in the Middle East are tells. As the name suggests, Tel Aviv is a tell; so too are the sites of earliest civilisation at Catal Huyuk and Gulpeki Tepe. Troy is a tell; the archaeology of Homer's Troy—all those heroes and bloodshed, the Wooden Horse—is Layer 7a out of about 13 layers identified so far, and they're not even entirely sure about that.

Iraq is covered in tells. Archaeologists love tells, as they are layer cakes of Middle Eastern history. They get super-excited if they find some coin or inscribed mud brick, and they learn a new king or emperor's name. But it makes me despair. How the fuck can you *lose* a king? Presumably he had palaces and lands and made bullshit speeches to his soldiers promising them eternal glory, and now it's all dust. How many times in the Cradle of Civilisation had we thrown our toys out of the pram? There are countless tells and ziggurats that stud the area like rotted termite mounds across an African plain: stalagmites of blood, sweat, vanity, folly and ambition; composted oaths, soured prayers to forgotten gods and boredom.

Somewhere between the endless Groundhog Day of whack-a-mole missions and the quicksands of Iraq's history you are confronted with this terrible thought: *I've been here before.*

I had that reeling familiarity on one of the first raids I went on that winter. At night it's hard to tell what century you're in.

It was the action of kicking in the door that struck me. Inside, our shouts and their wails. Small scenes in the cones of light from weapon-mounted torches; the colours washed out by their hyper-bright glare. A fat lady wearing about five dressing gowns—and possibly a suicide vest—is about to get her bawling head blown off when she reaches down again. *I know this will happen because I've been here before, 5 ... 4 ... 3 ...* Plastic roses covered in dust on a bedside dresser like a glitch, a repetition of a memory I hadn't had yet. A teen male in a shell-suit trussed in plasticuffs on the floor, old enough to be shouting back at the interpreter but young enough to be crying too. There were skeins of spittle between his mouth, nose and the floor; in the torch-light it looked like spun sugar. Gunshots and screaming. The muzzle flashes lighting up an inner courtyard where an infant is standing and looking up at me as urine streams down its legs. *I've been here before.*

I don't believe in reincarnation for the simple reason that no one ever has a dream about a past life that rings true. No one ever has dreams about eating termites with a twig or cutting themselves while knapping flint or herding fat-tailed sheep across the Zagros foothills or any of the boring shit that we've been doing all of this time.

But surely if you were to dream a past life it would involve kicking down a door in this land? How many countless genera-tions of humanity have had that experience? This is the cradle of civilisation; they invented buildings, then they invented doors and not long afterwards someone kicked one down. How many times had Sumerians, Akkadians, Elamites, Assyrians, Amorites, Babylonians, Chaldeans, Neo-Assyrians and endless dead twats kicked down a similar door? Was the first one barefooted, then sandal, now boot? The armour and weapons morph: bronze, iron, steel, Kevlar. Is that evolution or a costume change? The drama is the same; everything else is props. How many times has that child screamed the same universal cry that cuts through a Babel of tongues? How many times has that same urine puddle spread across the same trampled sand?

The killer déjà vu and the elongated moment are really the same thing—an explosive, reality-buckling thought: that all of us, the living and the dead, are experiencing every second of history simultaneously.

* * *

In the run-up to Christmas I opted to stay with an army unit. Their combat outpost was on the other side of the Mala'ab and it took ages to get to by Humvee. It was exposed to fire on all sides. As we drew up in our Humvee the soldiers inside shouted out 'SNIPER AREA! RUN!' and so we sprinted into the building, past the HESCOs and sandbags. There was gunfire, but then there always seemed to be gunfire. When I'd caught my breath, I had a cigarette with some of the soldiers on duty. By the time I had stubbed the cigarette out I knew this was the worst COP in Iraq and that I had to stay. The place broke my heart twice in 24hrs—once with sorrow, once with joy.

The morale of the unit was fucked. Sometimes you can smell it in a place, amidst the dust and mildew: sour ammonia, stale cortisol, clinical depression and endless cigarettes. These were kids at their wits' end ruled over by a bullying sergeant and a pale, polite officer who I met maybe twice. The officer barely left his room and the sergeant had a desk by the stairs but never went up to check on his men in their fighting positions on the roof. By evening I had broken up two fights—both involving the Sergeant attacking younger soldiers—and had other soldiers breaking down on me and crying.

At dinner we ate piping-hot chow and Ben & Jerry's ice cream, and then I watched the soldiers open care packages from the US. We chewed through cake bakes from small American towns I had never heard of and sweets from schoolchildren while we read their notes: 'Dear soldier, You are brave. Thank you for fighting for me, because of you I am free to bounce on my trampoline. God bless you. Meghan.' This one was written in crayon and there was a cute picture of Meghan on her trampoline with a bright sun like only a child can draw correctly.

Then Matty, the unit joker, started to read aloud from other letters: 'Thank you for protecting us. You are our hope. I hope you are safe at Christmas. My dad says you are fighting bad men. I am praying for you...' except he did it in a cartoon German gestapo accent. It was the hammy theatrics that made it so devastating: *For you, Ze War is never over.* The words Matty read were as old as war itself—hero, patriot, home—and it was darkly funny until he spat out modern phrases in that Hollywood propaganda voice—*War on Terror, Operation Iraqi Freedom*—when everyone flinched. Punchline: What had we become? Here was the Old Lie up and walking, bawdy, mocking and utterly obscene, schlock'n'awe; it was the ever-rotting clown speaking to us as Matty, as Nazi and as sweet Meghan on her trampoline. I looked around the table. A few guys were eyeing me nervously to see how I'd react as the new guy. A few were laughing in a terrible scared way, but several were crying. All of them had that panicked herd look I had seen at the memorial service: the look of too-young men faced with death through no fault of their own, finally wise to the killing joke that had brought them there. I wanted to cry then.

Later we went up to the roof and sat around a sandbagged machine-gun at one of the corners of the building three storeys up, facing away from the main street and over the ruins and wreckage of Ramadi. Everything we saw was in a free-fire zone; not a single house was lived in any more, apart from enemy, feral dogs and the dead. The fire-position was a small hut of plywood reinforced with green sandbags to about shoulder height, with scrim netting thrown over. The gun was a 7.62mm, which was set low, its firing port beneath a block of bulletproof glass that looked like it had been jacked from a Humvee's windshield. Inside the small hut, with its broad, pocked window, I felt as if I was looking out of a trawler's cabin: Ramadi was a vast grey sea of blasted buildings and twisted, rust-streaked steel, serried waves of rubble in lines where rows of houses had been, the troughs in-between where streets once ran.

There was occasional, light gunfire—none of it impacting near us—but we still kept our heads down; there was just enough light left in the sky to silhouette ourselves for a sniper. We sat on ammo boxes and bits of pallet crates, on the folded cardboard of ration pack boxes, as insulation against the cold floor. The clouds were low and grey like it might even snow.

Thad was manning the 7.62mm; he was straddled over several ammo crates that someone had duct-taped mattress foam to, making a saddle. On the plywood were biro scribbles in a dozen sets of handwriting: the musings of hours of boredom, tedium, fear and more boredom. One message read: 'This is the worst vacation ever'. Thad was keeping an eye out for dogs too. He shot them when he could. The dogs around here ate the dead quickly—body parts: theirs, ours. He'd seen a dog with the forearm of a friend of his after a bad IED explosion. Now, I'd heard this story before, but it was always a friend of a friend, an al-Anbar urban myth, or maybe the poor dead fucker just had a lot of friends. But here was someone who said they'd seen it, and that it was their friend. Thad was crying quietly as he spoke to me. Was it his friend? His story to tell? Did it matter? In the shared grief of combat maybe no one really owns stories. I can only tell you that those were definitely his tears.

And watching Thad cry I thought about the six ecstasy tablets I had hidden in the barrel of a pen in my pocket. I had been keeping them for myself as a little pick-me-up around Christmas.

I realise six may seem a lot, but the quality of Es was hit or miss back then—not always the golden disco biscuits of yore—and I wanted to be sure of a good time. I had planned on doing them in one of the transit camps, where it was safe and boring, but why not share? If anyone needed cheering up it was Thad and his crew on this shitty gun-emplacement. It would give the dogs a night off too.

I'm not entirely sure if I used the term 'Ecstasy' when I offered them. Dishing out pills wasn't unusual: many troops were used to popping Provigil, Proplus and a host of other uppers. From a legal perspective, in case any of these soldiers are still serving, let me just state that every time I offered a pill each soldier resolutely refused, saying, 'No sir, I cannot pollute this warrior's body while I serve my country at its darkest hour.'

After about twenty minutes, Thad had cheered up. He was chewing the edge of the ballistic plate in his vest like a berserker warrior in the Lewis Chessmen. Gonzalez was hugging himself and making 'oooooh' sounds as he peaked early. Bear just smiled and said, 'Oh man'. Everyone else was very intent on listening to music, but we only had a pair of earphones to share. But you know how ecstasy just *craves* noise? I could feel the drugs kick in too: hot and cold flushes like an invisible lover's caress; my jaw working overtime; I had a desire to tell great stories, share all that was marvellous, make it bigger, more fun. I put on some NVGs and then messed around with a thermal imager and watched a cat slink along a wall. Its body heat rendered it a perfect white, a ghost cat.

The Sergeant was on the radio every fifteen minutes asking for sector reports. By this time I was a bit bored and reported in some 'enemy activity'. I radioed in that there was a 'large bearded man, clearly some type of religious fanatic, moving along the opposite roof, dropping suspicious items down the chimneys'. No houses had chimneys in Ramadi. Most of them didn't even have roofs left. Other gun-positions were savvy and radioed in confirming the fat old man; you could hear giggling. Seeing as it was Christmas Eve you'd have to be moronic not to get it. But the Sergeant was a genuine moron.

'Engage!' he screamed down the radio.

And because it was Christmas and we were kinda in the Biblelands, but mainly because we were wasted, we all looked at each other with wide-eyed wonder and 'rejoiced exceedingly with great joy' (Matthew 2:10).

In 2006, an Italian neuroscientist injected rats with ecstasy and played them house music up to the legal volume for Italian nightclubs and watched various parts of their brains light up in scans. The louder the music, the more the drug stimulated brain activity. The experiment proved what most club-goers had long suspected: that ecstasy only gets better and better with volume. The legal limit for most nightclubs is 85 decibels. Anything over that risks damage to hearing. Some rock concerts reach 100 decibels, and the Foo Fighters were once picked up at a seismic monitoring station designed to detect earthquakes. But the prize for the loudest music goes to The Prodigy, who reportedly reached 135 decibels. At these volumes on ecstasy—where your teeth vibrate and the bass rinses sprays of sweat off your corybantic form—you are likely to lose your hearing and faith in organised religions.

However, the M240, with a muzzle velocity of 2,800 feet per second, delivers a volume of 185 decibels, and, with a top firing rate of up to 950 rounds per minute, is three times faster than Drum & Bass. As Thad unleashed burst after burst into the surrounding buildings, the concussive cones of pure noise it created felt like being spanked by the divine. The noise hurt, but it hurt soooo good.

We all wanted a go. There was a brief debate about whether we should keep the M240 in the position where the acoustics were amplified (sort of, but the gun's muzzle was outside the port), or set it up on the wall where everyone could watch. We opted for the wall. Thad offered Gonzalez the gun; they hugged each other. It was beautiful. They were wreathed in a kindly light. I could make wavy patterns with my hands, especially if I put the NVGs back on.

Standard NATO belt is 4-to-1 tracer, which means that every 5th round in the machine-gun link comes out burning bright or—if you're on ecstasy—like a fucking laser beam. On a medium fire setting, that's about two lasers a second. Bright red Photon blasting. Ricochets would tumble and whine into the night sky, leaving red-orange-yellow parabolas across our retinas. We immediately set about rearranging the link so that it was 1–1 and then pure tracer.

By the time I got on the gun I was rushing madly. I was the jolly fellow, trigger-happy, sharing molten love and friendly fire. I hadn't felt this good on ecstasy since the early '90s. I'm not sure I have even felt that ripped before or since. High? I was fucking Airborne. I poured endless fire into an adjacent building, the rounds tearing into the concrete and brickwork. A 7.62mm round hits with roughly the same force as a jackhammer. Shards of building and dust erupted everywhere. Others joined in with their M-4s. It looked like a waterfall of hell, strobed bright red dozens of times a second. The force of the weapons and noise brought my ascent to a peak. The barrel of the gun was red hot and glowing translucent so that you could see the individual bullets in the barrel, black and gelatinous, like demonic frog-spawn.

We were out of ammo after several passes, and the Sergeant was screaming on the radio again. We were told to hold fire until further orders. A couple of other Combat Outposts had decided to let off a few rounds, and their tracers erupted up like glowing fountains across the city skyline. When they stopped there was silence over the city again. The piles of brass were in drifts around our feet and tinkled like sleigh-bells when we stirred. We all hugged and wished each other a Happy Christmas. And then Bear started singing and Gonzalez held the radio up to his lips.

Most people know war through films, and soldiers are no different. But a few days in Ramadi are enough to wipe out any misconceptions about what war is really like. Soldiers singing on the battlefield only exists in old war movies, but Bear didn't know that. Somehow his voice soared above everything (and I promise you it wasn't just the E). Bear, a massive stone-cold killer, black and quietly handsome, with great, mournful eyes, raised by his churchgoing grandmother in the Baltimore projects, sang 'Silent Night'. I looked around and saw some guys laughing and hugging, some were crying and smiling but all of them looked like they were young men, alive despite it all, surrounded by their family at Christmas. I cried too.

6

THE GIFT OF GAME

If you bring forth what is within you, what you bring forth will save you. If you do not bring forth what is within you, what you do not bring forth will destroy you.

Gospel of St. Thomas

Flying back from Iraq and into London-Heathrow, I would always make sure I had a starboard window seat. As the plane made its final approach above the city, I could look down to my right onto an arching bend of the River Thames and see my home: an old sailing barge moored on the north bank of the river, the toy-town pubs along the riverbank, the rowers midstream, and the high poplars on the southern bank. If it was a very clear day, I might be able to see friends having a BBQ on the deck, and I would know I would be joining them in an hour or so.

The barge was just short of 70ft and just shy of 100 years old. She had a black hull and decks, white uppers and a band of duck-egg blue in-between. Inside, she was fitted out in maple the colour of set honey, and she smelled of beeswax, engine oil, Persian carpets and books. She floated twice a day on the tides, and I knew all her creaks and purrs: as the waters lifted her up or let her down, as flotsam & jetsam scudded her sides; the silly sound of ducks walking on the deck. She is the only object I have ever loved.

* * *

One bright Friday morning, I got up early and walked through the boat. My friend Ernesto was still asleep on a sofa and there was no sign of Rob Paulson, still in bed in the front cabin. I put on a pot of coffee and played with the radio, trying to get a frequency for Tramp FM, but there was just quiet. The sun streamed in through the portholes and glowed on the burnished maple. Over the years I had come to know the angles of those beams, from sunrise to sunset across the seasons, which floorboards and walls the sun would touch as it tracked through the year.

The coffee pot whistled and spat onto the hob, and on cue a lady emerged from Rob's bedroom looking remarkably composed. 'I'm late for my flight,' she said. I gave her a coffee, but it was too hot to drink; her name-tag said Becky, and she was in a rush. Becky had a beautiful smile and lots of fake tan. 'Stansted?' I asked. She nodded and said, 'See ya soon, I hope,' and nodded again in the direction of Rob's bedroom. Her heels reverberated on the iron deck, and then drummed several beats on the wooden gangplank. The noise woke up Ernesto, and I gave him Becky's coffee before heading up on deck to have mine.

It was a clear June day. The sun was up and the riveted steel of the hull made ticking sounds as it soaked up the heat and expanded. The tide was rolling out, and it would be low in a couple of hours. We were on big spring tides, and there would be a very low tide; good for 'mudlarking', AKA poking around the mud on the riverbanks for ancient rubbish.

For my friends, the boat had become a floating halfway house between Baghdad or Kabul and the real world. These friends brought their friends, and for one long summer it was a place for British, American and French soldiers between jobs, musicians between tours, documentary-makers between projects, clever folk between foreign postings, stewardesses on breaks from long-haul flights and actresses between jobs. And at night the boat would slowly fill up with other between people: chefs and waitresses at the end of their shifts, strippers when their clubs shut and the rest of the party crowd.

All of this was too tempting for Rob Paulson. He had turned up for a BBQ weeks before and hadn't left. Slowly I was getting to know more about him. Prior to the military he'd travelled the world (which he'd funded by robbing drug dealers) after a spell in prison (for weapons offences during a motorbike gang turf war).

I'd met Ernesto the year before at the al-Rashid Hotel in Baghdad. If you've never been there, don't go. It is, quite simply, an evil building. The ghosts of Uday and Qusay Hussein seemed to prowl the corridors. It has the lavish interiors common in those countries where homosexuals aren't allowed to decorate: a throbbing style of turbo-macho that backfires into the gayest shit you've ever seen, like Tom Cruise films. Ernesto had been too drunk to walk but was still very coherent. I introduced myself to him and we had a decent chat as he crawled along the marble corridors. Whenever he wasn't in Baghdad he came to stay on the boat.

Ernesto lived for women, and when he wasn't in love or heartbroken, he was reading feminist literature, attending women's marches or watching films about feelings. Ernesto was a lover to Rob's fighter. Both were utterly immune to reason in female company.

Rob had a vast lust for life and loved the world deeply, but it simply wasn't lined up right for him. He had his own code, which I found to be a complete mystery, although I sensed that friendship was his highest altar, and I was lucky enough to be his friend. Sometimes I'd ask him why he did something—pursue a girl, punch a guy, show mercy—and his explanation always made such sense in Rob-world that I felt stupid for having asked. Other times he'd just shrug and say, 'There's a bubble in my moral compass.' But deep-down, I don't think Rob really believed that. His compass was fine. There was no deviation. He was no deviant. It was just that his north wasn't the same slushy-frozen wastelands as it is for the rest of us. Rob was always pointed to a warmer place that was much more fun.

* * *

Tramp FM was our own radio station, one we had started by accident. I'd been on a job that required planting listening devices, and I placed a string of them under the benches along the Embankment and put a receiver up the mast. I wasn't interested in what people were saying; I chose the benches because they were evenly spaced and gave me some idea of signal strength in different atmospheric conditions. Once the experiment was over and I had selected which type of bugs to use, I took them all in. Apart from the one on Bench 5: the tramps' bench.

OK, 'tramp' is a little harsh, most of them weren't rough-sleepers, but they were all jobless and professionally alcoholic: 8% white cider; yellow, nicotine-stained fingers; first-name terms with the law. Most had that strange combination of fat-faced, babyish hairless skin and lustrous head-hair that occur in advanced, long-term alcoholism, when the body suppresses testosterone production and increases oestrogen output.

Their days would start when the thirst seized them, and they would commute to the bench by 0900, weather allowing. Tramp FM wasn't Radio 4, but it was a lot less boring than other local radio; it was hardly a chat-show until the first few drinks chased away their hangovers and they became more animated. They would talk politics (a surprisingly right-wing group) and relationships (AKA 'the b-b-b-bitch left me').

At around midday there was a barely detectable 'woompf' in the mood like the whispered ignition of meth-vapour. The alcohol had reached a critical mass in the group-think, and everything went mythic: friendships were patched, toasts were given, songs were sung and epic tales were retold with profound nostalgia, even though the events in the stories had happened that morning. Any few words or lyrics that had found favour within the group—often some hoary piece of wisdom or a saying of fridge-magnet banality—would be repeated endlessly. And everything was soaked in meaning, dripped with sentimentality or soared with poetry. It all rotated—mutating and doomed—around a black singularity of utter madness.

To a passer-by—hearing only 15 to 20 seconds of this—it must have sounded like apple-happy gibberish, but these men were engaged in a daily heroic cycle of friendship and betrayal that rivalled any opera or Norse saga. I'm not making fun of them. I only began to understand them when I realised that their sense of scale was vastly different. They had been so worn down by their addictions—the pounding hangovers and crushing guilt and regret—that the everyday had become legendary. Dung beetles pounding their breasts like Sisyphus. It usually ended in fighting, arguments and someone shitting themselves. It was better than a lot of Radio 4.

* * *

The three of us—Rob, Ernesto and myself—were standing on deck looking down through a hatch at our feet and onto Rob's bed in the cabin below.

'It's just like the Turin Shroud,' Rob said.

The sheets were imprinted with an outline, like chalk around a murder victim, but in fake tan.

'I really liked her,' Rob said, already slipping into the past tense.

'Becky,' I reminded him. He nodded.

On the sheets was an orange ghost. I was pissed-off, not so much at Rob; if anything, I was annoyed with myself for being angry about something as mincing as laundry.

'It looks nothing like the Turin Shroud,' I said.

It looked exactly like the Turin Shroud, but you couldn't agree with Rob; he'd take it as encouragement and then there'd be chaos. Like many social workers, army sergeants, police constables, prison officers and judges before me, I had come to the conclusion that Rob needed boundaries.

Nor was I going to rise to the bait. Often Rob would drop archaeological/historical/theological words into conversation just to wind me up. The previous week he'd been gobbing off about the Bronze Age and I couldn't work out where he was getting this knowledge from until I found him tearing pages out of my pile of *National Geographic* to snort cocaine with.

'It's like some distressing snow angel,' Ernesto said.

'And I doubt Jesus suffered as much,' I said. 'You disgusting fucking reprobate.'

That was another paradox with Rob. If you were a bloke and could stand your ground with him then you could call him anything and he'd be tickled. And I mean genuinely tickled—he'd have a physical reaction to your words—his chin would go up and his head would roll from side to side and he'd grin and try to spit out a retort in-between laughter. The viler the insult, the more it would delight him. In those moments Rob would remind me of my favourite dog breeds—Brazilian Pit Bull, Presa Canario, Bully Kutta—and how, when you play with them, there is a greater joy in their response because they are so stunned and delighted someone would dare knock 'em around like they were puppies again, but way at the back of your mind you're also thinking, 'I'm really glad we're all on the same page here because this fucker could kill me.'

But if a girl insulted him he would be genuinely wounded. *No Rob, I have no idea why she called you an emotional dwarf; it was mean and untrue.*

Maybe I was just angry because I hadn't slept that much. You know how when you're young and you and your mates hear a friend shagging away and it's funny? This was way past that. There'd been sounds—banging, slapping, howling, grunting, squealing, more banging—that no one should hear.

'It sounded like that time they accidentally shelled the Baghdad Zoo in 2003,' Ernesto added unhelpfully.

'The monkey enclosure?' I asked.

'The bad monkey enclosure,' Ernesto replied.

And Rob's head went back, and he laughed. And then he must have realised how hot the day was going to be and, ever mindful of hydration, he stumbled off to get a cold beer.

* * *

I had a long lunch with a girlfriend in town and by the time I got back to the boat it was late afternoon. The tide was vast and still coming in, flooding the towpath on the southern shore and lapping its way up the brickwork on the north embankment, and yet still it came in. It rolled in, perpetual and prehistoric, the colour of dirty mercury reflecting the baby-blue sky and the pale-green poplars. I pushed my way through the crowds along the Embankment: aimless tourists, brainless rowers and legless drinkers, many shirtless with a sheen of alcohol on them. There was the smell of beer on the hot pavement, greasy food and cigarette smoke. I climbed the steps over the river wall—clanging industrial metal—and caught fresh air at the top and the sight of my barge. There were almost two dozen people on my boat, a BBQ going, drifts of smoke and music. The tide was so high that the gangplank was level with the land. The boat tugged on her mooring lines and seemed to skate above the waters that gurgled and sang at her bow. She was happy.

Ernesto was playing with fire—an old steel beer keg that we'd sawed in half and hinged—cooking sardines and squid. Beside him was a metal bucket with almost two dozen steaks under an unholy potpourri of garlic and chillies and pungent marinade. 'Is that fish sauce?' I asked. He shrugged; he was stoned. Ernesto has grey-blue eyes, even when they are glazed. In one hand, he had BBQ-tongs; in the other he clutched a bong that looked like a penis-enhancer.

Rob was there with two new flight attendants: genuinely beautiful, endless legs, real tans. They drank iced beers out of long-necked bottles snug in neoprene blue sleeve-coolers stamped with the Winged-Dagger motif courtesy of friends in the Australian Regiment. The sky was the same colour. Rob nodded at the stewardesses, 'If you think about it, they're airborne too.' Rob-sense.

There were other friends too: a few lads down from Hereford, some US soldiers and Marines passing through; some mates back from surfing and climbing in Cornwall; a documentary maker and her boyfriend fresh off the plane from Baghdad; a couple of girls from jiu jitsu; a cage fighter. More on the way. This was a liminal space for them. A floating world between water and sky, nature and the city, the war and home.

I lay back in a hammock slung under the spar-pole. I could smell the oil I'd treated the wood with, BBQ smoke, spliff smoke too. I could feel the heat of the deck and the cool of the water. I watched the scene, the flotsam and jetsam of my social life. We were all in our late 20s or early 30s. I was 33 back then, Rob a few years younger, Ernesto a few years older. But it was one of the summers when you thought you might live forever.

Music drifted out of speakers propped up by a porthole. Heavy, drawling blues; electric guitar with plenty of feedback. Junior Kimbrough or R.L. Burnside, the latter once described as 'Blues walking like a man: the living personification of a guitar moan and a backdoor slam.'

The music spoke of chaos, distortion and feedback loops: flood waters on the Mississippi breaking through the levees, Katrina hitting New Orleans, the march of dark waters carrying everything with it into the night, an endless tide. Vast systems that didn't so much encroach but drag worlds into it. Flood and rebirth, fire and regrowth. It reminded me of war too: the ragged battlefront of an assaulting army; the mile-high red sand storms that would hit Baghdad and send the city into Mars mode; tendrils of dust that curled like fractal edges in the clawing downdraft of a Black Hawk.

The war and the dust, the burnt-out desert sun, it all seemed very far away in this world of cool liquid and lambent light. Yet almost all of us were intimately connected to it somehow. My friends stood on deck laughing; a girl demonstrated a fighting stance. She was a brown belt, but she surfed too. Maybe it was a surfing stance; the positions are interchangeable: jiu jitsu and surfing, boxing and war-fighting, rifles and pistols. Weaver-stance, lazy-weaver, so laid back, so slow-is-smooth. These people had that easy grace that comes with the balance of doing many things well. More laughter.

They looked like they were illuminated from within. I couldn't hear the joke, but I understood the trick of light: on the Thames on a bright day, with a full tide, the sun bounces upon the waters and makes the air itself a luminous thing. Conrad called it 'a benign immensity of unstained light'. It has drawn artists here over the centuries. On this stretch of river alone you could see William Morris's waterside home; Hogarth's house; Whistler and his wife were buried in the church nearby and, just around the bend, further upstream, Turner had painted, too. It is a phenomenon seen in estuaries and shallow seas that is beloved by artists. Think of the Newlyn School, the light of the Venice Lagoon. It is the light of the waterlogged Low Countries. It suffuses Vermeer interiors or gives imponderable depth to Cuyp's skies. I think it is the light of adrenaline—that glow from within, the light of life.

* * *

When they gave me my beret and I got to know the camp at Hereford, the first thing that struck me was how decent and friendly everyone was. I have spent time on hippyish boat moorings, squats, ashrams, monasteries, but I have never seen a place so free of petty hierarchies, sexism, racism or other big words. The camp was full of many incredibly cool and kind people, so many in fact that I began to wonder whether kindness wasn't their Top Secret. But while this gave me a warm'n'fluffy feeling, it also jarred with most of what I had been taught about violence while growing up. It fucked with my liberal resolve. How could this be?

I asked a grizzled old sergeant, and he shrugged. 'It's easy to be kind when you can kill everyone in the room'. But there's more to it than that. I'm not saying violence is the answer—pain, stress, chaos and trauma all help too. It's a case of dose and frequency. This is how it works:

At their core all my friends had gameness, a hunger for the ruckus. Here is a dictionary definition:

Gameness (noun): Adventurousness, audacity, bravery, coolness, daring, dash, determination, élan, endurance, firmness, fortitude, humour, insolence, grit, mettle, moxie, nature, resolution, substance, spunk.

In *A Fighter's Heart*, Sam Sheridan explains the concept: 'Gameness is a critical term to dogfighters, jiu-jitsu players, and fighters. It can be described as heart, as willingness to fight—a love of the fight stronger than a love of life'.

To understand what motivated their gameness requires stepping through the looking glass of Opponent-Process Theory. It's a clunky term for a counter-intuitive epiphany.

Opponent-Process Theory is one of those ideas that, once under my skin, I started to see everywhere. It tells us that the body is always seeking homeostasis, or balance. Any stimulus that effects the way we feel will be countered by the brain with an opposite response, to return us to neutral. Neutral is the ideal, zero level, against which all other incoming stimuli can be valued. Your brain isn't trying to make you happy or sad, it is simply aiming for a baseline—like your body's temperature or electrolyte balance—that it operates best at.

Imagine the input is pleasurable—Rob Paulson is swigging a beer, then another, several shots, and more beer. The alcohol will elicit an A-process: a feeling of relaxation, well-being, fellowship. His brain will step in to deliver the B-process, a flood of chemicals to counteract the alcohol, that result in hangover, anxiety, self-hatred, to the point he tries to flush his head down the loo.

Opponent-Process Theory also explains most of addiction. As Rob continues to stay on my boat and drink himself senseless for weeks on end until his next tour, he will develop a greater B-process which, in turn, requires more alcohol (A-process) to beat it. B-process always wins. This is why junkies develop tolerance to the very thing they desire the most, why many of life's pleasures pale with excess and why romantic love doesn't last forever.

Now the good news: if the A-process involves a painful stimulus then the body counteracts with a pleasurable B-process. Opponent-

Process Theory helps explain the joy of hot-sauce on food, the Runner's High, orgasm of sky-diving, religious rapture of self-mortification and the rush of combat. It's a trick of the mind that can be played back against itself: aim for the obstacle for peace of mind, expose yourself to the heat of action to be cool.

Those who engage in high-risk activities have been found to possess a more developed dopamine system. They score higher in novelty seeking and lower on harm avoidance because they get more reward out of it than regular folk—a bigger kick, a higher rush. Remember, it isn't the risk itself which is the goal, but that the type of activities that satisfy the need for newer and bigger thrills will involve jeopardy. Life has a way of placing the juiciest, most sun-kissed pleasures further out on the tall branches. And because fear enhances the senses, these pleasures are exponentially rewarding.

It gets better: not only does the body seek a state of homeostasis, it also tries to future-proof itself against further painful stimuli or stress by overcompensating. This is basic hormesis: a small dose of something harmful can bring benefits, whereas a medium- to high-dose exposure can be toxic. Hormesis is the basis of vaccination: a small dose of harmful agent provokes the body's immune response (conversely with bacteria, a small—sub-lethal—dose of antibiotics can lead to a surge in resistant populations).

Regular exposure to intense but intermittent pain increases our ability to tolerate it. Also, those who expose themselves to acute stressors more often develop greater pleasure from it and are less likely to suffer long term. Hormesis works for stress too. Subjecting our bodies to acute stress, with plenty of downtime in-between to recover, builds up our tolerance. Folks who have inoculated themselves against stress are a pleasure to be around.

It doesn't have to be fighting; others surfed, climbed or ran endurance races. They pushed themselves to the edge. They knew their limits but never got to know them really well because they kept excelling beyond them. Pain, suffering and adversity became the engines of their personal evolution. Going through an extreme state can feel like an evolutionary leap, as if the rush comes from the accelerated learning itself, a g-force growth-spurt towards a higher plane of existence.

An academic paper published a few years ago linked flow-states to the higher realms of personal development, or, to use Maslow's term, 'self-actualisation'. The study focused on Olympic athletes and found that the more frequent their peak experiences, the more likely they were to make ethical and empathetic decisions in their lives.

I'm a lousy fighter, but there are few things that give such a complete workout to so many primitive systems as a well-detonated fight-or-flight response. It's a flow hack, a shortcut to kindness.

If you doubt this, please take a trip to your nearest boxing gym or Brazilian jiu-jitsu club. The values and principles of a jiu-jitsu club (respect, integrity, excellence, personal development, a deep camaraderie that feels familial) aren't unique to jiu-jitsu—they are shared by most religions—but in fighting sports they are drilled into the conscious and sub-conscious, in that deep-learning that occurs at the extreme.

There is a deep spirituality in these Temples of Fight-or-Flight. I find more good nature on the sweaty canvas than I've ever seen amongst all the church pews, prayer rugs or yoga mats.

Maybe it's just 'heart'—that soul of fighting. Maybe they are all the same thing. Perhaps I'm just dumb. I would love to be able to absorb humility and perseverance from large books, but I need to have it spelled out for me physically in the primordial calligraphies of neurotransmitters. I can't get the words into my head praying on my knees; I need to be thrown on my ass. Repeatedly. Daily. The world is a candy-store with a blind store-owner and I can fill my head with all manner of dozy, sugared conceits; on any given day I can tell myself a dozen big-headed lies before lunch easily. I'm simply not strong enough to fight my inner asshole on my own; I need help choking the little fucker. I want to submit to a higher power, but when I tap out, just before I black out. Then, and only then, do I feel much surer about my place in this world, and I am a much better person for it. As Steven Kotler wrote, 'Altered states lead to altered traits'.

* * *

Is it possible to be addicted to violence? Or rather to the B-process flood of endorphins and their heroin-like qualities? Erin Pizzey, a feminist activist, believes so. She set up the modern world's first domestic violence refuge not far from the boat, and in her decades of work there came to two startling conclusions worth repeating here: firstly, she believed that women and men were equally violent. Secondly, that early childhood abuse had the power to rewire our neural circuitry and that almost two thirds of her clients were addicted to the endorphin rush of violence, the B-process. They sought it out unconsciously and repeatedly in dangerous and abusive partners. They were, in the title of her book 'Prone to Violence'.

I've known men who would qualify as being prone to violence through early trauma but all of the ones who made anything of their lives had learned to channel these urges into acceptable forms, through the military or martial arts. The endorphin addiction was there and they were conscious of it—some would go into cold-turkey if they couldn't get a sparring fix—but they had found a way of managing it. I doubt they would have taken a cure had one been available. They weren't merely 'functioning addicts,' for their addiction was one of the principal drivers of their incredible abilities to function at the highest level.

* * *

But here is something else from behind the mirror of the Opponent Process Theory: the comfortable world can begin to look incredibly cruel. Sometimes the less danger and genuine stress—the safer the space—the more hysterical the outrage and viciousness. I first became aware of this through a Resistance to Interrogation course, a NATO-standard briefing on what to expect in the event of capture. The syllabus is based on vast amounts of data gathered over many wars, but the dark conclusion is this: a soldier can expect increasingly vicious and horrific treatment the further he is taken from the front lines and the deeper into the enemy's rear-unit territory.

This was true of my experiences in Iraq: abuse to Iraqi prisoners of war wasn't done by front-line troops but occurred in the Enemy Prisoner of War (EPW) units that operated to the rear. EPW units tend to be manned by the dregs, psychos and saddos who can't be relied on in battle. Abu Ghraib wasn't done by infantry but by redneck reservists, while the institutionalised cruelty of Guantanamo is meted out by soldiers about as far from a battlefield as is possible on this earth.

A similar inverse rule applies in civilian life. 'War hath no fury like a non-combatant,' as Charles Montague wrote. For many of us, the most difficult part of a war-zone trip was the last leg of the return home. I loathe the moving walkways at the airport. I once counted two dozen pre-recorded security announcements and safety notices before I made it to passport control. Large LCD screens belt out rolling news of terror alerts; newspaper headlines are full of third-rate politicians lionising some Third World terrorist and leveraging fear for petty advantage. I feel like I'm in a re-education camp of learned helplessness.

* * *

Of course, some of us got the dose of violence wrong and saw too much. *So it goes.* It is said that men don't talk, but that's not true. It's just that men don't talk to the type of people who say such things. On the boat, I couldn't get them to shut up. At first it annoyed me; I'm not proud to write that now. I tried to make the boat a place of good times, a refuge from the war; that was my antidote. I was well beyond hearing the same nerve-shredding story about some fuck-up during a job in Iraq, again and again and again. (Hear it once and you'd do anything to unhear it.) It killed my buzz. But the boat—due to its proximity to the airport and the people it drew—became an ad hoc psychological first-aid station.

Post-Traumatic Stress Disorder is a vastly overused term for a little understood condition. It's a shit-show cluster of symptoms that might include intrusive thoughts (flashbacks), shame, depression, insomnia, emotional numbing, hyper-vigilance and avoidance of anything associated with the trauma. From a neurological perspective, the brain is perpetually primed for a fight-or-flight scenario: the amygdala is overstimulated and in a constantly activated loop of both looking for, and perceiving, a threat everywhere, like it is on a spin-cycle. At the same time, the hippocampus is underperforming, its job being to consolidate the memory and shift an event into the past tense. The neocortex, which should step in to regulate—'hey you guys'—is side-lined. Lastly, the highly activated sympathetic nervous system churns out stress hormones that ramp up that tired/wired feeling towards fraying and snapping. Like a panic attack—a spasm within Shrew—dark and elemental thoughts from the most ancient parts of our brain are mutinying like emotional epilepsy.

For the sufferer, a miasma of generalised anxiety sparks on even the mildest cues, triggering responses similar to those caused by the original trauma. And it is this feedback-loop or spasm that makes it so very difficult to treat: most forms of psychotherapy rely on revisiting the memory of the trauma, which, in the case of PTSD, is precisely what provokes an episode.

None of my friends ever got to this stage. Now, I don't have many friends, so it's not exactly a vast dataset, but I suspect we were on to a good thing back then: early intervention, community and great drugs, but luck too; I have very lucky friends. And very positive ones: we reframed these traumatic experiences as the trials and tribulations of an extreme life. We saw trauma as a means of development.

Most important, we caught them early. All my friends are decent people. By that I mean that they were initially fucked up by the appalling things they saw as much as any other ordinary, healthy souls would be. Post-Traumatic Stress is normal, and after a few weeks most people recover; Post-Traumatic Stress Disorder is the few people who don't. The boat operated as a decompression zone for folks between the pressures of war and the expectations of civilised life, like a pause on an ascent from the deep to the surface, to stop the Bends.

The boat also formed a tribal setting where trauma could be discussed openly. By tribal, I simply mean a small collective of people with similar experiences and world-views. You didn't need someone who was in the same unit or same battle as you, but rather someone with the shared language to bear witness to your stories. Mostly that language was silence.

Our group consisted mostly of guys who had been to war, but it wasn't exclusive; the only proviso was you didn't ask any dumb questions. In that situation, every question is a dumb question. To ask a question is to try to understand. That isn't the point. There isn't a point—you just listen.

In a major scientific study published by ... oh fuck it: we gave them MDMA. Shitloads of the stuff. If someone was burnt out after a job and we decided we were going to go 'there' then we went hard; everyone on the boat had to drop their wrap before noon—a heroic dose, Odin praised us—then we all monged out in the sunshine and not only *heard* the story but really *listened*.

If you have been to war you realise that all war stories—but especially the ones that fuck you up—are incomplete. Even to call them 'stories' is misleading, for they often lacked narrative; they were non-linear, splinters of something either too horrific or too vast to conceive of as a whole. Events which, as James Lee Burke wrote, 'can only be seen correctly inside the mind of a deity'.

Such fragments also don't make sense, because they are lodged down deep, beneath reason. The fragments would tumble forth like emotional Pictionary—flashbulb memories of horror—and our job wasn't to guess the word or discern a narrative, but simply to be there.

All of this is pretty basic Standard Operating Procedure for what friends do, but the MDMA is the really clever bit. MDMA delivers knockout levels of serotonin and dopamine to the central nervous system. Its effects include euphoria, increased empathy, a sense of inner peace, relaxation and reduced anxiety. Why is this helpful to those with PTSD other than a brief holiday from the self? Because it allows sufferers to talk about their memories without provoking a fight-or-flight scenario and, by doing so, breaks the feedback loop of horror.

On the boat, not only did MDMA help the sufferer, but it made us a far better audience. It takes a lot to listen to a friend's nightmares. I'm not a great listener, even on a good day. I have loved three or four women enough to ever listen to their dreams, and even then I wasn't exactly holding both their hands across the breakfast table as they shared their stories.

But MDMA is a dose of pure empathy: on it I deeply cared for my friend's stories, their dreams and their nightmares. Being jacked on Class-A narcotics is frowned upon in traditional group therapy, but we listened-the-fuck out of what was said. We walked with them through the retelling, through every drop of the horror, every single drop, we absorbed it all and we did it with love.

To be in the grip of PTSD is to be owned by an event, to be forced to reenact it. MDMA gave my friends a chance to rescript the trauma. Each retelling gave them ownership over the event, rather than it over them. They could self-author who they were.

* * *

While we're on the subject of fight-or-flight scenarios and MDMA, let me add this: they make for a powerful cocktail when taken simultaneously.

I took MDMA before jumping out of a plane very early one morning. I was peaking as we reached the jump altitude. I don't think this was lucky timing; the adrenaline acted as a propellant charge to the MDMA: the higher we got, the higher I got. It was my turn to jump first. The instructor opened the outer door to this roaring world of colour like a furnace of pure creation: the top of the sun peeked its head above the wine-dark Cotswold Hills and enflamed the gentle bank of lilac cloud. It blasted golden light and the plane hung in the sky like a bug caught in amber. England stretched out beneath me: a grey gauze hung over the land. It glowed. Here and there, church spires and copses poked their dozy heads out. I could make out the darned edges of hedgerows, the patchwork of fields, the tapestry of this great land. I wanted to sing hymns, or jerk off, or both. Far below me, a glow-worm of headlights in the mist as sleepy-eyed motorists smiled through their commutes to artisanal jobs in nameless towns. I wanted to speckle their windshields like an overly patriotic pigeon. I wanted to share, love from above.

I could feel the roar of the engines through my ribcage. If I opened my mouth my lungs filled in the wind. I knew the pure pleasure of a dog hanging out a car window, and got intense visuals off the sunlit fuselage and vast propellers like the chromatic glint off a dragonfly's wing. But I loved the landscape more. I stepped out into heavens of mad beauty.

A slipstream at that speed on adrenaline and MDMA is like being cuddled by god. Molten, candy-coloured winds hugged every inch of my body tight. My flow was pyroclastic. I was alive. I was cared for. I arced out above this earth. I knew its span and felt pure love as I reached out to hug it.

*　*　*

Where were we?

Oh yes. PTSD.

PTSD gets too much press these days. There is also something called Post-Traumatic Growth, or PTG, which barely rates a mention. In fact, there are far more reports of PTG following trauma than resulting psychiatric disorders. Up to 90% of trauma survivors show some element of PTG. The two are not mutually exclusive, and the former may help engender the latter. PTG is not the direct result of trauma; rather it is how the individual perseveres with a new post-trauma reality and how they can forge positive personality changes from this struggle, such as a deeper appreciation of life, empathy with others and a sense of purpose. PTG is not a new concept; early Jews, Christians and Muslims, as well as Greek and Roman philosophies, speak of the transformative power of suffering. But it is new to the field of psychology. Partly this is because traditional psychology is reactive and focuses on treating mental illness. It judges its success by returning sufferers to their former baseline and then stops measuring.

The term Post-Traumatic Growth is relatively new. It was coined by two researchers, Richard Tedeschi and Lawrence Calhoun, in the mid-1990s after interviewing bereaved parents and spouses, cancer survivors, veterans and prisoners. Clearly no one was happy with *what* had happened to them, but the majority reported that they learned profound lessons that had eventually changed their lives for the better.

PTSD and PTG can be plotted on a graph. Those who suffer trauma and do not return to their pre-trauma level have PTSD. 'Robustness' describes those who remain unmarked by trauma. I've never met any of these people and don't want to. Individuals who suffer a downturn and then return to their former levels of well-being are said to be 'resilient'. PTG looks exactly like resilience to begin with—the dip of trauma and the return to the baseline—but then they keep growing and exceed their former baselines going on to form fresh insights, new attitudes and personal strength. These people are said to be 'thriving'.

In nature, thriving is the new shoots after a forest fire; it is the survival of the fittest, the very engine of evolution. It is building muscle after lifting the heaviest weights you can. It is the Blues, it improves with obstacles and heartbreak and your baby's Judas-like duty to bring you gasoline instead of water. It is also the driving force of historical growth, or, to quote Harry Lime, 'In Italy, for thirty years under the Borgias, they had warfare, terror, murder and bloodshed, but they produced Michelangelo, Leonardo da Vinci and the Renaissance. In Switzerland, they had brotherly love, they had five hundred years of democracy and peace—and what did that produce? The cuckoo clock.'

In psychology, it is a process akin to hormesis, or, to use Nassim Nicholas Taleb's term, 'anti-fragile'. 'Some things benefit from shocks; they thrive and grow when exposed to volatility, randomness, disorder, and stressors and love adventure, risk, and uncertainty.'

Who gets PTSD and who gets PTG depends on belief and pre-existing personality traits. Belief works by shaping our understanding of what is possible. How we perceive the future can be a self-fulfilling prophecy.

Let's say all you know about the mental effects of trauma is PTSD and your knowledge is gleaned from films or media reports of veterans going crazy and then life bitch-slaps you a truly terrible event: the next day you're a wreck, trembling, tears—you're going to think that you have PTSD and that you're descending into depression and madness—which creates a vicious circle because these thoughts and feelings worsen the symptoms which are then played back to you and increase your chances of going under.

But there's another way. Martin Seligman is one of the pioneers of positive psychology (the term was coined by Abraham Maslow). It's a movement that studies happiness and has created a bridge between rigorous scientific method and ancient spiritual wisdom. He explains that PTSD is not a given:

> If, on the other hand, you have just a little bit of medical literacy and you know that crying and mourning and feeling very down are typical, normal reactions to being fired, to combat, and that the usual response is resilience and sometimes growth, that stops the downward spiral. So it's very important for people to know that the normal response to very bad things is not going under.

Pre-existing personality traits play a huge role too. Researchers modelled PTG rates against the Big Five personality traits, and found that it was associated with agreeableness, openness and extraversion, and came up with hypothetical reasons for this. Agreeableness (trust, altruism, honesty and humility) may mean that survivors are more likely to ask for support and—more importantly, being kindly souls—are more likely to receive it. Openness (inventive, curious, seeking new experiences and having emotional situational awareness) is thought to help survivors absorb, reappraise and reframe their traumatic experiences and remodel their worldview as a result. Finally, extraversion (outgoing, energetic) promoted PTG because extraverts are more likely to use problem-solving methods and engage in coping strategies. They are also more likely to seek help.

* * *

Lastly, here is something else I discovered on the boat that summer. Once you have been through several trips to the wars, and learned to ride the horror, a bright truth begins to emerge that you might struggle to explain to those from the other end of the safety spectrum, who garner their world-view through screens and nannying algorithms: there really isn't that much trouble out there. In fact, it's the reverse. When your profession is violence you begin to understand what a very small job market there is. There are just not that many conflicts in the world and their numbers have been decreasing for decades. Even the most 'war-torn' countries have vast areas of peace. You need to get dust on your boots to prove it, but the world is an extraordinarily lovely place and humans are far, far better than we're told.

* * *

The kindness of my friends came from deep within. Even a small bit of good nature could be leveraged and multiplied through the processes mentioned here. Gameness and Opponent Process Theory explained why they were so blissed out after a hit of hardship; hormesis mapped a mechanism by how they grew; and PTG showed how some people are more likely to thrive from the slings and arrows of an extreme life. Mentally, emotionally and spiritually, they understood—what most fighters know physically—that flexibility was key, and tolerance was strength. None of them were brittle spirits; they could reframe any adversity into a lesson, or any obstacle into a path.

It wasn't the winning that made these friends so chilled, but the intimate, deep knowledge of losing again and again and again. They embraced error. As Nelson Mandela said of boxing, 'I am either winning or learning.' My friends bench-pressed their trauma. They fed off failure, stress and chaos, and by doing so, banked huge quantities of motivation and willpower. It was a practice that gave them an ever-increasing appreciation of and appetite for life. They had resolve—that profound, self-strengthening resolve you can only develop by being that person, with skin in the game, who figures your way through real-life problems. Above all, suffering gave them a form of self-contained, transcendent cool that bordered on a simple, elemental nobility. As Primo Levi wrote about noble elements, they are so happy in their disposition that they refuse to react with any other element.

* * *

And that evening, just to ruin this completely beautiful vision of my friends, Ernesto, Rob and the other lads went out on the lash, on the pull. They'd invented a stupid competition nick-named the 'Clark Kent' game, which involved trying to attract girls using the most boring chat-up lines they could devise, vying for girls' attention by pretending to work in marketing or finance. I refused to play, partly because I'm terrible at chatting girls up, but mainly because my dad was a journalist, looks a bit like Clark Kent and is one of my heroes.

Instead, I stayed on the boat and watched the sun rise and the tide come in again. There is a strange phenomenon right at the top of the tide on the Thames that only a handful of people know about, but is filled with a subtle, protean magic. It happens just at the switch between incoming tide and outgoing tide. As the last of the tide surges in and loses its strength, it meets a buildup of river flowing down. For a few moments, it's not one thing, nor the other; neither flow nor ebb. The current still has power in the middle of the river but, already, at its edges, it has started to curl and go out again. Just then, a deep and mournful shock of water moves through the river. The boats rock sleepily and tug gently at their mooring lines, the pontoons groan and yawn quietly, the tide goes out again. And life goes on.

7

TWO COLLECTORS

On days when the beers were going down a bit too early on the boat, I would excuse myself and head down the river to mudlark. It's the closest I've ever got to a healthy hobby. I'd pick a good low tide and cycle or paddle down to the City—the ancient heart of London—and look for old coins and curios amongst the mud and shingle of the riverbank.

Most of the times it was a chance to be by myself, but sometimes I teamed up with Stan, an old man who taught me some of the tricks of the Thames. He showed me how the river deposited its loads: lighter material such as pottery, bone and oyster shells at the top; flint, metal and denser loads towards the middle. He taught me how to spot old metal clusters where coins, jewellery or pilgrim's badges might lurk by looking for old pins (old pins have handmade heads of coiled wire rather than the modern moulded variety). Once he even showed me where there was a medieval shipwreck that slowly gave up her cargo of pea-sized garnets from India or Sri Lanka.

But despite his generously sharing all that hard-earned knowl-·edge, I knew very little about Stan. He had been in the military and was about the right age to have served in the Second World War, but he never spoke about it. I'd assumed this was because he hadn't done much worth retelling. This is just a matter of odds. Send ten people to war and one goes to the front lines and the other nine stir soup, drive trucks, fold blankets and do all the other jobs they don't make computer games about. Nine out of ten returning soldiers 'can't talk about the war' not due to the horror but because they didn't actually see anything. All ten of them probably serve their country far more than I ever have, or intend to, but it's hardly a gripping yarn, and while I was fond of Stan, I didn't like him enough to hear the hilarious exploits of the Queen Alexandria's 3rd Auxiliary Catering Unit.

But a few years before, Stan had shown that he was still connected somehow. He knew when I'd passed Selection, and texted, 'I hear congratulations are in order'. I was equally impressed he could text. I wanted to know more about him, but I never pressed him.

Stan and I sat down on the north foreshore with our backs to the Embankment wall, facing south. We were down on proper terra firma, where the city began; familiar landmarks loomed over us. The morning sun was coming up above London Bridge to our left. The occasional train rattled over Cannon Street Bridge to our right. The river currents had piled up a loose mound of oyster shells and brown, water-worn bones that dried out before the shingle further down the shore's slope. It was comfortable and peaceful. I smoked a joint. Stan didn't have any; it 'played havoc with his heart medication'.

The embanking of the Thames was a grand Victorian project. Prior to that, it was a natural riverbank, ad hoc piling, countless wharves and jetties, warehouses and storerooms, running north to Upper Thames Street. The oyster shells were native (*Ostrea edulis*), dredged from the estuary, a fast food of London since Roman times. Many of the bones—ox and mutton—bore butchery marks.

TWO COLLECTORS

Stan was wearing a beanie hat, NHS glasses and several jumpers under a battered green field jacket with endless pockets. He had shaved that morning, but had missed bits in his wrinkled, weathered face. I liked him for that; I had this image of Stan prodding Death in the chest with a fine, bone-handled, badger-hair shaving brush.

I had been to Maria's Market Cafe across the river beforehand and brought bacon and bubble'n'squeak sandwiches with plenty of brown sauce (having correctly predicted the onset of the munchies), and we shared them. Stan had brought his collection of pilgrim badges he'd found in the river over the years. They were neatly packed into individual glassine bags, and several had small card inserts with identification notes and dates.

He had an extraordinary St Albans pilgrim badge that fitted into the palm of my hand, and another from the Shrine of Thomas Becket. Both were late medieval. But best of all were several small scallops from the Shrine of St James in Spain, which reminded me of my own pilgrimage there.

I loved holding them. They were warm with adventure and connected me to my favourite pilgrimage routes and this river that I loved so much. Each one had been won hard: days, weeks, maybe months of walking or riding to some distant shrine and then the same journey back. What had driven the badge owners to make those journeys? Was it to give thanks, seek a miracle, do penance for a sin—or simply for adventure? The site of The Tabard Inn in Southwark was just across the river. It gave me itchy feet.

There were several perfect, delicate ampulla (tiny decorated lead flasks) designed to carry back Holy Water from a sacred shrine—hydration for the soul. The Thames mud can spit out items from a thousand years ago that look like they were dropped yesterday. I looked through them while Stan spoke.

'There are just two bits of advice I have for you.' I sensed what was coming.

'Firstly: Hate all officers...'

I told Stan I'd heard this speech.

'OK. Secondly: Never talk to women about killing.'

This was new but a little obvious.

'Because they'll be disgusted?' I asked.

'No, because you'll be disgusted about how turned on they get over it.' Not so obvious; this wasn't the rose-tinted, Brasso-fumed march down memory lane I was expecting. I took another drag from the joint.

'I remember the first two men I killed; they were officers,' he continued.

'Wehrmacht or SS?' I asked brightly, in my best Enid Blyton voice, thereby exhausting my entire knowledge of Huns with Guns. I was also a little stoned—OK, I was completely fucking baked.

'No, English.'

I waited.

'They were two toffs. Did no work themselves. Wankers. Sent the men out on dangerous patrols. We were getting chewed up out there. I was the sergeant.'

This was not a man unburdening himself. I wasn't sure why he was telling me this story. It felt more instructional.

The tide was still going out. There were old wooden piles down on the foreshore, black with slime and flecked green with duckweed. They steamed in the morning sun. A pleasure boat went past, and the gravel sucked and hissed in its wash. It looked set to be a good tide. The Tide Tables had said it'd be really low, but the fine weather—a good high pressure system—squeezed just a little bit more water out of the river.

'It was when they started to punish the men—dock their pay, demote them—that I decided they needed sorting. They were short-term Charlies from some posh regiment, and these were men's careers they were fucking with.'

'So you shot them?'

'God no! I sapped'em, unconscious, and let the niggers finish them off with their bush-knives.'

We were quiet for a while.

'You look offended. You think I'm wrong?'

'I just hate that word,' I said. (Is racism the opposite of being stoned? The pebbles were pretty.)

'How 'bout "Locals", or "Indigenous forces"?' He was taking the piss now.

'Much better.'

'I guess that's what I'm trying to tell you. It's not so much "Hate all officers" as "Always trust your sergeant." It's our job to look after you. We'll kill anyone to protect our boys and make up some shit to tell the kids when they go to the Palace to pick up their dad's medals.'

'That's it? No trouble for you? Misplacing two officers?'

Stan laughed.

'Not a word of it. Everyone loves a good war story. Heroes both of them. Much better for all involved.'

The tide rolled out. It was very low. I got up and brushed myself off. Stan looked up at me.

'No Gods, no Masters and all that?' he said.

'Yes mate, I get it.'

I gave him a hand up, and we began searching the shore.

* * *

All my life I have ached for the beauty that I see in high-adrenaline moments—a way of seeing where knowledge falls to the wayside and the world is revealed like the Eden I know it to be. That unfiltered, pinpoint clarity and rich colour that comes with danger or great drugs. It's an illuminating blast of loving light that seems to come from heaven but—being greedy, vain or just plain insensitive—I have to get up close to Death's Door for maximum effect. Many times I have wished I didn't have to get myself into so much trouble just to see like that. I'd kill to be able to see big ideas in a flower or a grain of sand. So too with art: to be able to approach an object and get a dose of beauty from it, no altered state required. I would love to be that guy.

Luckily, I met that guy. His name was George Ortiz and he was an extremist. 'I have a need for beauty, for the absolute.' He taught me how to see; he taught me how to forget.

Ortiz phoned me out of the blue one day and told me to come to Geneva. Just like that. We'd never met, and I'd never spoken to him before. The tickets were waiting at the airline counter. I wasn't even looking for a job. He'd got my number from a female friend who'd told him I had studied archaeology and was getting to know my way around the Middle East.

I didn't know much more about Ortiz than he knew about me. All I had heard about him were legends: an aesthetic genius, the last of the great collectors. I hit the books and phone hard to find out more: George Ortiz was born in Paris in 1927, where his father was the Bolivian ambassador and his mother was an heiress. Ortiz's grandfather was the Bolivian 'Tin King', Simon

Patino, one of the richest men in history. Ortiz grew up in Paris, studied philosophy at Harvard and was a radical Marxist—in a way that only the children of the rich can afford to be—until he fell passionately in love with Ancient Greek Art in his early 20s, just after the war. It was this fusion of scholarship, fanaticism, a desire for beauty, and extreme wealth that made George Ortiz such a formidable figure, and his collection of ancient and tribal art one of the greatest on earth.

I got hold of the catalogue of Ortiz's exhibition at the Royal Academy of Arts, London, in 1994. I studied it overnight and on the plane. He had collected not only Greek Art but Roman, Etruscan, Celtic, multiple periods across the Near East, and far and wide across African, American and Polynesian cultures. The objects were incredible in their own right, but as a collection it didn't make sense. Most collectors focus on a specific period or type of artefact. Ortiz had gone the other way. There seemed to be a method, but I couldn't discern what he was thinking. I didn't have the time to ask myself big questions, so I concentrated on memorising everything I could about the most impressive-looking artefacts. If you want to flatter the world's greatest collector, I thought, go for his biggest pieces.

And so I found myself ringing a doorbell on the gate of a grand house set in large gardens on the outskirts of Geneva on a bright summer's morning. A voice on the intercom told me to come through and walk across the gravel drive to the house. The wisteria was in full bloom. Vines with young grapes twisted through sombre cast-iron railings. A small, old man waited at the door: Ortiz. Bruce Chatwin had nicknamed him 'Mighty Mouse' on account of his size and legendary energy. Even at a distance I could sense this. It turned out to be anger.

The first thing Ortiz did was scream at me for being early. This had never happened to me in my life—I mean the 'early' part. I apologised and told him he could go fuck himself and call me a taxi. This wasn't a bluff. I had just met a girl named Susanne who was waiting for me in Amsterdam; I had better things to do.

Once we had reset, he showed me to an apartment in the house where I could drop my bags and freshen up. I remember brushing my teeth and being stared at by the bust of a Roman emperor, in pale marble: blank eyes of eternity like shelled quails' eggs. I felt a pang of stoicism and splashed cold water on my face to fire up some resolve. I repacked my wash-kit into my travel-bag because I didn't think I'd last the day.

When I ambled downstairs Ortiz was the definition of charm. We chatted over a coffee and I told him a bit about my studies in archaeology. I didn't embellish, but glossed over many of the important details, such as the fact that I was academically sub-normal. Before we went downstairs to see part of his collection, he complimented me on how good I looked. Perhaps the man really was an aesthetic genius after all? I was wearing light Church shoes, Balmain linen trousers, a blue Voyage shirt and a raw silk and linen jacket by Dunhill: kinda Eurotrashy, but I made that shit look great. In particular Ortiz liked the jacket. He wanted to see how it looked on him, which I thought was odd given the difference in our sizes, but I humoured him. It was only after he put it on, turned to the mirror and patted himself down that I realised he was—very charmingly—searching me for listening devices or weapons.

Ortiz was very security conscious, and had every right to be. In 1977, his five-year-old daughter Graziella had been kidnapped and was missing for eleven days until Ortiz himself dropped off the $2 million ransom on an autoroute. Graziella was released unharmed; one of the kidnappers was caught, another was found shot dead and little of the ransom money was ever found. But it wasn't just criminals that Ortiz was worried about: his warehouse had been raided by police looking for looted antiquities.

Truth is: I actually was wearing a wire. I'd agreed to carry it for a friend of mine who was part of a concerned circle of folk who were interested in how money from looted antiquities in Iraq and Afghanistan might be used to fund terrorist organisations. Back then, only a handful of analysts and academics had made the connection. Everyone else saw looting as a victimless crime, and it was almost impossible to get support for operations targeting it. Nowadays, it's a cause célèbre, and archaeologists, law-enforcement and military organisations have spent far more on conferences than ISIS ever earned from looting.

I digress.

I was wearing a wire—I'm not proud of that now—and Ortiz found it. He took it from my lower inside jacket pocket and held it up to me. It was disguised as an iPod. By that, I mean it was an iPod, but one of the earphones had been converted to a microphone, and it could be powered up remotely with a car-key alarm-fob, which was in my other pocket. It recorded, then encrypted the audio file and hid it beneath the operating system. (This is showing my age, but iPods were new back then, and hiding a listening device in one was considered beyond sexy.) Ortiz might have been an expert in ancient art, but he knew diddly about the latest music technology.

'Rap music,' I said guiltily.

Ortiz looked disgusted, hurriedly put the iPod back in the suit pocket and handed my jacket to me.

We descended a flight of long stairs towards a basement. Ortiz walked down in front of me. My thumb rested on the car-alarm fob in my pocket, on the button that would trigger the recording. I remember rubbing it, but I didn't press it. It felt too much like shooting a man in the back.

At the bottom of the stairs, a corridor opened into a vaulted basement beneath the house, where it was cool, dry and dark but for a few lights, each aimed at a display case or cabinet. I had read that Ortiz was obsessed about lighting and the exact height of his displays, so that people 'met' the objects in an ideal setting. We stopped in front of a cabinet that held an Achaemenid drinking vessel and stunning Byzantine silverware. Each object glowed in the gentle spotlights. I'd rehearsed clever facts about all these objects. Instead, Ortiz handed me one that I hadn't noticed.

'Tell me about this,' he said, putting a dark, egg-sized object in my hand.

I could feel its weight, that otherworldly heaviness of precious metals: it was two gold-hoop earrings, entwined together and embedded in an oxidised nest of baser metal that looked like a rusted scrap of chain-mail. The gold hoops were large, the bodies coiled with plain and beaded gold wire. Each one ended in bull's-heads, horned but sightless, sockets where jewels once stood for eyes. The tiny bulls nestled each other. I knew they were Hellenistic, but beyond that I couldn't say much.

'Tell me the story,' he said.

The Iliad? Hansel and Gretel? I didn't have a clue.

There was a long pause.

'A woman goes to bed,' Ortiz said. 'She takes off her jewellery.'

And he mimed a lady taking off her silver chain necklace and putting it down first. He acted this scene out like it was nothing—which it was—but he did it with such gentle respect that I knew he'd watched his wife go through the same motions 10,000 times before. His acting was done with love. Then he mimed taking each earring off and joining them together, so they didn't get separated, and placing them on top of the necklace.

This wasn't art, it wasn't archaeology—it was somehow far, far better than both. It felt like alchemy, but with time itself. Ortiz didn't just see the gold or the baser metal but transformed them into a living thing: a simple gesture from over two thousand years ago, a moment of intimacy that had been preserved for ever. For just a moment, I felt I knew her. I thought of the women in my life, those gestures, of my mother, my grandmother, a ripple in time and a deep connection.

'Next,' Ortiz said, selecting a tiny bronze deer. It was less than three inches high in my hand. My mind went to work sorting through years of archaeology studies, excavations, museum visits, auction catalogues...nothing.

'It's a tiny bronze deer,' I said.

There was silence.

'Tell me the story. Why do I like this particular object so very much?'

Ortiz wasn't quite losing patience, but his voice had a hint of steel. I wasn't worried about his anger, but I was having fun and didn't want the game to end before I'd had a chance to win.

I held the deer up close and at least tried to look clever.

'Know less and feel a bit more,' he said.

The deer stood in my palm. It felt scared, but this seemed a very stupid thing to say. I didn't want to look any more stupid than I was feeling. I may have even tried to put on an 'awestruck' face, the type you're *meant* to have around great art. I just wanted the silence to go away.

'It's a doe,' he said plainly. 'Look at how fluid she is. She is perfect, she is young and alive with spirit, the spirit of being a deer.'

And with each word the deer felt a bit more than just an object. It felt innocent rather than mute.

And then Ortiz did his deer impression.

'I saw this once on a hunting trip in Spain, with the King— the King of Spain.' He spelled it out slowly, watching me.

It wasn't that he was name-dropping; he was just being precise. Ortiz had always lived in a world of lots of hunting parties with lots of kings in different countries; it was easy to get confused. Now we had cleared that up, he continued.

'It was very early in the morning, on the edge of the forest.'

He held out his hands in front of himself and made two fists, knuckles down. Then he splayed his fingers down the middle, two each side, so that they resembled the cloven hooves of a deer. He bent over and planted his hooves on the imaginary earth and straightened himself up, alert, and sniffed—sniff, sniff, sniff—twitching his nostrils.

I stood there too, not alert, probably a little slack-jawed, watching a billionaire therianthrope, in his gilded cave, shapeshift into a deer.

'The doe stopped suddenly, ears pricked, eyes wide, scenting the air, attuned. It could sense the danger instinctively. Look at that object—can't you see that?'

I said I could, but we both knew I couldn't: yes, a bit, no, nah not really. I tried to change the subject and didn't really think before I opened my mouth.

'I bet the king liked your deer impression.'

Ortiz stared at me with the compassionate pity only the very stupid should receive.

* * *

I stayed at Ortiz's house for a few days. I got to know his wife Catherine. I saw all of his collection. And I watched him. Each time he handled an object he went into a rapture, like the beauty itself was an essence or a form of communion. He was addicted to form, shape, to the aesthetic. He lost all sense of reason in the presence of beauty. He was devoted to it, he gave himself over to these artefacts and they gave him spiritual nourishment.

For me, it wasn't just the beauty, but the impossible age of the objects, the mad otherness of the cultures they represented, like far-flung constellations in the night sky. Across the gulf of time, they were both wildly distant and heartbreakingly familiar. It was ego-dissolving. I looked at my own reflection on a silver Sphinx, on a gold armlet; I stared face to face with ancient gods and heroes and I felt cleansed by the flux of human history.

* * *

But Ortiz didn't offer me a job. Instead we agreed to meet in Italy a month later.

I next saw him in Tuscany. I'd gone there with Susanne for a friend's wedding. It had been a long weekend, there had been a few parties, the sights in Florence. We'd gone riding too: pushing our horses into a gallop on trails above the valleys. All I saw of Susanne was a cloud of dust and the sparks from the horseshoes in the gathering gloom.

Susanne was very clever—she is the smartest person in this book—but she was also stunning; she had that form of beauty that doesn't seem of this world. Walking down a street with her in London was a jarring experience: a tunnel of silent howls from men and razor whispers from the women. That's the weird thing about extremes; being far outside the bell-curve either way can feel freakish. Extreme beauty and extreme ugliness provoke very similar reactions amongst the rest of us.

In Italy, Susanne provoked traffic accidents, two in four days. I watched them all unfold in slow-mo: we'd be walking down a street and the male driver—one in a car one day, another on a moped the next evening—would lock eyes onto Susanne and ignore where he was going.

Ortiz phoned me and invited us over to lunch at a friend's villa he was staying at. He gave me elaborate directions and made it sound like it was hard to find but it turned out to be a palace that was in every guidebook. It was a seventeenth-century building set in Italian and Spanish gardens, with a lemon grove, a lake and a nymphaeum, or grotto dedicated to Pan. When we arrived there was an informal lunch by the pool, but Ortiz insisted there were formal introductions. I remember a pair of contessas, a foreign ambassador and a few senior priests up from Rome, including a cardinal, although I should probably list them in a different order. It felt a bit like Cluedo, if Cluedo did an Illuminati version.

I sat next to a Monsignor who was also in the Vatican's diplomatic corps. He was one of the most charming men I have ever met. Do you know how—very rarely—you talk to people who so utterly embody what they do, that it seems like part of the divine plan? That was this guy: if God had been looking for someone really charming to represent him He would have picked the Monsignor. Which I suppose He did. We were halfway through an incredible conversation when Susanne decided to skinny-dip. She stripped then and there at the side of the pool and it reminded me of a Chandler line: 'It was a blonde. A blonde to make a bishop kick a hole in a stained-glass window.' When the Monsignor saw what was happening he burst out laughing and got up to leave with his colleagues—I guess they had to—but he was smiling and shaking his head. I watched him walk up the stone path trying to catch up with the other priests who were in panicked retreat from the naked girl in the water but, somewhat ironically, heading towards the Pan's nymphaeum. Then the Monsignor turned to me and held up his hands like he was weighing his options, or juggling heaven and hell, and shrugged and laughed again.

Ortiz and his wife Catherine headed for Pisa for the afternoon with me and Susanne in tow. We visited the Campo Santo to see the sarcophagi. Ortiz and Susanne argued all the way around. The corridors echoed with their shouting. At times it was so loud that the guards intervened. Not only was Susanne incredibly clever, but she also knew her history of art. It was fascinating to watch, the best fight ever: in one corner was an aesthetic genius; in the other was absolute beauty itself. Susanne disagreed with everything he had to say; she had a way of jabbing with questions and then delivering an upper-cut statement: stick and move. Ortiz couldn't handle her. It was like one of his objects was talking back. It sent him apoplectic. Catherine and I followed them around and admired the sarcophagi and the frescoes.

At the end of the day, Ortiz offered me a job on a few projects, but nothing came of it. The few times he needed my help I was abroad. As for looted antiquities from war zones? I never saw anything that made me suspicious. But I did see Ortiz many more times, in London mostly. We'd have lunch or dinner and visit the British Museum or the galleries of Mayfair. Other times he would send me books he thought I should read. He was incredibly generous with his knowledge and his time.

To this day I try to summon his way of seeing when I am faced with an object. I try to block out the din of signals and meet the object on its own terms. I try to feel the spirit of the piece, to see the beauty firsthand. It's a paradox: in order to remember everything he taught me, I must forget everything I know.

* * *

I only truly understood what Ortiz was saying about the deer years later in a far away place. I was with a team keeping eyes on a small river crossing from a scratch observation post (or OP) in a small stand of trees 500m away: people hunting, though sadly no kings of any description. We had been there for several days, and the guys with me were tired and grouchy. Personally, I love certain kinds of surveillance work when I get paid to do fuck all. Sure, I like watching the world flood past in a city, the tiny soap-opera eddies of urban life. But I love rural OPs far more. Think about it. When was the last time you lay on the earth and had a deep look, a proper listen? How long did you do it for? Imagine doing that for days: being part of nature, we were so still and quiet, eye-level with the ground, so filthy that we felt part of the earth; life thrived around us. It is incredible what you learn when the spatial scales fall away: the epic shit that insects get up to. I'd spent the days in that OP watching amber ants do Babylonian things in the dust.

It was very early in the morning, first light. I had just swapped my night-vision scope for a daylight one on my rifle, and was watching the river while my buddy swapped his. The river was more of a brook, snaking between dry meadows and spiny bushes. At one point, on a small bend pointing towards us, the river slowed down and the current cruised lazily over a small bar of golden and brown pebbles. And that's where I saw it: a doe stepped out between the bushes and tip-toed down to the water's edge to drink. I could feel how perfect the deer was. I could taste the water she drank. Then it sensed something and stood upright.

Down the rifle scope I saw the deer, and I saw the little statue. I saw George Ortiz being the deer, I saw him as a young man hunting with the King of Spain. I could see even further back: I watched the same scene on a morning in Greece about 700BC. I looked at the original deer over the shoulder of the sculptor who made it. For a brief moment we all saw the same thing. It was a shot of beauty, godlike in delight, arcing across the centuries, connecting us all. It hit me right through the eye and I knew a lot less.

8

HE'S NOT THE CALIPH; HE'S A VERY NAUGHTY BOY

Niaz was very jumpy. He was deeply suspicious of me, and had every right to be. Most people would label him a terrorist. Terrorists, though, thought he was a traitor. I thought he was a dickhead, but couldn't work out if he was a hero too.

How bad are terrorists really? I don't mean evil. I mean crap. Should the new ones even be called terrorists?

I was thinking these thoughts as Niaz drove us around the deserted backstreets of Manchester in the rain. We looped and switchbacked down empty streets, past boarded-up restaurants, overflowing wheelie bins, off-licences and bingo halls. *Is he run-ning a counter-surveillance drill that he has been trained to do, or copying something o   the ilms—or is he simply lost?* I made small talk for a bit, then went quiet and let Niaz create some distance between himself and whatever he saw in the rearview mirror. Niaz's story was always about running away from what he saw in mirrors.

I wanted Niaz to be settled. I wanted to try to get inside his head so I could simulate an attack on London. I'd been tasked to try to either buy or build a nuclear weapon, to see if the terrorists could do it too. It wasn't as exciting as it sounds, I promise. Part of the brief was trying to find out how terrorists thought. Were they capable of it?

Niaz Khan should not have been in the car with me. He shouldn't have been alive at all. If the plan had gone right he should have died hijacking one of the planes in 9/11. His journey is one of the most fascinating personal stories I have come across since the towers came down. Not least because Niaz himself has the personality of a dial-tone.

Niaz was average build but there was a tension in his physique that made me think he'd be tricky in a fight. He drove and he talked. This worked for me. If you're interviewing someone with something to hide, it's best to get them engaged in a task, however mundane. It redirects their critical faculties elsewhere, and with it, their ability to self-edit. It's a rawer product. But so is blood from a stone.

By the way, this is a test. For you.

Try walking a mile in Niaz's shoes. Consider it another form of Selection; it was certainly his. If you get to the end of his story and have no empathy for him then you've failed. Try again.

I am often struck by people who refuse to empathise with radicals as if it was a point of principle, and how, through that weakness posturing as strength, they are much more like their enemy than they can conceive. You should practise being wrong; it's where your natural weakness is: if you are good at boxing, work on your ground game; if you're right-handed go southpaw; if you're southpaw ... you get the idea. The black-belt level for this exercise would be the Ideological Turing Test, a phrase coined by economist Bryan Caplan. The original Turing Test was designed as a test for artificial intelligence: in a blindfolded experiment a person has a chat with a robot; if the person thinks they are talking to a human, then the robot has passed the test. If you genuinely want to understand terrorists, you should be able to articulate their worldview so fluently that you could be mistaken for one.

But here is the cheat: you don't even have to be able to quote dusty tenth-century Muslim scholars—most of them can't. Instead you just need to be able to empathise with their frustrations, hopes and despairs. The processes of radicalisation are the same if you wind up a Nazi, a Communist or a radical Islamist. It's not about where you are going, it's about where you are coming from; it is a journey from the self. Most people sign up for reasons universal to us all: a sense of purpose, direction, empowerment, excitement and belonging. It is impossible to stress how important the latter is: extremism feeds off alienated and atomised individuals. The desire to belong is really a desire to lose yourself in a compacted mass of people.

As part of your empathy training, try watching ISIS recruitment videos side by side with the Army recruitment ads, the ones they show mid-morning on weekdays. The production values might differ, but the message is the same: here is a place where you belong; you will have friends; excitement is waiting for you. The mulch of history is young men mistaking depression for oppression. Getting 'out of it' through drugs or extremism is often more important than where you are going.

Perhaps the single most useful book to understand Islamic terrorists doesn't even mention them. *The True Believer* was written by Eric Hoffer in 1951 and concerns the nature of extreme mass movements. Hoffer lived as a drifter through the Depression in California as a migrant worker. For a time he slept rough on Skid Row. One winter, while panning for gold, he was snowed in for months in the mountains with only Montaigne's *Essays* to read. Hoffer understood the desires of the frustrated more than any writer before or since, because he had lived them. He wrote some of his most profound philosophical treatises while sleeping in railway yards. It wasn't simply because he knew gnawing hunger, but because he had tasted hope.

As Hoffer said, 'The chief burden of the frustrated is the consciousness of a blemished, ineffectual self, and their chief desire is to slough off the unwanted self and begin a new life.'

Are you ready? Let's get back to Niaz.

Niaz Khan was born in the UK but spent most of his childhood in Pakistan, where his family was from. He returned to the UK when he was seventeen with dreams of studying English and going to university. It wasn't meant to be. Instead Niaz wound up as a curry-waiter in Oldham, near Manchester, slinging poppadoms and pints to drunks. And every night he took his meagre earnings down to the local casino, for Niaz had a chronic gambling problem. On Fridays he would often attend the local mosque, partly as a self-imposed penance, more out of loneliness. It was a mosque with a strong radical following, and he told absolutely no one there of his addiction.

It was a struggle to get these details out of Niaz. Fragments of his story would come out, then nothing, then a bit more. The windscreen wipers were on low, to clear the drizzle, but they also seemed to provide the cadence of his narrative. As for the direction his story takes: sometimes he would backtrack from important points or deadend into silence when I thought we were about to get somewhere interesting. His storytelling was a lot like his driving, and his driving was ... well ... I can see why al-Qaeda didn't want him flying the planes. There was a bleached quality to his language, as if the gambling or the extremism stole the warmth from his voice. In all the time we spoke he never mentioned any family or friends.

I could've murdered a kebab but we didn't agree on where. Anywhere Niaz felt safe had bad food; all the 'dangerous' places had the best food. This is possibly a metaphor for the War on Terror. He continued with his story:

Oldham 1999, about as far from the gardens of paradise as you can get; there probably haven't been 72 virgins in the town's entire history. In the charts, Boyzone, Atomic Kitten and Cliff Richard vie for the Christmas No. 1. Picture yourself in a polyester uniform and clip-on bowtie serving endless lagers and dayglo-dyed, roadkill curries: the drunkenness, looped sitar muzak, constant racism, teeming ropes of neon lights, flock wallpaper and vomit. At closing time, a walk down the high street where every other shop is a bookies or a baker: a Breughel of fights, urine and binge-drinking collapse. Niaz would either hit the local betting machines or take a trip into Manchester to the casinos there. Bigger slot machines, more bright lights and dinka-dink sounds like a dark call to the unfaithful. Then—possibly—a trip to the mosque for *Salat al-fajr*, the dawn prayers, fluorescent lighting, that sour-sweat smell of the night-shift, worn carpets, and talk of salvation. And finally a bus ride to a bedsit while the England that Niaz dreamed about wakes up, just as he falls asleep.

Niaz Khan had dreamt of a better life, and suffered profound frustration and existential crisis when his hopes weren't met.

Niaz had always tried to be a good Muslim. As his sense of alienation and misery increased, it was only natural that he turned towards the local mosque, a safe space away from the casino, from the drunks and the crippling alienation. The Imam, a firebrand preacher, thundered about the black flags of jihad. He took Niaz under his wing, but didn't try to recruit him—yet. And that was the infernally clever bit.

I watched a group of kids—mostly Asian—in hoodies settle on a bench in the park nearby. They were more a gaggle than a gang, but they made Niaz nervous. We drove on. I wanted to know about the flags he talked about. After the British flag, then the Pakistani, then British again and finally the banner of jihad...

'Did you really think that another flag would be the solution you were looking for?'

'It was for the cause,' he said.

I suspect at the beginning Niaz was gambling because he had hope for his life in the west: that his number would come up and all his dreams would come true. A slang definition of insanity and also addiction: doing the same thing a thousand times and expecting a different result. But odds of a thousand to one also pay out big—life-changing cash.

The casino provided a microcosm of the world outside that Niaz could relate to. At least there was a reason to his losing, the unfairness of his life reduced to dice and roulette numbers. There was also the discipline an addiction provides. Above all, the casino provided a brotherhood of sorts, an equality under the odds, against the house. Khan was still losing, but at least he wasn't alone.

Niaz went back to the casino night after night. His world was a schizoid wheel between slot machines and prayer mats. Some mornings, in a fit of shame, he took his winnings from the casino and put them in the mosque's collection box for the Taliban.

On the night of 18 March, 2000, after a series of very bad losses at a Manchester casino, Khan was approached by two men who knew him by name. He was terrified. He had every right to be: Khan was £9,000 deep in gambling debts to loan sharks, and Manchester has some of the most brutal debt collectors in the country.

In many ways it was worse: al-Qaeda was staging his intervention.

'They say to me, "You are good Muslim but you do gamble. You should feel ashamed. But you can do something to make God forget this, to make God happy. We can help you."

'And I say, "What can you do for me?" and they say, "You hear Osama's name" and of course I have heard of him many times from the Imam, who says he is a great man.'

This was not a random encounter. It was a very specific and clever targeting by men associated with the mosque. They knew every detail of Khan's life. They knew his triggers—how and, more critically, *when* to exploit them. Few Western intelligence agencies can match this degree of psychological profiling. And none come jangling the keys to paradise.

The two men said they worked for Osama bin Laden. They offered to clear Khan's gambling debts and give him enough money to fly to Pakistan. Khan was being offered an addict's moment of clarity: a clean slate and a route to salvation, all in one. Khan went home, packed a few possessions and headed for the airport without telling a soul.

'Just like that?' I asked.

Niaz squirmed like he was reliving the hook.

'Ben, they are al-Qaeda,' he said. 'They got inside my head. They could get inside *your* head too. They could make *you* do anything.'

'Niaz,' I told him. 'If terrorists were this good-looking they would be getting plenty of blow-jobs, and then they wouldn't be terrorists any more, would they?'

Niaz sighed. Humour is not one of the precepts of al-Qaeda. But then again, neither is getting laid. It is a strongly held belief amongst many people battling Islamic terrorists that peace could be achieved in the Middle East with several airborne battalions of sky-diving Ukrainian hookers. And imagine how much fun that training would be?

'What happened when you landed at Lahore?' I asked.

Niaz says that he waited at a hotel for 24 hours before being met by a contact, and then he was blindfolded and driven to a safe house. Niaz has told different investigators different versions. Some describe a building on the outskirts of the city, others a site within Afghanistan. The log for the hotel in Lahore suggests he spent a week there before being collected. His inability to recall details or timelines made him an infuriating subject, but I don't believe it changes the veracity of what happened next.

'There were many people there from all over the world,' he said, 'from Philippines, Bangladesh, Saudi Arabia and Chechnya. We were all interviewed, and they said, "You will hijack a plane and 99% chance of blowing it up and are you OK with this" and I said "I am here to die"'.

Niaz looked at me when he said these words. A chill wasn't even *ambling* down my spine. I'm not trying to big-up myself in the retelling. I liked Niaz; I still do. Somehow this curry waiter and gambling junkie had been sling-shotted into the heart of the greatest terrorist attack in history. Four planes in a row. That's a jihadi jackpot.

What I was not impressed by was the whole willingness-to-die punchline, because it begs the question: why are you still on the stage? Yet, I've heard it countless times from would-be terrorists. ISIS are forever banging on: 'We love death more than you love life'. Well, yes and no.

As Hoffer put it, 'They see their lives and the present as spoiled beyond remedy and are ready to waste and wreck both hence their recklessness and their will to chaos and anarchy. They also crave to dissolve their spoiled meaningless selves in some soul-stirring spectacular.'

'Did suicide bother you?' I asked Niaz.

'No, I don't mind because this world is no good,' he said.

But even in death there was a pecking order. Niaz was never destined for flight school in the States. He was never going to pilot the planes. Those jobs were left for men like Mohammed Atta, an articulate, Westernised college-kid. Niaz was still just a curry waiter. Niaz was muscle.

'For two weeks, we had more talks and much preaching and also lessons,' Niaz says.

They were taught the art of hijacking. Niaz learned hand-to-hand combat and how to use a variety of weapons that had been disguised so they could be smuggled onto a plane. He was shown how to blind his victims with an aerosol (a pepper spray disguised as Lynx deodorant). Niaz was taught how to turn the pop-up handles of carry-on cases into a hidden, lethal, double-bladed sword. Then they were trained together in four-to-five-men teams to use blades and spray to drive the passengers to the back of the plane. All of these types of weapons and tactics were used on that day. The house even had a mocked-up cockpit of a 767, the type of planes used in the attacks.

Most importantly, Niaz was taught how to wield terror itself: to strike early on in the flight, 'When no one was expecting it,' and to slit the throat of a stewardess at the front of the plane to cover other passengers in blood.

Old Trafford loomed into view, and we stopped at the traffic lights. Football. 'Fan' is just a shortening of 'fanatic'. I looked at Niaz, trying to imagine if he could have carried out such butchery.

'Were you happy with those instructions?' I asked.

The windscreen wipers squeaked, and there was the metronome sound of the turning signal.

'Yes, it's war. Anything is OK in war.'

'No feelings?'

Niaz shrugged.

Slowly it was dawning on me why they picked him. The compartmentalisation, the disassociation, all the qualities that made him so frustrating to interview were the same factors that made him so perfect for the job. Al-Qaeda were aware of his abilities long before he was.

After three or four weeks training Niaz was given $35,000 to set up a new life in America and await further instructions. His route was Lahore to Doha, then London to Zurich to London again, and finally to New York. The reason for this zigzagging route was to give Khan as much airtime as possible before the hijackings so he could familiarise himself with various airport security systems, and those on board the planes.

At JFK his instructions were to wear a skullcap he had been given and find a man wearing an identical skullcap at the taxi rank outside. There the man would twice greet him with the words 'Are you Babu Khan?' and twice Khan was to reply, 'Yes, I am Babu Khan.' But something went wrong.

Khan said he waited and waited, and as he did so he began to reflect on his journey and his family back home. He prayed for a sign. 'I think that Jihad is in Afghanistan with the Taliban', he thought. 'This is where I want to fight. Not in America'. But Khan didn't go home, nor did he go to a local mosque or even to relatives who lived nearby. And there, above the teeming crowds of the arrivals hall, he saw the sign: a path to another paradise that he yearned for, one that was calling him back, a gigantic billboard for the casinos of Atlantic City.

It took Khan three days to gamble away all of al-Qaeda's cash.

And then he did something truly extraordinary and brave: he phoned the police, and they handed him to the FBI. The bureau questioned him for three weeks and submitted him to two polygraph tests; he passed both. A report was sent up to HQ, but it was never acted upon. After three weeks, the FBI flew him back to the UK, where he was handed over to the British authorities. This time he was questioned for 45 minutes and released. The next time authorities heard from Niaz Khan was a year later, on 9/11, when he called *Crimestoppers*. No one ever bothered to return his call.

* * *

My lousy joke about blow-jobs to Niaz was more than a flippant comment. Extreme religion and addiction are mutual enemies, but only because they are fighting for the same customers. I am endlessly fascinated by this, not least because I find it very funny—but mainly because it fills me with hope: we are going to win this one.

Chronic gambling is a behavioural addiction—no substances are involved. It relies on the reward pathway that we met during military training. It is one of the most powerful learning engines in the brain. Its job is to provide a cone of attention and motivation towards a certain goal, which it does through the release of dopamine. Dopamine is a neurotransmitter; it is pure desire. The more motivation and repetition, the more likely a habit will be formed. If you have plenty of motivation towards a goal, you need less repetition; low motivational goals require lots of repetition. This is why my DS only had to scream at me two or three times amidst the gunfire and explosions for me to develop a good habit—nothing is as rewarding as survival—but Mr Williams, my French teacher when I was a teenager, had to repeat himself twenty times for any word that didn't involve seafood, alcohol or chatting up French girls. Which was every word in French business-language studies.

Ironically for Niaz, researchers say gambling 'hijacks' this very primitive part of the brain. Remember, the brain isn't doing anything *bad*; it is simply doing what it evolved to do: learning to chase life's acorns. Gambling is all about dreaming of a magical reward amidst endless repetition, especially on the fruit-machines that were Niaz's favourite. Each time that connection is made, the dopamine pump squirts a dose that paints the target with desire, like lighting up a tank with a laser for an airstrike. The heart of addiction isn't the target but the bright path down the laser beam. Dopamine isn't pleasure but the anticipation of pleasure; it's the journey, not destination. Dopamines forms mental narratives and imbues them with drama regardless of how those stories end. The playwright William Archer said 'Drama is anticipation mingled with uncertainty'. Pathological gamblers get almost the same dopamine hit whether they lose or win. The renowned neuroscientist Robert Sapolsky refers to this dopamine jackpot as 'the magic of maybe'.

But just as dopamine lights up the target, it also masks input from other parts of the brain, specifically those devoted to judgement and decision-making. Constant repetition reinforces the desire for gambling and mutes the voice of reason.

I have never 'got' the rush of gambling for money. (But I do get a kick out of gambling with my life.) Money simply isn't my thing; it doesn't motivate me. I don't like cash enough to miss it if I lose, and it doesn't make my day if I win. I can't look inside Niaz's head, but I suspect his jackpot target was loaded with the glitter of acceptance into a society that ignored him. Fast cars and faster women are a flight from self. Every other shop on Oldham high street is a Paddy Power, Betfred, Poundland or Quicksilver Casino.

I have been around war and weapons most of my life, and I'm still constantly surprised at the ingenious ways we have cooked up to kill each other. But even I was creeped out by the ruthless sophistication and manipulation of the machines inside gambling joints. Many are specifically designed to chime with dopamine cycles within our brains to promote addictive behaviour. The bright lights and ascending tones ramp up and pay out multiple 'credits', which trick the player into thinking they have the advantage in a phenomenon known as a 'loss disguised as a win'. This creates a smoother form of gambling that further lulls the gambler into the repetitive cycle, all the while draining their money reserves—not too fast to notice, not too slow to be boring—like a bilking machine. The resulting hypnotic state has been labelled 'dark flow' by psychologists studying gambling addictions. It shares some similarities with the flow-state in fight or flight we saw earlier, namely tachypsychia, where hours pass without notice. And under the cloak of this reverie, the relentless repetition re-stitches and reworks the neural pathways further: revising the lesson, carving the habit, burning the bad program deeper.

Most critically for Niaz's story, the reward pathways that engaged his gambling addiction are precisely the same ones that are used in religious experiences. In the USA, brain imaging of Mormons showed increased activity in the nucleus accumbens at points the volunteers reported 'feeling the spirit'. This part of the Shrew brain is fuelled by dopamine, and is responsible for impulsive action and anticipation. Whether Niaz yearned for the jackpot or jihad, this part of the brain continued to fire profound feelings of desire and yearning within him.

Addiction carved new pathways in his mind and made him ripe for recruitment. Every time he hit the casino or the mosque he entrenched these patterns further, creating a feedback loop. As Marc Lewis wrote in *The Biology of Desire:*

> The repetition of particular experiences modifies synaptic networks. This creates a feedback cycle between experience and brain change, each one shaping the other. New patterns of synaptic connections perpetuate themselves like the ruts carved by rainwater in the garden. The take home message? Brain changes settle naturally into brain habits—which lock in mental habits. And the experiences that get repeated most often, most reliably, and that actually change synapses rather than just passing through town, are those that are the most compelling. In fact, desire is evolution's agent for getting us to pursue goals repeatedly.

Most religions make some use of spiritual euphoria in their practices, but the repetitive, self-reinforcing use of religious ecstasy in radical Sunni Islam is particularly ideal for re-hijacking the wiring of a gambling addict. Niaz's gambling addiction helped prepare him for indoctrination like a low-budget Manchurian Candidate—a Mancunian Candidate. The slot-machine—its dark-flow hypnotism and magic jackpot—meant his recruiters didn't have to work too hard to present suicide as a glorious victory, the ultimate loss disguised as a win.

That's what I like most about Niaz's story: al-Qaeda battling a fruit machine in the cockpit of his brain and losing. His salvation was a nightmare plot; his relapse was possibly our salvation. Sadly his warning was never acted upon with all the catastrophic results of that fateful day. But I also wonder this: how many other people were waiting for Niaz to show up? Was he the missing man of another team, one that was tasked for a fifth plane that was never hijacked because of his actions or inactions?

Had Niaz not fucked up his contact meeting in the taxi rank it is likely he would have found himself with other hijackers— many of whom were addicts as well—in Las Vegas. Mohamed Atta, Egyptian, 9/11 ringleader and pilot of the first plane to hit the World Trade Centre, visited the Olympic Garden Topless Cabaret in Las Vegas with other hijackers a number of times that summer. Hijackers from another team visited the Pink Pony, across the street from the House of Leather, on Florida's Daytona Beach.

Sometimes it's refreshing to see cataclysmic world events through the eyes of a stripper: Samantha, 29, told a newspaper that she gave a dance for Marwan al-Shehhi, pilot of the second plane to hit the towers. She said the terrorist gazed at her blankly while she ground her crotch just inches from his face. 'Some big-man terrorist, huh? He spent about $20 for a quick dance and didn't tip more. I'm glad he's dead with the rest of them. But he wasn't just a bad tipper—he killed people.'

* * *

I liked Niaz. A small part of me admired him too. He had the balls to make his pilgrimage. It's a shame that his prophet living in a cave turned out to be Osama bin Laden.

As for me, I never got my hands on a nuclear bomb or even a dirty bomb. We tried everything: shady deals in Paris for uranium; dud test-bombs from Kazakhstan; and something from Bulgaria that barely glowed in the dark. Eventually we wound up getting stung for some Strontium 90 in a botched weapons deal in the Caucasus. I loved the chase, the thrill of working undercover. I was furious when they pulled the plug on the project. It left me itching for a fight. I wanted to hunt a big target. I wanted to take down something dangerous and genuinely scary. Through that desire I became a lot more like Niaz than I could have ever conceived.

9

TIE ME UP, DON'T TIE ME DOWN

Whipping and abuse are like laudanum: you have to double the dose as the sensibilities decline.

Harriet Beecher Stowe

When I was young I was taught that women hated violence. I was taught the story of Lysistrata, written by Aristophanes, where a woman ends the Peloponnesian War by persuading all women to withhold sex until their men stop fighting. It was so boring that I took it seriously. I only realised it was a comedy when I joined the military.

Hereford is a damp market town on the Welsh borders. The river is always swollen with rain and at opening hours the streets flood with mobility scooters between dole office and pub doors. The few jobs are in the cider industry; the main profession is drinking. The architecture is drab, Victorian and funereal, soot-blacked, streaked with arsenic-green algae from overflowing gutters choked with moss. The large, dour buildings are built with a local red sandstone the colour of livor mortis.

At night you understand the link between fucking and fighting. This isn't clever sociology that I could demonstrate with a whiteboard and arrows. You live it. If you've never spent time in a bar where there are regular fights then you're just going to have to trust me on this.

My favourite person to go out on the town with was Paul Stout. He was happily married and never strayed, but he loved fighting—loved it like the artist he was. He was a gifted, generous and funny man who had honed his talent in Muay Thai rings and hundreds of brawls. Between work and play we would go to the gym on the base and spar. Sometimes, I'd hold the heavy bag, and even though I saw his punch a thousand times I could never get my head around the sheer force of it. I seem to spend a lot of my time in war zones just trying to get savvy with the turbo-physics of violence—shrapnel buckling lampposts like bendy straws, cranial ejection in head wounds, the delicate splashes of a depleted uranium round through a tank—but I still can't get Paul's punch, the maths of it. It came out of nowhere, you couldn't see it coming, but its effects took weeks to leave.

I can't even remember the name of the pub. Or which night it was. I wasn't pissed. We didn't bother with the queue; inside the bar it was three deep with men in pressed shirts with prominent labels, muscles and menace. Women were in clusters facing each other, straws in their drinks, too much lipstick and sideways glances that could launch a thousand riot vans if it kicked off. It always kicked off. The women controlled the violence, but I couldn't prove that in a court of law. And that's my point. One wink or whisper from a woman was all it took and a fight would break out. I see it all in a burst of silent CCTV footage; the music was so loud everything was unsaid. Any time a good-looking female headed towards you her boyfriend would be seconds behind. How could you tell us all apart? It was Hereford for fuck sake: anyone not in local high-street clothing was from the base. Anyone with a tan, or with a nice car, or who was in good shape—proper shape, not gym-pretty—was from the base. And anyone from the base was a ticket out of that town. Or at least a ticket to a good first marriage and a nice farmhouse up the road.

This next bit sounds so backwards I'm embarrassed to tell you, but the women had a test to see if you were the real deal. They would tell you their telephone number but you couldn't punch it into your phone—oh no—you had to remember it. The thinking was that only we—we few, we happy few—could digest an eight-figure map reference; it was beyond the ken of locals. An eleven-figure phone number, that's what counted for a knight's errand in Hereford. I thought it was just some joke about the locals until it happened to me: this lovely woman giving me the memory challenge on the dance floor covered in broken glass with her boyfriend out cold and bleeding—Stout, not me, I swear—and her mates looking on as she tells me her number like it's the most romantic shit they've ever seen. Her friends had so much wonder in their eyes that I felt I had to make a special *thinking* face like it's a challenge or something. Her and her mates looked at me—as those eleven digits slid down—like I was a medieval sword swallower.

And it must have worked—sort of—because she came back to the Green Dragon Hotel with me. 'Sort of' because by the top of the stairs I couldn't remember her name. By the time we got to the room I wasn't in the mood and tried to go along with it because I had nothing better to do.

The only light came from the streetlights outside, where the columns of rain looked like citrine quartz, and the curtains were nicotine yellow. The room was cold but the radiators were blisteringly hot, and every now and then the pipes rattled and honked like geese. It was hard to feel sexual in the Green Lion, but it was the sexiest place in Hereford.

'You're in the Regiment, aren't you?' she asked.

'I'm really, really not,' I said, mainly because I felt like a fraud, a part-time boy-scout at best. I'd only ever seen the military as a hobby, not a source of identity.

'You're my first soldier. I can't wait to tell my Dad,' she said as she undid her boots.

I don't remember what I told her; sometimes stuff comes out of my mouth that is so boring that even I zone out, and then I come to with a jolt and get all worried that I might be on the spectrum. It hadn't been a good day. We'd been training in a torrential downpour at a mocked-up building on some shitty base nearby. No one had a clue what they were doing and—I kid you not—the part-time DS in charge spent most of the afternoon under his poncho trying to download grainy online footage of the Iranian embassy siege to try to figure out how to abseil through a window. I'd spent my time smoking cigarettes and watching rain drip from the barrel of my weapon, feeling like I was in a military reenactment club. I tried to tell all of this to the girl: that we weren't Special Forces, that we were barely diet SF, that I use fabric softener when I wash my balaclava—anything not to be this girl's fantasy.

'Would you please just shut up and fuck me?' she said, unhooking her bra, laughing like I was the big silly.

And that was the only time, in my entire military career, that I remember genuinely saluting anyone.

* * *

That was the first and last time I got laid for any association with the military. It felt fraudulent, and creeped me out. The uniform always felt like someone else's costume—an illusion of strength—and I didn't love the women it attracted. I liked that lady, but her expectations felt like baggage. In my limited experience, when women are attracted to strength it's a set-up for lots of emotional heavy lifting in the future, and I'm very lazy. In relationships I yearn for neutral buoyancy.

I have always been painfully shy. I was weak and shy as a kid, but in my 20s I did a few press-ups and then—Kapow!—*weak and shy* becomes *strong and silent*. I've never had a problem being stereotyped or objectified, if anything I appreciate the handrails of such tropes: it means I don't have to think so much. But being silent seems to be a mistake emotionally, and some women project illusions on you. It's not always about strength either; if you're as silent as I am, mute even, then some women mistake you for a good listener, and that can be like being waterboarded, but with feelings.

Uniforms felt like the dressing-up box; period drama, paint-by-numbers of a dull world I'd assumed we'd left behind some time before I was born. I never believed my role in role-play and, paradoxically, uniforms require lots of imagination to get into: you have to really believe in the power of institutions to find their garb titillating. I've never felt strongly enough about religion, the law or school to find females dressed as nuns, police-women or schoolgirls erotically charged with potential transgression. It all left me cold. No, it made me think I was weird for missing out. I didn't like *not* liking it. I felt like I was autistic, a fizzy static, like fleas were jumping on my face, my not understanding something others found so obvious.

I'd always wanted to be a sexual extremist, but I wound up being a slag. A massive vanilla slag. Each hook-up was like trying to hitchhike away from myself or into myself, and no one took me as far as I wanted to go. I didn't know where or how far that was—the edge I guess, as usual—or maybe just somewhere I didn't feel like I was being left behind. I was jealous of people who had kinks. I confided this to a friend, and she suggested I try Japanese rope bondage, because I lived on a boat and was good with rope, but I found the knots more interesting than the result. And besides, why would I want power over someone else? That was the day job, even if it *was* only a hobby.

I didn't find it shocking, and I badly wanted to feel shocked—to *feel*. What were the boundaries of sex? What was the sexual equiv-

alent of jumping off a cliff on a bright summer's day into deep
waters? I wanted totality across the senses. I wanted it spelled out
for me on my nervous system. You can't make-believe oblivion.

A kink is similar to a habit. It is a form of training involving
desire and repetition. Kinks and habits get under your skin with
multiple exposures to stimuli, sneaking and snaking into the
mind. I was hanging around with lots of female medics in those
days—another perk of violence—and I find smart, capable
women very attractive. I like the intelligence of female A&E
doctors and nurses, the chutzpah and humour of paramedics. The
biggest dramas of existence are their day jobs—they have a gauge
for what is drama-worthy that I find settling. Their work gave
them the emotional ballast that comes with doing life-and-death
shit—and the confidence and resolve of doing that shit very well.
It's a turn on. I've gone out with a few doctors, and they have all
been great, but I never saw it as 'a thing'. The first time I thought
'Oh, maybe there is a pattern here' was on a gurney outside an
operating theatre. She was a hot anaesthetist. Let me say that
again: *she was a hot anaesthetist.* How can you argue with anything in that sentence?

* * *

As the orderlies wheeled me down hospital corridors for an operation (damage to my face from getting repeatedly rifle-butted with
a couple of AK-47s), it occurred to me that I'd seen this point-of-
view shot of similar ceilings many times before in medical dramas
on TV: the square tiles scrolling past and fluorescent strip-lights,
an upside-down man smiling at me as he pushed us along, nee-
nah-nee-nah. Beside me—keeping pace—a tracking shot: a
blonde woman walked alongside the gurney in light-blue doctors'
scrubs, which were worn low, and her skin was tanned somewhere
between cinnamon, gold and garnet. Her scrubs had a bright-
yellow drawcord that made me think of the Swedish flag.

The trolley stopped in the prep room, and she dismissed the orderlies and filled a disposable cardboard tray from the shelves. When she turned around I saw how beautiful she was, so I didn't look at her, and instead admired her handiwork as she tourniquet'd my arm, swabbed a fat vein, inserted the cannula and then deftly slipped a pulse oximeter on my finger. I watched her hook up a three-way tap on the IV line and then fill a syringe from an ampoule that was so small it looked powerful. She was very capable. Slick drills—that sweet-spot overlap between intelligence and practicality in medical women that I find insanely attractive but is rarely reciprocated. She plugged the syringe into the cannula-line in her left hand and checked the oximeter.

'You have a resting pulse of 45. You're really fit,' she said with indifference.

I struggled to say something very witty and charming, but she cut me off with a series of hand gestures worthy of a Hollywood SWAT team: holding her index finger to her lips in shush, pointing to her name tag, making the call-me phone sign and then waving goodbye, and—just as I tried to take all this in—she fired the syringe in her other hand like a detonator and the room instantly overexposed with those burned-out colours seen at extreme altitude, the edge of space, and then the black-diamond perfection of the rushing void.

And one thing led to another.

* * *

That scene from another perspective: on a base somewhere, we practised house assaults endlessly, fighting from room to room in the darkness and taking fake casualties—'man-down drills'— where one of the team would pretend to get shot and in-between blasting away it was my job to jab the 'wounded' and get IV liquids into them. Again and again. It was hot outside, and bright, which made the dark Kill-House seem more like a crypt, with bare, pocked walls. It was cold, and there was a smell of mud brick and the chemical tang of gunsmoke. One day it was a female medic, a tough blonde, who volunteered to play dead: 'woman down'.

We reset the scenario for the Nth time and fought our way through, and I found her in the third room of a corridor slumped like bad drama against a wall. I cut away her uniform and felt for a vein in the blackness. I was very good back then; I mean I could've probably injected a hummingbird mid-flight in perfect darkness. But in those rooms, with the concussive waves of automatic weapons and stun-grenades, I struggled. Her whole skin seemed to have a beat. I found something—that line of bounce in flesh that hints at the pressure of the vein underneath—and aligned the cannula. I looked at her. She nodded. I stuck her. I remember looking very closely into her eyes as the needle went in and the gunfire discoed around us. She had blue eyes too, but they strobed green in the yellow-flamed gunfire. As someone unloaded a 3–4 round burst nearby I saw her retinas ratchet open, in jumps, like an aperture of a lens going 3–4 stops. Flashbulb memories lit by muzzle-flash.

And if you repeat that enough, adrenaline becomes an aphrodisiac.

* * *

To become a better combat medic I did a civilian paramedic course, with a long attachment on the ambulances to get more trauma experience. The closest thing to a war zone in the UK were the Welsh Valleys on a weekend. I loved every blue-lit second of it: the roller-coaster in the back of the ambulance careening to some call-out with the sirens blaring into the night.

Opening the ambulance doors each time we stopped was like channel-surfing: soap opera, health warning, action film, tragedy, comedy, karaoke, all acted out by the toughest and funniest people I have seen in my life. Pub closing time in Merthyr was a cross between a medieval battlefield and a midnight carnival, with men and women swinging broken pint glasses, bottles and pool cues. My stitching was Savile Row within days. I yearned to tick off injuries like I was catching Pokemon.

I finally got a sucking chest wound with a 16-year-old kid who'd been stabbed with a screwdriver minutes after dropping LSD. But it was only a tiny electrical screwdriver, so the injury was more like a wheezy zit, and I only slapped on a chest-seal because it looked cool. Most of the treatment was talking the saucer-eyed kid down from his trip as we sat on the kerb together. I hooked him up to a heart-rate monitor and consoled him whenever his pulse began to climb. Then the sun came up over the housing estate and he was tranquillised by its beauty; he wanted to know if I could see it too. His first sunrise on acid and my first sucking chest wound. I felt like we'd bonded, but he practically went into tachycardia when I tried to hug him.

There were heart attacks, car crashes, suicides, births and overdoses. One minute, a farmer with his severed arm across his lap and his stump tourniquet'd with baling twine, joking and apologising for the bother. The next, having a cup of tea and lemon drizzle cake with some ancient biddy at 3 am and holding her hand because ... well, just because she was lonely and didn't know who else to call, and that's brave too.

The medics were part of their community, and they looked after their people. We got called out to a woman who had been slapped around by her husband. It was nothing too bad, and she refused to press charges, so instead we asked the husband to come along in the ambulance. 'But there's nothing wrong with me,' he protested, and everyone laughed. Twenty minutes later he had to be stretchered off. With one ambulance man driving, the other listed the husband's injuries into the radio, like calling out bingo numbers, before we gave them to him.

In the midst of all of this death and mayhem, fucking is an act of resistance—life, life, life, life, life—Eros/Thanatos, petit mort/Grand Mort. Adrenaline and desire were a snaking path in my mind, like the empty road rushing towards us in the head-lights—the familiar hills—saturated snapshot memories lit by blues'n'twos, head torches, surgical lights, streetlights, moon-light. I've never seen so much sex and death compressed into such a short period of time. The female nurses were Valkyries, hard as nails, belt-fed humour. It makes my heart yearn now, and I want to blame adrenaline, but I suspect it was something else too: those valleys, the people, their utter fearlessness to be them-selves, and *fuck you* if you didn't like it—and fuck you if you did.

Richard Burton, who came from the Valleys, had this to say at the height of his fame: 'Here am I, as rich as Croesus, married to the most beautiful woman in the world, but what I'd give for a pint and a shag up against a wall in Merthyr'.

* * *

Back on the boat: a girl who was deeply into pain and into blood (always mine), which hadn't really emerged on the first few dates—at least I don't remember her flagging it up, but she was so beautiful I couldn't concentrate. We were falling in love, and she wanted to weigh my desire by how much pain I could take, a nightly trial by ordeal, and big questions don't occur to me when I'm having fun. (If I'm having lots of fun the little questions don't get a look-in either.) Equally, I was interested to see how far she would take it, to see if I could map her limits in a get-to-know-you kinda way. You can only see what people have when they let it all out. I wanted to see what she had. That something, I wanted it. I wanted her to give it to me. Love does that. But most of all I wanted to win. It was a game and I wasn't going to blink first.

It started out in a fairly DIY manner, small stuff first: she would smash a handy champagne flute and drag it across my chest. (Counterintuitively, cheap glass delivers a more stable edge than crystal, and costs less to replace; please try this at home.) I got to admire the levels of my own epidermis, dermis and more; flashbulb memories of such searing clarity they looked like the pages of medical books.

We moved on to razor blades—the fancy pearl-handled straight ones you buy in old shops near St James—which scored less for pain but were easier on the scarring. She developed a thing for drawing off my blood in a syringe beforehand and spraying herself at the point of orgasm, which, sure, seems a little odd to tell you now, but at the time, like I said, I was in love and eager to please.

Yes, it hurt, but nowhere as near as much as you'd think. Previously, on the hills, I had struggled to relabel pain as anything other than what it is was. In the face of beauty, in the grip of desire, it simply wasn't a problem. Pain felt like an opinion.

But really Dear Reader I was doing it for you. Because that's what valour is. Self-sacrifice. No, don't thank me. It's what I do. More Victoria's Secret than Victoria Cross, but jihad comes in many forms.

Beyond the blades and blood, porn and pain was an infinite world of calm, an altered state.

What we're talking about here is a fight-or-flight response in a sexual encounter producing a flow state and that—to me—is fascinating. And fun.

Until recently, the *Diagnostic and Statistical Manual of Mental Disorder* stigmatised BDSM as a paraphilia that caused stress-inducing disorders. In the US, even admitting to it was grounds for divorce or denial of child custody. It was seen as a mental aberration, and beneath the purview of scientific enquiry. But in the last few years, there have been fascinating studies that shed light into this world and what is going on in the brains of its acolytes.

There are a number of reasons why pain can enhance sex. As we saw early on, during fight-or-flight situations, the blood is sent to vital areas and away from sexual organs. In the right dosage, fear and pain can be used to brake orgasm, prolonging and extending the sexual act and allowing the body to fill itself with all the great endogenous drugs we have already met.

Endorphins, are often the result of painful stimuli. But while endorphins mute the pain, these endogenous opiates also help us lose our inhibitions by suppressing shame and hushing any inner critic. Social mores, self-awareness and even time itself are no match for opiates. BDSM delivers a lot of B-process juice. So much so that a clinic in Siberia is prescribing beatings to help alcoholics and addicts overcome their addictions (thirty lashes for an alky, sixty for a junkie). The professor in charge believes it is the endorphins which help reset his patients' minds.

Oxytocin is the hormone of bonding; it works in bondage too. It gives salience to social situations, separating the wheat from the chaff. It links social cues to the reward pathway.

Dopamine runs the reward pathway. It is the engine of desire and learning. It forms chunks. It carves habits. It bends kinks. It is why BDSM can be addictive.

Lastly, just as there can be decreased blood flow to the sexual organs, there is also a down-regulation of activity in the Prefrontal Cortex. We are back into Transient Hypofrontality and Flow-States.

In BDSM the two main roles are top or bottom, referring to whether a person is dominant or submissive, active or passive (an interchangeable person is known as a 'switch'). The two roles each produce their own altered states: top-space is a flow-state associated with performing a focus-based task; toppers describe the feeling as being 'in the zone'. Alternatively, 'bottom space' shows a different, dreamier, deeper flow, like a form of trance. Bottom space is also known as 'sub-space'.

Dr Staci Newmahr, in her groundbreaking book *Playing on the Edge*, was the first to link BDSM to flow states:

SM participants speak of their play in terms of ecstatic experience, or what can be understood as flow. They speak of weightlessness: of grooving and flying, of the cessation of cognitive process and of the disappearance of the world around them.

She went on to distinguish the difference between top and bottom flow.

Tops achieve flow through mental focus, particularly when engaged in activities that require intense concentration, such as knife play, needle play, and advanced bondage.

When bottoming, players experience flow as a result of intense rhythmic sensation, sensation or pain itself, unrelenting focus on a particular task or concentrated effort to endure a sensation or circumstance.

BDSM practitioners are masters of the art of reappraisal. They can take painful signals and relabel them, rather than attempting to ignore, suppress or focus on the pain. Meditating on spectacular levels of pain, they find compassion and deep love. Margee Kerr, in her book on fear, labelled this type of people 'emotional ninjas.'

A study of a BDSM group in the *Journal of Sexual Medicine* found that BDSM enthusiasts displayed more favourable psychological characteristics than a control group: less neurotic, more extraverted, more open to new experiences, more conscientious, less sensitive to rejection and higher subjective well-being.

These are also some of the defining traits of what flow-godfather Mihaly Csikszentmihalyi labelled as an autotelic personality: people who find reward in life through flow-states, and have little care for material reward. There is a such a strong bridge between autotelic experiences and 'spiritual experiences' that they may be different terms for the same thing. Many people within the BDSM community believe that not only does their practice make them better humans, it brings them closer to a spiritual force. This intersection of pain, sex, altered states and spiritual experience is known as 'sacred kink'.

BDSM contains within it many elements that have been used for centuries by men and women seeking divine knowledge: ritual, ordeal, pain, surrender and visionary experiences. All major religions contain some form of painful ritual designed to bring us closer to our deities: the penitents in Easter celebrations in Seville, Spain, the self-mortifying Shia Ashura celebrations or the Native American Sundance ordeal. It is within our myths too: the god Odin hung himself from a tree and impaled himself with a spear to conceive of writing in runes. It may even be recorded on the walls of the cave at Peche Merle: the pierced man, in an agony or ecstasy of spears.

Not only do painful ordeals have the ability to make us better individually, they also have the power to make better communities. Dimitri Xygalatas is an anthropology professor at the University of Connecticut who has studied extreme rituals: fire walkers and flesh-piercers. He was also the first to quantify the link between extreme rituals and prosocial behaviour, between the painfulness of an ordeal and the empathy and altruism it fostered.

At the Hindu Kavadi rituals in Mauritius, where devotees impale themselves with needles, skewers and hooks, he set up a simple experiment. Xygalatas interviewed hundreds of worshippers to measure their religiosity, some of whom had done the full extreme ordeal, others who had joined simply in prayer and song, others who had just watched. Afterwards he gave each 200 rupees (average daily pay for manual workers is 100 rupees) and asked whether they wanted to donate any of the money anonymously to the Kavadi temple. The average for the pain group was 134 rupee donation; those of the non-pain group was 81 rupees. It wasn't that the more religious were more likely to undergo the ordeal and give more money; it was that the pain had increased the generosity of the participants. Even amongst the watchers there was an increase in generosity amongst those who had witnessed a painful ordeal compared to the watchers who had merely witnessed the prayer and song.

Xygalatas also did other experiments amongst fire-walkers in Spain using heart-rate monitors on both people undergoing the extreme ritual and the spectators in the crowd. He recorded a 'spectacular degree of synchronicity in heart-rate patterns' between sufferer and spectator. And the closer the bond— stranger or friend or family—the more similar their heart rate activity was. Familial and social proximity correlated into physiological harmony; pain and empathy knotted people together.

* * *

On the boat that summer were quite a number of strippers. I'm not sure how they got there, maybe the musicians brought them along. I dated a few of them. They tended to show up on the boat in the late afternoon. Counterintuitively, it was the highest-paid girls who worked the daytime shift and barely had to dance. Instead, each had a stable of suitors who would turn up during office-hours lunch breaks. In return, the girls would run them down the brutal shopping gauntlet of Bond Street. It wasn't unusual for the strippers to be clocking a couple of Rolexes a week, and many of them managed to buy their own homes after a few years working the clubs. But that's not interesting.

The group that fascinated me were a clique within the strippers, a subset of professional BDSM girls, dominatrixes or Pro-Dommes. They existed at an intersection of extreme wealth, pain and sexual desire. Their clients were hedge-funders, CEOs of major companies and so on—mainly men, but a surprising number of women too.

The Pro-Dommes were the Special Forces of extreme sex. They ran missions into altered states and operated under a veil of secrecy, signing NDAs with their clients that cut both ways.

They had incredible psychological knowledge and a therapist's ear for their clients' needs. They operated within a rigid framework of 'safe, sane and consensual' as their rules of engagement. These three words were the protocols or standard operating procedures that governed behaviour within the professional BDSM community. Many had more medical knowledge than I did. As backup they had a doctor on speed-dial, a gay Scotsman who wore immaculately tailored suits cut in a 1950s style, with ties and handkerchiefs bearing the McQueen totenkopf. He lugged around an ancient crocodile-leather travel case with a defibrillator inside, and if you asked nicely he would write a prescription for just about anything. (If you are heterosexual, never discuss your 'extreme' sex life with a BDSM homosexual; they tend to yawn.)

One of the ladies asked me, as a favour, if I would like a go with her. Did I want to go 'tops'?

No.

I'm quite happy to subject myself to all manner of exercise or punishment, but doing it to another person, for her pleasure? That was way out of my comfort zone. I didn't want to have anything to do with it. But this girl was cool, smart and funny. And very persuasive.

The instructions were very elaborate: a four-point suspension from the ceiling by wrists and ankles, face down, so she floated at waist high 'to anyone standing'. I asked her to draw a diagram on a napkin. She did, and then jotted down a few items to add to her pleasure: the exact number of candles she wanted, which brand and scent; the type of cane and other items. She wanted everything to be new. It hadn't even occurred to me that there might be a secondhand market, and I shuddered at the thought of that particular car-boot sale. I was left with a very expensive shopping list scrawled next to a diagram that looked like a spider bumming a swastika.

The cane wasn't a cane but a long shoe-horn. She'd insisted it was real horn, with a suede cord at one end. It was quite old-school deviance, and I had to go to Jermyn Street to one of those last-of-a-breed gentlemen stores to get them. I guess if you mix with ladies who eroticise power then you have to do your shopping in these places but they're not to be cheap. They even kindly wrapped it up in crepe paper and a heavy paper bag with ornate cord-loops like the aiguillettes on admirals' shoulders. I unwrapped it outside the store. It was over a foot long, white-grey opaque and curved very slightly, like a sabre. I made a few practice strokes in the air between passing shoppers; it was surprisingly light, with a good weight-to-surface-area ratio.

The candle store was hideous and expensive. I staggered out reeking of flowers I'd never heard of, feeling violated. So far, the only thing that had been spanked was my wallet. I was broke and still only halfway through the list of handcuffs, shackles and Japanese silk rope. 'Improvise, adapt and overcome,' I thought. The boat was rammed with rope and sailing equipment. I was sure I could jury-rig something. Mid-caning, in the near darkness, lit only by silly-smelling Parisian candles, would she be able to spot the difference?

That afternoon, Rob Paulson and Pikey Lee dropped by with a few of the lads and insisted that they help. The system they built was so simple, yet so perfect, that it made me proud of our military: four points, each fastened with ropes and cable-ties to four deck-hatches in the cabin's roof; elastic ankle and wrist fixtures made from mountain-bike inner-tubes, with secure velcro quick-release cuffs. They even stress-tested it, bouncing around and laughing, fag packets and 9mm ammo spilling out of their pockets, making fun of me like I was some sort of weirdo until I got rid of them to the local pub.

Rob stopped by the hatch.

'Be careful mate,' he said. 'That bondage stuff, it's like eating broccoli.'

I waited. It sounded like some bit of prison slang, like 'tossing salad'.

'My mom made me eat broccoli when I was a kid. She said it takes 28 meals before the brain rewires, and then you crave it. You're mad for it.' And his eyes did look a little crazed.

'But I've never seen you eat broccoli,' I said.

'No, I hate it,' he said. 'But I think it works for everyone else.'

'Rob, please fuck off.' And he did.

And it would've all worked brilliantly, but there's a lot of difference in the physics between a 6'2" 220lb SAS trooper and a 5'5" 105lb BDSM warrior. Her ass was my head height. It felt like using a rolled-up magazine to swot a bug on the ceiling; frustrating, too. Eventually, after a few adjustments, we got into the swing of it.

The candles flickered and gave the rite a feeling of being done in a cave. It felt primitive.

I've seen a lot of people eat up pain and pressure in the military and extreme sports. I've never seen anyone do it with more style. This woman used breathing techniques I've only ever come across on NATO Resistance-to-Interrogation courses. She bellowed encouragements to savagery that would have left my military instructors blushing. This woman had more mind over matter than most fighters I knew. She had the gift of game.

She went full-tilt through the looking glass and transformed herself, strobing between human and animal states. She turned pain to joy, humiliation to liberation, submission to empowerment. I've never seen someone so utterly helpless have such total mastery over themselves. She wanted more. It was like feeding a fire. The more pain, the filthier the talk, the tighter the restrictions, the more she seemed to thrive, the more voltage she embodied, flying and flowing until she was glowing and goddess-like.

TIE ME UP, DON'T TIE ME DOWN

It was a beginner's mistake to release her hands first, but she was pretty forgiving. She fought to get her breath back amidst her laughter. Watching her peel the wax off her skin made me think of a snake shedding its skin. There was something wildly and darkly archaic about her metamorphosis. As if to underline the point, she sported a hand-outline on her ass which glowed red on her skin like rock art on a cave wall.

Did I get much out of it? Sexually: nah. Just not my thing. It was fun being a sorcerer's apprentice for a bit, but all the transformative magic she wielded was within her own head and her own body. It was cool of her to give me that trust.

She had also brought over a bag of tricks—the tools of her trade—an eye-watering array of whips, shackles and sexual toys some of which were hooked-up to an electrical device that delivered limb-spasming levels of voltage; and a raccoon penis bone. The latter isn't as unusual as it sounds: in fact, many mammals have penis bones. Racoon penis bones are particular in that they are finger-sized and j-shaped. They are also known as 'Texas Toothpicks' and were once worn as good-luck talismans by Mississippi steamboat gamblers. Nowadays they are used by homosexual rent-boys—known as 'Lot Lizards' who work behind gas stations in the US South-West—to massage truckers' prostrates during fellatio.

It was a long weekend. We became friends; bondage can be bonding.

* * *

Within the fairly extreme world of BDSM was another, more radical, subset. They believed that the altered states of sexual ecstasy allowed them to reprogram their consciousness. They came to this conclusion from a dark place; many of them had been abused in the past.

Trauma Play involves taking a traumatic event and replaying it in a 'safe, sane, consensual' way. They do it again and again.

It involves lots of pain, endorphins and dopamine. By replaying, reframing and retelling what happened to them, they believe they can write a new version of themselves and 'reauthor' their fate.

I can't decide whether this is one of the darkest extremes I have touched upon or one of the bravest, brightest and most redemptive.

The only person I know who has tried it is a friend of mine, Katherine X. She is a Pro-Domme and has a clutch of degrees in psychology, speaks five languages and has modelling good looks. She got involved in BDSM after a protracted relationship with an abusive boyfriend. She ascribes to the 'Femme Forte', or strong woman, school of BDSM.

I met up with Katherine to get her story. I got a table at the back of the restaurant so we could have some privacy. I couldn't see the door but knew when she had arrived the way the other diners stopped and stared. She was wearing a designer dress, thigh-high boots and a raccoon-fur Davy Crockett hat. Katherine plonked herself down, ordered a coffee and started talking. She doesn't do small-talk, this is what she had to say:

'Polite society is freaked out by pro-dommes, we derive income and pleasure from our work, we are the embodiment of the independent, sexually motivated woman in full possession of and exercise of her sexual citizenship.'

She continued as I scribbled and misspelled the big words.

'BDSM heals where all traumas register and reside: below consciousness ... in the body. The abuse was irrational, so the cure had to be equally irrational. Like cures like.

'In my case of emotional and physical trauma, BDSM allowed me to experience a role reversal in power exchange, instead of giving away my power—my control and agency—I was in charge, in control of the *scene*, and was healed by receiving the submission and surrender of my subs in a way that my submission in my abusive relationship had been "taken" from me.'

Katherine signed quotation marks around 'taken' with her fingers; she had perfectly manicured nails. I don't think I've ever noticed that in a woman before, or since.

'In BDSM we have choice and agency; in abuse I didn't have choice or agency.'

I kept jotting this down.

'The change in context, the flipping of roles combined with the altered states of consciousness I would experience when I could exercise my intense sadistic desires, was ultimately healing for me. I reclaimed what I had abdicated.

'In this kind of play your *edge* is pushed towards something akin to instinctual panic.

'At the edge, BDSM carves out new neural pathways and changes consciousness through the body. It's the ultimate biopsychosocial reprogramming, powerful because of its erotic context.'

'What was the rush like for you?' I asked.

'Top space and subspace felt like doing ecstasy, but I was dead cold sober—all the body sensations heightened, there was a flow-state sense of focus, and euphoria. It then expanded to something I can only describe as a connected collective global awareness from the other humans in the room to humans deceased to plants and animals, like a psychedelic experience times ten.'

Katherine paused before continuing:

'BDSM—she said—allows us to 'hack' panic. There aren't many opportunities to run naked through moonlit forests any more in our automated, tech-ruled world. We live so much of our daily lives in our heads, with our inner dialogue of fears, insecurities, imagined slights or victories. BDSM yanks you out of your head and into your body with a snap of the whip, the close of a buckled cuff around ankle or wrist, the gag in your mouth.'

To Katherine BDSM wasn't just an endorphin rush but deeply therapeutic. It reconnected her to her world, to her body. It recharged her, it gave her power over past events in her life.

Trauma Play sits at a crossroads of personal choice and society's consensus on what is acceptable, between healing and hurting, victim and abuser, psychology and religion. But the real issue is one of agency. Altered states offer us the chance to remake ourselves, by ourselves. That can make them very threatening to large portions of the status quo.

In the past, in the West, and in much of the world today, religion has had a monopoly on suffering and redemption. Organised religion controlled people's access to altered states and their ability to purge sins and better themselves. At a neurological level what is the difference between a man scourging himself during Holy Week on the streets of Seville for his sins and a woman like Katherine X being whipped in a dungeon? If anything, Katherine is more brave and less blameless for she is engaging in redemptive suffering—not of her sins—but of sins done to her. Which, if you pause to think about it, is a whole lot closer to the message of Easter.

Nowadays in the West, it isn't religion but science that is the arbitrator of how you heal. Classical psychology would maintain that these BDSM women are still beholden to their trauma. I get that. But who owns trauma, or the means to dispose of it? Is it possible to recycle it into something useful, maybe even something positive or thriving? Does it always have to go through the acceptable channels? Who is more qualified: the men in white coats or the women in black leather?

Talking to Katherine X and reading the small amounts of academic literature on the subject (sometimes research is just grind, grind, grind), I came to believe that many of the women were using sexual ecstasy to reset and rewrite their trauma in a similar way that my war-going friends used MDMA to replay and reframe theirs. Both groups sought power over their trauma and the dark lessons that had been gouged into them in those moments within the altered state of fight-or-flight. They believed it required an altered state to reset an altered state.

Both religion and psychology require a fully paid-up priesthood, and altered states are incredibly difficult to monetise if people start visiting them solo. We have known about the therapeutic effects of MDMA for decades, but it took a huge private initiative to fund the research that opened the way for clinical trials (and a glut of PTSD cases caused by the War on Terror who refused to be ignored). No one has a patent for MDMA; there is no money in that cure. Who is going to fund further research into the therapeutic effects of BDSM? A hardware store?

* * *

Flora is at the end of this chapter because she was the very opposite of everything we have so far discussed. She was 'polite society', and at the very top of it.

Flora was part of a gilded set. They were very beautiful extremists—in the sense of extreme wealth—and by almost every metric of twenty-first-century Western values these women were the big winners. They were too out of my league financially to be girlfriends, but I enjoyed their company. They were smart, witty and well-informed. It was always a visit to a museum or gallery and then lunch; they kept me cultured.

It was like hanging out in a Swiss watch advert. An A-process of parties, private jets, endless yoga, cashmere, freckles and unpronounceable fruits for breakfast. Yes, of course it was fun. It was the road of excess, which led to a palace, but not of wisdom.

Neither Flora nor any of her friends worked, but they had intimate knowledge of the markets and used financial terms that had me reaching for the dictionary. Flora mocked me for dating strippers but I suspect this was driven by what Freud described as the narcissism of minor differences: the difference between contract and pay-as-you-go. Socialites and pole-dancers might seem poles-apart but it's the same pole. Flora had a cold, mercenary edge when discussing wealth—especially other people's—that would have given my real-life-mercenary friends goosebumps. And she used enough zeroes to give Stephen Hawking the wheelies.

Technically, some of them were young mothers—the most important job in the world—but they had outsourced the day-to-day work to nannies, housekeepers and tutors. In fact, they had outsourced or delegated everything that might cause stress, adversity or frowns, and that was where the problem lay.

Their beautiful and celebrated world was too perfect. Eternal sunshine creates a desert. That's the trouble with hedonic happiness, it habituates; soon the pleasures pale into insignificance, new ones are required and with that much money and connection you are going to run out at some point. Their extreme wealth insulated them from the very stressors, unpredictability and trauma that induce growth. It was a zero-sum game that created a mental and emotional state equivalent to the Hygiene Hypothesis. The latter is a theory that overly sterile environments are causing a rise in allergies and autoimmune diseases, because the immune system has nothing to train itself against, and so overreacts against everything. Similarly, anything that these women found stressful was cleansed from their lives, but their resilience, their ability to adapt and grow, went with it. They became brittle spirits.

Like any addiction, it robbed the user of self-control. These brainy women surrendered their empowerment to their wealth. The nannies, mannies, cleaners—the help—made them helpless. And all the well-meaning staff, doctors, psychiatrists and therapists only robbed them further.

They were caught in a feedback loop: just as doing something hard makes everything else seem easy, only doing what's easy makes everything else hard. It was a velvet-roped, fast-tracked path of least resistance. Every time they reduced the stress in their lives, they could cope less with the next cycle, unwinding to a point of infantilisation. The merest hint of stress could trigger a huge emotional reaction.

The B-process of wealth wasn't pain but a deep malaise, an ennui that was almost impossible to place. But I could taste it like dust in every pixel they posted, down a glittering vortex that ended in an immaculately polished depression.

* * *

I met Flora when she was resting between marriages, and after I slept with her I thought she'd want to get rid of me. Instead she said, 'Are you retarded? Let's have some fun.'

So we flew to Paris one Friday evening and went straight to a funfair in the Jardin des Tuileries, and I know that sounds wanky but if you don't have one gooey paragraph in your life's tale about a girl in Paris then you've fucked up. The Ferris wheel felt like Fortune's Wheel, an intricate jewelled tourbillon at the heart of the city: at the bottom there was the remaining heat of the day, fairground lights and music, smells of candy floss, lime trees and the calciferous dust of the pathways. And up: the colder, cleaner air, Paris skyline, icy stars, Flora's perfume, her laughter clear above the muted din below. And again and again.

It was one of those nights when Paris is raw sex. The heat amping the smells of cafés and cigarette smoke, the stench of the piss on warm ancient stone, echoing laughter and arguing, the meltwater guttering off the ice on triple-tiered *fruits-de-mer* like a waterfall, music thumping off the bateau mouches, parties of revellers every step along the Seine, a medieval miasma of cooler air on the river like the ghosts of heretics, club-goers in high heels clattering down cobblestoned alleyways and the scent of early-morning bakeries.

And later, in some grand bedroom off the Place Vendôme, looking at Flora naked, in wordless come-hither, I understood the powerful conjunction of obscene wealth and weaponised pleasure like a diamond bullet to my Shrew brain. She was a grande-horizontal, much like the portraits we'd seen in the Musée d'Orsay earlier that day. Her regular retinue of suitors— cold-blooded billionaires, lispy priapic tweeds and rosy-faced generals—wouldn't have been out of place in the background of some Belle Époque ball. Flora had perfect legs which she pointed to the ceiling and spread like some golden astrolabe aimed at the glittering constellations of the chandeliers—astrolabia. Her pubic hair was ink-black, like the smallest dash of Japanese calligraphy, and writing about it now, even years later, makes me harder than Chinese algebra.

I'm telling you about Flora now because she was the last of the good ones and the first of the mercenary ones. If there is a tipping point in the narrative arc of this book, then it was at the top of that Ferris wheel.

Prior to her, I was lucky with my girlfriends: they had all been very clever, beautiful and kind people who left the world better than they found it through art, photography, medicine, music or good deeds. Their balance was healthy; they were in credit with life, for they gave more than they received.

The girls after Flora were takers: faster, easier, looser and more ruthless. And so was I.

I lost my humility. I was too busy looking at myself, and didn't see the warning signs. I didn't feel bad—quite the opposite; I felt indestructible.

10

THE GREAT HEROIN EXPERIMENT

I'm not sure what you're expecting from an SAS locker-room scene, but you're going to be disappointed. The lighting was wrong for starters: bright fluorescent strips that glowed in the steam from the showers and gleamed on the sweating tiles. The place smelled of sweat, body odour and cheap shower gel, of mud, mildew and military kit. I was expecting something a bit more *Top Gun*—men with high cheekbones and low waist-towels looking intense—but there wasn't anything even vaguely homoerotic about it, unless you counted Rob Paulson, and then you'd have to be super-desperate.

There was tough talk for sure, but it wasn't for show—these men had little left to prove to each other or to themselves. Instead it was about that unsaid truth that fresh challenges were needed, to keep the edge sharp.

Of an evening it was common to find a group of lads discussing doing Everest, or some obscure killer-peak in the Karakoram, or an invite-only ultra-running race. And I enjoyed the chat, in abstract, because I'm lazy like that. I'd just ear-wig: which peak was the hardest, which route the toughest, who had died and how; or a kayak trip across a wild ocean, a first-contact tribe, and so on and so on. What was the ultimate test? And one evening, amongst the clanging locker sounds and banter, the fug of steam and deodorant, one lad—whose dad was a committed junkie with a three decade habit—said, half as a joke, that coming off heroin is the hardest. And that was where I felt *The Idea* go into me, to the bone.

That's how I saw The Idea at first: the reverse of a mountain peak—an abyss.

Why would I want to do that? Same as they said of Everest: Because it's there.

And that's where it sat for a while, for weeks, maybe months. Could it be done? And how? How much heroin would I have to take to know addiction, to touch the bottom of the abyss, and how long would it take to resurface?

The more I thought about it, the more it appealed to me on a number of levels.

It was heroin because my mate in the locker-room had said 'heroin'. He could just have easily said 'crystal meth' and I probably would have gone for that. I didn't really care. I was thirty-four and felt the urge to risk it all. I just wanted really big game to hunt, a bete-noire to take down; I'd display its head on my wall and smile at in my dotage. Is that too much to ask for?

From what I knew of heroin addiction, I pictured it as another piece of endurance: parachute in, long march out. I wasn't interested in the oblivion of the drug, more the journey home.

But I also liked the idea of coming face to face with this substance. I'd never tried it but it had a staggering reputation as the ultimate drug, an agent of misery, enslavement and death. I wanted to 'interview' the molecule like I would a terrorist, like I had interviewed Niaz. What was at the heart of the experience? What made it tick? What was the nature of addiction?

Another part of me was up for the fight. I liked the idea of battling something that had so many KOs to its name. Fine: let's see how hard you are.

THE GREAT HEROIN EXPERIMENT

I also liked the undercover element of it: becoming a temporary junkie, wearing their skin, if only just to walk a mile in their shoes. These were people shunned and marginalised by society; that seemed unfair to me. I didn't know any heroin addicts personally other than a few street junkies in my neighbourhood; I would occasionally give them money or stop for a chat. They seemed like nice people, or no different from anyone else. What was their disease? Could I catch a glimpse of what it felt like and report back?

But the main reason was exploration. I was raised on a diet of books filled with tales of far-flung tribes and lost civilisations; I devoured Tintin, Indiana Jones, Monkey Magic. My father, a foreign correspondent, sent me postcards from exotic lands and brought back knives and gourds, masks and art from his travels, many of which I had seen in comics or films, and I took these as proof of the exciting world that was waiting for me.

By my early teens, *National Geographic* had taught me that the world was fairly well mapped out—still teeming with wonder, but with the blank spaces having been filled in. The great days of exploration were over, and its ersatz replacement was adventure. The difference is huge, but subtle: it is to do with the people back home. If you bring something back that changes or adds to the sum of knowledge about our world, then it counts as exploration; otherwise it is adventure. It could be almost exactly the same journey—let's say to some far-flung island off Papua New Guinea—but if you come back with a discovery, however small, you've added to the sum knowledge about this fine world we live in. It could be a new species of leech or bug—it doesn't matter—it is enough, your account is in credit. But if you return home with only a selfie, then all you're trying to change is how the world sees you, and all you have managed is an ego trip. By the time I left school, it was all adventure: fevered egos with double-barrelled names hauling themselves the wrong way over an ice-floe because 'it hadn't been done before', but in truth, because they hadn't been hugged enough as kids.

The idea of heroin withdrawal as a feat of endurance and adventure appealed to me at the beginning, but the more research I did, the more I began to see it as exploration. There seemed to be much ignorance and fear around the subject. People spoke about heroin in the same whispered terms the medieval world reserved for the lands beyond Christendom, those liminal spaces at the edge of maps, where geography slips under myth and ignorance and the points of the compass are less cardinal than moral. If heroin was a kingdom it was one wrapped in taboo, populated by shuffling zombies, criminals, outcasts and extremists of different sorts—a hellish nether-space, a limbo of enchantment, entrapment and lost souls. It was Here-be-dragons and Abandon Hope. In short: it sounded fucking great.

I'm not denying there was a dark and destructive streak to my thinking. Up until that point I had pushed things, sure, but all my adventures had been of this world, in three dimensions. I wanted to take enough drugs to make the mountains melt. I wanted to get into the biggest battle of my life—on my own. The idea frightened me, and that was attractive. How much can you say about yourself until you have had a good kicking? How much fight do you have in you? What do you understand about luck until you have chanced it all? How can you know how sane you are until you have thrown it all away and given yourself over entirely to genuine oblivion? Seriously, who are you? What do you see in the mirror? And how do you know your reflection is true until you have crawled through the carnival funhouse and stared at all the other mirrors there?

I wanted enough money to buy the drugs, rent a cottage by the sea, and pay for a medic friend of mine to stay there 24/7 in case I overdosed. As usual, my brain started whispering dumb-fuck thoughts again: *Come on, how tough can it be?*

All of this might have remained wishful thinking, but a few months later a TV channel got in touch saying they wanted to film someone taking cocaine, ecstasy and skunk-cannabis as an experiment. The inspiration behind this idea was the BBC Panorama 'Mayhew Experiment' from 1955.

If you have not looked into this experiment, then please do; the footage is online. It is a message from another era, a world brimming with confidence, optimism and kindness. Two men in suits sit in a drawing room together on high-backed chairs with a small table between them. On the table is a lamp and a glass of liquid. One man is Christopher Mayhew, who served in the Intelligence Corps in the Second World War and was selected for the Special Forces before becoming an MP and Under-Secretary of State at the Foreign Office. The other man is Humphry Osmond, a psychiatrist who invented the term 'psychedelic' and also gave Aldous Huxley the dose that caused him to write *The Doors of Perception*.

The two men chat for a while before the cameras; their language, accents and mannerisms are archaically beautiful and soothing. Osmond asks a few clinical questions to set a baseline, and then Mayhew drinks the glass of liquid containing 400mg of mescaline. An hour passes, shown on an old carriage clock, and then the cameras return to the two men and the utterly wonderful sight of a sitting MP of the House of Commons (later the House of Lords), apologising for his 'poverty of language', trying to describe the beautiful colours of the curtains before going on to experience 'strange excursions in time' and 'years and years of heavenly bliss', all while sitting next to the doctor.

The film was never shown. The BBC was worried about controversy, and convened a special board made up of psychiatrists, philosophers and clergy. Amongst the latter, Canon Bessett from Cambridge University felt that Mayhew's mystical journey had been obtained 'on the cheap' (as opposed to—I would hazard—via the church collection tray), and with other board members ruled the experience invalid. Later in his life, Mayhew had this to say:

> I think the experience was valid ... you can dismiss it as a dreamlike hallucination which lasted for a fraction of a second owing to the disintegration of my ego and so on. Or, you can say, with me: it was a real experience that happened outside time ... By a shortcut, I did visit the world known to mystics and some mentally sick people and therefore ... it is valid.

Of course I was intrigued. Cocaine, ecstasy or skunk weren't particularly tough challenges, but I liked the chutzpah of the channel for suggesting it. When I met the team assigned to the project, I realised that none of them would have volunteered themselves. They were all over-friendliness combined with a lack of direct eye-contact. Their idea was to do three experiments in laboratory-style conditions within the studio. I'd get hooked up to a few machines which doctors would use to monitor the changes the drugs produced. Meanwhile I would describe how these changes felt: science versus experience. I figured I'd use their project as a series of test flights to see if I wanted to take on more serious highs. My role was more lab-rat than psychonaut. It was unlikely the experiments would produce any profound insights like the Mayhew Experiment, although skunk can have a spiritual kick. Street wisdom suggests that, while it might not throw open the Doors of Perception, it does let you have a long look through the catflap.

I asked for a few weeks to research the idea. The main hurdle was the channel's own lawyers. The problem was not with the illegality of the drugs—that could be dealt with under a public-interest defence—but with the location I was to take them in. The lawyers were in a panic over a clause of the *Anti Social Behaviour Act 2003* which meant that any premises where Class A drugs were taken could be classed as a 'crack house'—including TV studios. I'm not a lawyer, so I let them fight it out amongst themselves and continued to talk to doctors, police, addiction experts and regular drug-users. And after I asked about cocaine, ecstasy and skunk I threw in a fourth question: what about heroin?

* * *

Heroin comes from the opium poppy, *Papaver somniferum.* Remains of the plant have been found in almost every single ancient culture, back to the cave mouth. Opium appears in *The Odyssey,* stirred into a cup of wine by Helen herself, as the supreme antidote to sorrow. Statues of Aphrodite were adorned with poppies; so too were those of Thanatos (death), Nyx (night) and Hypnos (sleep). The Eleusinian Mysteries—the most famous mystery cult of the ancient world—focused on Demeter's descent into hell to search for her daughter, Persephone, their reunion and the return of spring. Demeter was an avatar of earlier Minoan poppy-goddesses who wore diadems of poppies as symbols of nourishment and narcosis, scarlet flowers that spoke of blood and resurrection.

The earliest cultivation of the opium poppy was in Mesopotamia by the Sumerians, who called it *hul-gil,* or 'plant of joy'. Earlier still, poppies have been found in over a dozen Neolithic sites across Europe, the earliest being the 'Cave of the Bats' in Spain, dating to 4,200BC, where poppy pods were used in burials. As Nick Tosches wrote in *The Last Opium Den,* 'When God put His mouth to the nostrils of Adam, there was probably opium on His breath.'

The word 'syringe' comes from that of Syrinx, a handmaiden of Artemis who was renowned for her chastity. One bright morning, on a typical day in the Greek Bronze Age, Syrinx was being chased through grove and glade by the god Pan, hell-bent on raping her. She fled to a river's edge, where the water nymphs took pity on her and transformed her into hollow water reeds. The horny goat-god arrived at the water's edge panting with exhaustion and thwarted nymphomania. As he exhaled his feta breath across the hollow reeds he was so entranced by their plaintive notes that he cut them down and fashioned the first pan-pipes. I'm not one to victim-blame—syringes have saved more lives than any other invention—but being responsible for Pan-pipes is unforgivable.

Perhaps the earliest forerunner of the syringe is the Witches' Broomstick. The drug was Mandrake, one of the chief drugs of European shamanism, as central to its ceremonies as ayahuasca is in South American native practices. Mandrake is a powerful hallucinogen that gives the initiate the sensation of aerial flight or spirit travel, but as a member of the Solanaceae family it also contains potentially toxic alkaloids which cannot be orally ingested. Instead the plant is rubbed along the shaft of a broom and administered via the vaginal or anal mucous membranes and into the bloodstream. Bedknobs could also be used—bedknobs and broomsticks.

As an interesting example of how history comes full circle, over a decade ago the toy manufacturer Mattel released the Nimbus 2000, named after Harry Potter's broom (batteries not included). Sadly, it didn't fly, but it did vibrate. The incredibly positive reviews on the toy-store websites don't bear repeating.

* * *

Heroin is commonly taken one of three ways: snorted, smoked or injected. Snorting sounded pretty horrible. It is bitter and heavier than cocaine, so that much passes by the nasal membranes and is lost down the throat. Smoking is the most popular means—place heroin on a piece of foil and run a lighter underneath to melt the powder into a liquid so that it gives off a sweet vapour, which is then inhaled through a foil straw. But this method is also very wasteful: not all the heroin vapour is hoovered up, and much is lost on the exhalation. Which is why injection is king—it is a matter of economics, more bang for your bucks. Every molecule is delivered into the bloodstream.

How much do you have to take to get addicted? There is a vast library of medical opinion and addicts' testimony, but the truth is that no one knows. Physical dependency sets in after three days of use, but it is harder to get an exact figure for the mental side of addiction. Most of the experts I spoke to estimated fourteen days of continuous use would give me a genuine experience of addiction and cold turkey.

I had coffee with a renowned addiction expert from a famous London clinic and told him about myself and my plans. 'Nine-to-one odds you're going to find this easy,' he said. 'But there is a small chance you will be in trouble. You will be in a fight with yourself—all of your strengths will be used against you. You will be your own worst enemy—which, in your case, will be a hell of a fight. Good luck.'

* * *

I tried for ages to get that film made. There was always a problem; lawyers mainly. I tried to get a scientific research license. I tried to find a suitable third country. I tried to build indemnity between the production company and the risk of it going wrong. At one point, a production company did go for the idea, but they wanted me to live in a council flat and beg for money, because 'that's what junkies do'. I told them to fuck off. I wanted this to be my journey. I didn't want to be a tourist in someone else's nightmare.

For two years I tried every angle, but nothing worked.

In the end, I thought I'd do it myself. No cameras, just myself, some drugs and a notebook. There are lots of fights, battles and wars that simply don't interest me. This wasn't one of them. It felt made me for me; I had wanted it for too long. I simply couldn't walk away from it and still be the same person. A part of me, my favourite part, would have died.

I had to know.

Whether the next part of this book is exploration or adventure depends on you, and whether my journey has changed the way you think about addiction. The experience certainly changed my mind. It changed my brain too.

* * *

So let's get high.

I doubled the dose and the length of time to 28 days. If I was going to do it, I wanted to smash the fucker.

I arranged to get my drugs through a friend of mine, Johnny, a chef at a local restaurant on the river. He introduced me to his dealer, then brought me a few bags over and showed me how to smoke heroin. He also said he'd look after me for the first few hits. Keep an eye on things.

Oblivion, serves two
Ingredients:
Six small bags heroin
Steel kitchen foil
Lighter

Technique:

Take an A4-size piece of foil and partially fold it, so that a gentle valley runs down the middle. Set aside. Always use steel foil; the aluminium can give off fumes when heated that cause brain damage. This may seem churlish when taking highly addictive Class A drugs, but enjoying drugs—like enjoying life—means reducing the risks while still trying to have fun.

Next, take a pencil and roll some foil around it three or four times—*I am getting a bit excited writing this*—then slide the pencil out so that a tube remains. This is your straw. It should be firm enough so that it can be held in the lips without crimping.

Place the contents of one bag of heroin at the top of the dimpled A4 sheet, heat it with a flame from below and tilt the sheet slowly. All the while you should be breathing in through the straw—not enough to inhale the powder, not too little to lose the vapour. The heroin powder should melt and begin to run down the foil, releasing its vapour. There is a Goldilocks-zone of heat: if the flame is too close, it will burn; too far away and it won't budge.

Like a lot of simple recipes, it took a short time to get right, but ages to master. Johnny was well-practised and dextrous. He made it look effortless. Johnny had an easygoing way with the foil. I'm not sure if this was due to his time served in a professional kitchen or the length of his heroin habit. He had 'moves'; prepping the straw and the foil—it was like watching a master-stoner roll up a perfect three-skin joint. Then it was my turn.

Up close, the powder looked like a filthy lava: brown lumps dissolving in a piss-yellow stream, impurities swirling black across the Martian surface of the foil that reflected like a fun-house mirror. Vapour and smoke snaked up from the edges of the molten droplet and curved into my straw as I inhaled and chased it down the foil.

The vapour isn't unpleasant, but it's hardly the elixir of life—to the tastebuds at least. There was a slight vinegary smell, a caramelised taste verging on the burnt. The drug hit my nervous system after five to ten seconds. After that, taste was no longer a concern. Nor was anything else.

Given that I was going to spend most of the next five years addicted to the stuff, I would love to be able to paint a vivid scene of my chemical apotheosis. But it wasn't a revelation, a home-coming, mother's love or the ambrosia of the Gods. Heroin created an absence which was hard to gauge. A muffling of life's static that allowed me to go further within myself, but not with introspection—instead it was a place of comfort and dreamy reflection. I was hoping for more, much more, but was too blissed out to care.

And that was it. It wasn't love at first sight. The memory of that first hit doesn't sit alongside my first kiss, first joint or first wave on a surfboard.

Johnny assured me it was very good stuff. He was nodding and nodding off. I had a few more hits and vomited everywhere.

* * *

And?

And: not much.

For the first week it was like partying every night without a hangover the next day. Heroin felt like a cousin to alcohol, but without any of the negatives. It was lush, deep and sedating, but fairly single-track. It lacked the love of MDMA or ecstasy, the excitement and ego of cocaine, or the philosophy of weed.

By the second week I noticed the symptoms of withdrawal during daytime. The timing of my first dose slid from the evening to the mid-afternoon as I developed a physical dependence on the drug. It felt like the earliest signs of flu—congestion in the eyes, aches and pains—and was chased away by a hit of heroin. There was zero emotion in my choice. It was as obvious and about as sexy as taking a cold remedy.

Over the same period, my tolerance increased and I was able to take larger amounts of the drug. Able, and willing too. I doubled the daily dose and got similar effects: euphoria and contentment. Remember, in Opponent Process Theory, the drug is input A, and the body's reaction is the B-process opposite. Increasing tolerance is the B-process to multiple exposures to heroin.

This continued for Weeks 3 and 4. Throughout the entire time I was surprised by how little effect heroin had on the rest of my life. It didn't create a ripple. I went about my day and no one commented on my behaviour, state of mind or noticed anything unusual about me. When people asked me how the experiment was going I told them it was about as exciting as a course of antibiotics. I enjoyed getting high but—all in all—it didn't strike me as the adversity I had been looking for. That is part of the cunning of heroin: it makes you feel fearless and intrepid in a way that you don't rationally associate with a chalky powder.

On the last night, I did a final dose and said goodbye to the drug. It wasn't a wrenching farewell. I slept well, had a fairly decent morning and then felt the flu-like symptoms come on. I took to bed, drank plenty of water and watched endless documentaries. By day two, the symptoms were worse. I had terrible shits and feverish chills, but nothing much worse than that. These largely went by day three.

* * *

But physical dependence is only 1% of addiction. The other 99% is invisible, because it is everywhere. It isn't within you, it has become you. It is habit.

When I finished the cold turkey I lurched around for a week or two, and it was bad, but I managed to trudge back slowly towards normality, and rejoined the world I had left five or six weeks before. Except it wasn't the same world, and I was no longer the same person. I couldn't register it consciously, but everything had changed, as if a wrathful god had taken every single pixel in my vision and tilted it ever so slightly back towards heroin. The world was a brightly lit labyrinth, and every turn seemed to lead back to heroin.

My fuck-up in one word: neuroplasticity.

I wasn't the same person I was at the start of the experiment. I hadn't taken account of the brain's spectacular ability to change, even over a short period of time.

All my previous drug-taking had involved single-dose events: I would take a substance, savour the results, and then the drugs would leave my system and my mind would return to normal. I had expected the heroin experiment to be more of the same. The most glaring flaw was the notion that my mind would remain a fixed constant, and that I would battle through the physical dependency as I had battled through other adversities in my life, maybe even with some grit and panache. What I hadn't factored in was how malleable the brain is, and how rapidly those changes can take place.

Addiction felt like a beautiful panic. One of delight rather than fear. For just as fear can rob us of reason, so too can desire.

It didn't occur in a single, mad moment, but slowly, imperceptibly, by degrees. This is why addiction is so hard to describe to a rational person. It was less about the victory of desire than the creeping surrender of reason.

Addiction was a bloodless insurrection of the animal forces, a sense of being overwhelmed by irrationality without a struggle.

Like panic, addiction creates a split at a neurological level, between Monkey and Shrew and Lizard. Under a narcotic stupor, my prefrontal cortex had begun to decouple from other parts of the brain as desire ran amok.

In short, Monkey was sidelined and began to waste away, and Shrew got the upper hand.

Monkey: critical, reasoning, analytical; able to crack jokes, keep time, self-analyse, assess risks, delay gratification, say 'no'.

In his place, Shrew: impulsive, immediate, love, lust and wild desire, craving.

Addiction was hard to comprehend, because the very tools of understanding became neurologically harder to access.

Addiction was like transient hypofrontality (when our prefrontal cortex down-regulates and goes temporarily offline), except it wasn't transient. Fight-or-flight responses stop when the threat has passed; flow-states are over as you cease to engage with a hard task at your very best. Addiction just picks up speed.

It felt like panic, and it felt like flow: a sense of timelessness, being lost in the moment, feeling so engrossed by the experience that other concerns fell to the wayside. It had many of the good qualities of flow, but not the best bits: no merging of action and awareness, because there was little of either. Nor was there the feeling that I was my best self, carried on an incoming tide towards something greater than myself. Instead, addiction felt soul-draining, like being carried away from myself. It was water flowing downhill, the tide going out. It was ebb rather than flow.

Weeks after the experiment, long after I'd gone cold turkey, I knew, like a matter of profound faith, that I would return to heroin. The fight wasn't over. Those drug-free weeks weren't a bright drug-free future, but time in the corner between rounds. I knew the bell would ring soon; it was only a matter of time.

Addiction was a long slide down the totem pole—Monkey-Shrew-Lizard—that stripped the better parts of my humanity first, peeling back reason, revealing inchoate emotion and animal desire.

And what better place to start a slide down a pole than with a stripper?

The evening Abby arrived on the boat, I knew she'd have heroin with her. Somehow, I just knew. She was a stripper, and wanted to party after her shift. She was petite and blonde, a manga-cartoon version of a stripper, if the illustrator had zero regard for the laws of decency or physics.

I guess we all choose the means of our destruction. I could pretend she was some outside agency, some *belle dame sans merci*, but I phoned her.

Abby lay on a couch in a thong and one of my T-shirts and worked the foil like origami into simple shapes, with a practised flourish. We listened to desert blues.

Did a flutter of concern and future regret shadow my thinking as I watched her sprinkle the powder onto the foil? Nah. I was mesmerised by the immediate reward. Shrew had the upper hand, and Shrew doesn't do foresight.

If there was a rational thought, it was glittering arrogance. Remember how endogenous opiates (endorphins) suppress shame and self-criticism? Well exogenous opiates (morphine, heroin) do exactly the same thing. Watching Abby, I might—and that's a big 'might'—have listened for the voice of reason, *but answer came there none.* I didn't hear anything, and so proceeded to get high. Instead all I heard was: you've beaten heroin once. It was a cake-walk. You can do it again. I didn't hear my inner critic, because Monkey was duct-taped and plasti-cuffed in the boot of the car.

The next hit? Two musician friends piling in at midnight after a gig. How can you not do drugs with rock stars?

The next? I don't know. I can't remember. It was like a drop, then a patter of raindrops, then a downpour. After a while I couldn't remember a world that wasn't soaked with heroin.

Fuck it. I asked for the ride. I wanted to follow an idea off the edge of the world. And that's precisely what I got. I wouldn't have had it any other way.

11

DESELECTION

One morning—one of a hundred mornings—I sat at the table in the galley of the boat. It was an Edwardian table with heavy mahogany legs—I'd never liked it—and six matching chairs. I sat alone. The table was covered in books and notebooks, guides and maps. There was a little clearing in the clutter where my drugs kit lay, a 'work station' including syringe, cooking pot and gauze. Maybe I had a wrap of drugs on the table; if I didn't, then I had one on the way. Sunlight streamed through the portholes, so I must have been high. I cannot recall a high-memory without sunlight, just as I have no withdrawal-memory without darkness, gloom and rain—smack weather. And so the sun shone in at 45 degrees through the portholes, making soft poles of light in parallel upon the maple planking which had once been polished to a sheen but now looked mute under a patina of pale frost. In better times there would have been motes drifting in the sunlight, but the boat was too damp for dust back then. In places, water had swollen the planks, and they heaved away from the hull like a tumour. The wood on the table needed a polish too; the damp had lifted several layers of veneer in the corners, and a length of brass inlay poked up and twanged a blues note like a Jew's Harp. With enough heroin it was a comedic sound to tail a punchline: waa-waa-waa.

On the table my mobile was vibrating. The caller-ID told me it was a good friend. I felt shame. A debate played in the front of my mind whether to answer the call, but this was only mental ping pong to keep me absorbed until it stopped ringing. It's not that I *didn't* answer it, but that I waited just long enough so that the decision was taken away from me. *I'll call them back later*, I told myself. If heroin addiction had a sound, it's that: like a trapped bug against a pane of glass, mechanical panic, an unanswered call, a possible connection falling silent. No amount of heroin ever changed that noise, or could mute the despair I felt. Heroin is the mass of missed incoming calls from friends and lots of out-going calls to dealers; dealers never call you.

When had I become a junkie?

The Ship of Theseus Paradox is one of the oldest thought experiments in Western philosophy. *I didn't enjoy writing that sentence, but please bear with me.* Theseus spent a lifetime battling chthonic bandits, kebabbing monstrous boars and journeying to the heart of the Labyrinth with his ball of thread so as not to lose himself—turning neither to left nor right, always down—to slay the minotaur in that chambered pit. Afterwards, he voyaged back to Athens under black linen sails, became king, ruled wisely and passed into legend. The Athenians kept his ship in the harbour as a memorial to the great hero-king. As time passed and the elements had their way with the vessel, they replaced cedar planks that had broken, the rotted oak tenons, oxhide fixtures, until not a thing was left of the original. The ship lay in harbour for several hundred years, and great men saw it and stroked their beards. At what point, the philosophers asked, was it no longer the same ship that Theseus sailed? And what if every broken and rotted piece of wood was stored in a shed and centuries later a new technology allowed for those pieces to recover their true and original form and be put back together again? Which then would be Theseus's ship?

It's a lot harder to answer the paradox when on heroin, mainly because the answer is heroin. My boat was in a shit state, but looked ship-shape after a decent jab. A bad habit is not a single hole beneath the waterline but hundreds of bad choices—substitutions, temporary stopgaps, deferrals—that occur under a stupor. The realisations come long after the stages have passed—if they come at all—in waves, like the stages of grief: denial, anger, bargaining, depression and acceptance.

I was in denial. On the surface, I was still an explorer, not an addict; the tide was still coming in, not ebbing out. I never did 'anger', because even a truckload of smack wouldn't have made me lose sight of how this was all entirely my doing. I owned the mistake but, at that stage, I still couldn't grasp it, nor realise how fully it held me.

Only occasionally, I would catch glimpses of the enormity of what I had done to myself, and then I felt shame. Shame was new to me. I had never suffered from pride—never really had much to be proud about. I had no defence against shame. My chief shame was of having fucked up the experiment so badly, the sheer stupidity of it all. But I was also ashamed at being so helpless, and so very bad at being helpless. The horror of realising how thin my civility—my dignity—really was. And nothing—I mean nothing on this entire earth—washes away the stain of shame like heroin.

The triumphant metamorphosis that addiction wreaks, from man to junkie, is like fight or flight spread over countless days.

The drug reworked my character, stripping it, by degrees, from human reason to animal craving. It is a gradual process—thousands of tiny choices—where desire for heroin and the attendant behaviours are substituted for the better things in life: friends, exercise, a healthy diet, spiritual self-worth. A patch, a mend, an abbreviation, a fix.

You don't need to be able to read an MRI scan to see inside my head. I could demonstrate this with my phone records: the slow disconnect from rational and reasonable friends and family who challenged me, and a shift towards acquaintances who didn't. I spent my time with damaged people who didn't ask questions, or who were so lonely they would share their drugs in exchange for company. It was a slow slide from positive buoyancy to neutral to sinking down into the abyss. And for the first time in my life I felt alone—more alone if there was a girl in bed next to me—but no amount of junkie company would cure it.

I remember lying in bed with a girl holding me in her smacked-out sleep, watching dawn creep through the sky, feeling her waxy, hot skin, fake tits against me and a three-day stubble on her cunt marking the time she had last been up the pole at the strip club. I had to go back to the table, and cook up a dose. Using her stockings as a tourniquet, I jabbed, and there was something in the size of the vein and the way it rose below the skin that I thought, 'the early bird catches the worm', and because I was up early, I told myself I was a good person.

I watched that phone ring silently countless times: Rob, Ernesto, Flora, other friends, more Flora. I never made a conscious choice to give up on any of them. And just as I didn't reach for the phone to take the call, so my brain no longer called these friends to mind. Why didn't I pick up? Maybe there had been concern in their voice the last time we had talked. Or maybe I couldn't remember the conversation at all, and there was a surge of panic that they were waiting for me somewhere for a meeting I hadn't shown up to. Or perhaps it was a nagging anxiety that I would repeat the same conversation and reveal how out of it I was. Good friendships seemed uphill; they required too much motivation. I deselected them and my better parts with them. In their place I picked people whose mental health and well-being wasn't an affront to my own decay. Smack friends won by default. The path they offered—the one of least resistance—was downhill.

As good friends faded, so did good habits. I had no idea how damaging the soft life could be. I stopped going for runs, and got lazy with my diet. I deferred chores, delegated tasks and shrugged off responsibility. I avoided adversity and stressors, and became increasingly fragile. This was the very opposite of hormesis, where a little of what is bad for you encouraged growth. Instead I was atrophying because of the deep bliss of drugs. A jab of heroin is like a shot of extreme wealth: it is a land of luxury, free of stress, responsibility, adversity ... the very things that give us character. And with each retreat into weakness, I would double down, and cull anything else that caused anxiety or discomfort, chemically gliding towards a sweet abyss that felt good but starved any of my higher systems of the very volatility that kept them sparking.

Every injection changed the contours of my social landscape; each repetition made the next injection slightly more inevitable. The funnelling of attention is incredibly subtle—it is almost impossible to distinguish the lip of the event horizon—cues become signposts. I can't say what came first: the tramlines in my mind or the track marks on my arms.

It is a 'way' as in a 'way of life' or 'being carried away'. What had started as a path became a way, a pathway, a one-way, a groove, a gouge, a rut, a trench, a gorge, until it was a tunnel, where all my attention was focused on the next score.

With my narrowing and mutating social life, it wasn't that my good friends weren't at the front of my mind. That is precisely where they were. The problem was that I wasn't talking to my prefrontal cortex much those days. 'What fires together, wires together', as neuroscientists say, but also 'What fires apart, wires apart,' and I wasn't dialling in those synaptic numbers. This is how friendships die: lack of communication. Addiction is a lack of connection—between me and well-meaning friends, or between my craving and well-meaning neurons.

And so much guilt. But not once did I think of it as leaving a friendship in the past—it was never like that. I was simply post-poning it to another day in the future, when I was in better shape or had more money; then I'd treat them, I'd show them a fine time, when I was back on form, not long now. And to bide me over until then, I'd have another shot.

Not only did heroin change my ability to map my life, it also completely rewired my sense of time. As we saw in fight or flight and Transient Hypofrontality, time is experienced across the prefrontal cortex. As my PFC went increasingly offline during addiction, my sense of time collapsed. The 'now' of instant gratification became everything, I was mesmerised by immediate rewards, and I shunted all of my remaining hopes into the near future. Tomorrow became a real thing, as tangible as yesterday is to you now.

'Tomorrow' was a repository for all those things I was going to do. At any other moment in my life a 'to-do list' would fill me with trepidation and boredom, but not on heroin. On heroin, 'to do' became a sunlit museum of my bright future, the plans in them as irrefutable as any artefact in a glass display case, capable of stirring pride and self-belief. My table heaved under the weight of guidebooks and research. My notebooks were crammed with detailed schemes of journeys I was going to make: training plans, kit lists, reading lists, maps and route outlines. I would read local weather reports of villages in high valleys, on obscure pilgrimage routes, half a world away, to work out exactly what type of sleeping bag I'd need, and then bask in pride at my meticulous research. I spent ages combing the Internet for the next boat I was going to buy—an expedition yacht, to get me away from here—and devoted days to poring over satellite imagery and nautical charts to find wild and far-flung moorings for her.

These plans were proof that I was going places. I was enthralled by them. I waved them in the faces of friends who questioned how I lived: How can you argue with this? 'When,' they would ask. 'Tomorrow,' I would say, and believe myself. But they didn't.

So fully could I inhabit this future space that the present was a hiatus that would be over by the end of the day. I lived this conviction with a passion akin to some cultist in a permanent state of jubilation for a second coming or a transport saucer. I knew I would go to sleep and wake up in a new world full of great adventure that I was rushing towards. It was like a permanent Christmas Eve. Some nights I was so excited that I had to have another jab just to get to sleep.

When friends confronted me with the truth—that I was going nowhere—I reacted with genuine distress. I was shocked at their use of cheap logic, the wounding unfairness of it all, and I couldn't understand why these people—who were meant to be my closest friends—had so little faith in me or my plans. Couldn't they see I was trying? And so I shut them out further, and in doing so refashioned my network further away from sober people and more towards drugs. Addiction is constant revision—re-vision and re-visioning—until drugs vision was all that I saw.

12

DISCONTINUATION

The chains of habit are too weak to be felt until they are too strong to be broken.

Samuel Johnson

After my denial and dreaming phase, I became a raw recruit in heroin bootcamp. It was like old-fashioned military training: moronic and endlessly repetitive, boring, dull, mindless, monotonous. I unlearned everything about individuality. It slowly stripped away my character, my rational self, and left me unquestioning and obedient. There was no uncertainty in my day or disorder: just a singular purpose, a challenge I sank to meet. The less self I had, the less self-control. As my faith in myself decreased, my belief in the power of the molecule over me increased. We are what we do daily.

In heroin bootcamp, my sense of humour was the first to go. I started to take everything seriously. It was a long unwinding of everything I had become. Self-discipline leached out of me, and instead I gave myself over to the relentless discipline of chemical half-life—fix, withdrawal, fix. 'Withdrawal' is another word for retreat; I was in constant training for defeat. I was endlessly drilling myself, square-bashing in ever decreasing circles. I could strip and reassemble my syringe kit in the dark, my movements slick—slow is smooth and smooth is fast—as I sped to cook a dose in the rush to be numb; working parts forward, the bolt, the firing pin ...

Instead of going 'over the top' at the whistle, I would march off at the merest trilling ringtone of a friend who was going to score. Marching away from myself. Marching towards a bench in a park. Some days Mark would be there. Kindly Mark, who was a committed Christian and would always bring an extra can of strong cider for me as we waited for the dealer. He had that long-term junkie smell, somewhere between an ashtray and a crypt. We'd chat and he'd make jokes about the quality of the gear, the dealer being late, the crap new syringes at the needle exchange—what passes for smackhead humour, plucky and whimsical. It was still funnier than military humour.

Biologically, Mark should never have been a heroin addict, because he had the fewest surface veins of anyone I have ever met; he was just a good-natured lump of grey flesh. Sometimes he would sing hymns to pass the time. I enjoyed those moments, the camaraderie, the tang of the strong cider, and not once did it occur to me that I was listening to 'Songs of Praise' live on Tramp FM.

To the outsider, the life of a junkie might appear diametrically opposed to soldiering. But it is the most regimented, repetitive, narrow and mundane world I have ever encountered. It's more militaristic than the military. Junkies only appear to be chaotic when our lives intersect with normality. Sure, we forget to turn up for social meetings, or to work, or we lie and steal, but I've never heard of a junkie failing to meet their dealer on time. It only looks crazy to you because you can't hear the barked orders of our animal urges. Us? We're on a secret mission, for fuck sake.

It's the very opposite of chaotic. We have true singularity of purpose and unswerving loyalty; nothing gets in our way. By comparison, even the most ardent soldiers, suicide bombers, are one-time wonders; junkies are so devoted to the cause that we self-destruct every day.

* * *

After I lost my sense of humour, humility was the next to go. I became more of an asshole. As I devolved, and parts of my personality collapsed, other traits bloated and sickly bloomed.

My diaries of that period remind me of sociopaths I have dealt with: an endless stream of mewling narcissism and an engorged sense of self-importance. I saw myself as a dispenser of praise and damnation on all before me—either swaddling them in sentimentality or consigning them to hell for some imagined sleight. My subconscious seemed to be overcompensating for my own staggering failure, with delusional levels of judgement on others.

As my ego swelled and inflamed, the jotted entries became increasingly pompous, and I developed that passive-aggressive tic of manufacturing shocked confusion: spluttering in ink that *I was at a complete loss* to understand why others treated me poorly, *I didn't know what was going on*, *I honestly didn't know what to make of it*, *I was at a complete loss as to why ... why oh why*, written with all the impotent rage of the letters section in a suburban newspaper, or a viewer's complaint about the daytime soap opera my life had become.

I huffed and puffed into my diary, full of wounded outrage, trapped between being consciously unable to understand a social situation and unconsciously—but profoundly—aware that I was too weak for genuine confrontation with the person who had 'wronged' me. Or—more importantly—to face myself and the deeper truth of just how bad my situation really was. I saw betrayal everywhere; I would manufacture feuds and co-author crises until they reached that flashpoint of suffering necessary to warrant a call to the dealer. Everything was always other people's fault. As the alcoholic comedian W.C. Fields once said, 'I always have a bottle of stimulant handy in case I see a snake, which I also keep handy.'

The question I still ask myself is this: did the addiction cause personality changes as it decoupled the better parts of my reason and judgement? Or have I always been a total asshole, with only a thin veneer of sociability, which I easily blowtorched off with Class A drugs? The disease model of addiction tells us that junkies are sick, and not the moral failures that they were previously viewed as in the past. But can both be true? If long-term addiction causes the parts of the brain associated with reason and rational choice—those areas that govern morality—to switch off, then isn't that both a sickness and a failing?

I'm not sure why I continued to scrawl such drivel into my diaries, but it seemed very important to some part of my vestigial character, to prove to itself that I had some semblance of an inner life. It was pure emotion, without any rational thought to temper it or achieve insight. I knew nothing and felt everything. Without the ability to reflect, I couldn't see what I was becoming.

And still the phone vibrated: mates in Afghanistan fighting; the deep shame of not being there with them. But worse was Stan, alone and dying in an East End nursing home asking me to visit. Every week for months I promised him I'd come to see him—I meant it every time—but I never did.

* * *

The Ronin Miyamoto Musashi also wrote, in the *Book of Five Rings*, that 'Today is victory over yourself; tomorrow is your victory over lesser men'. Nowadays it is something of a fridge magnet of self-improvement, but its corollary is also a koan of self-destruction: I was losing against myself, and every day of failure engendered more failure, bad habits that spawned offspring and fed back on themselves. The curve of disaster is exponential, multiple points of no return plotted in needle marks down my arms. Each step backwards was a step down in cognitive ability. As I slowly devolved, degenerated and regressed, it became increasingly unlikely that I would be able to get back to a drug-free life, or, as Albert Einstein said, 'No problem can be solved from the same level of consciousness that created it.'

* * *

After I became a dreamer, then a mindless recruit, then an ass-hole, I slid further down the years to became a teenager again, both emotionally and neurologically. It used to be thought that brains were fully developed by the time a child reached puberty, and that teenagers were prone to mood swings because of the surging hormones in their systems. Recent advances in brain imaging has shown that, while the brain has fully grown by puberty, it is only by the late teens and early 20s that it is wired correctly. This wiring process begins at the back of the brain, and works its way to the front. The prefrontal cortex—responsible for decision-making, planning and self-control—are the last bits to get fully plugged in. The connections are there, but not at full capacity; they don't have the bandwidth to dial in, regulate and override emotions.

As addiction down-regulated connections to my prefrontal cortex, I became impulsive, petulant, emotionally hypersensitive, less able to rein in my feelings and prone to bouts of rage. I shirked responsibility. I believed passionately that I was right about everything. In that overly emotional state, ungoverned by reason, I gave huge amounts of meaning to trivial events. I felt unfairness keenly in my dealings with others—the type of unfairness only teenagers and children feel. I didn't clean my room either.

Instead, I sought refuge in box sets and computer games; I wore a tracksuit for months because I was always about to go running but never did, and wore them like comfort-wear: daytime pyjamas. I even found myself watching soap operas with a stripper-girlfriend, and being emotionally drawn in by the characters. The show gave us something to talk about other than price and dosage.

And after the teenage moods a long, slow toddle towards infantilisation. Mewling for the needle like a nipple. Then the climb into womblike oblivion. And as I undid my development, I had still further to go: from upright man, to junkie shuffle, to bellowing and whimpering animal craving.

The terrifying nature of the labyrinth wasn't being lost in its complexity. It was the fact that I was becoming the minotaur. The really clever trick: I was just that fraction too animal-stupid to realise it. I couldn't quite remember what the ball of thread was for, or what it was doing in my hand. In the same way I would stare at the vibrating phone and see a friend's name and not understand the life and the love they were trying to summon me back to.

13

MONKEY, SHREW AND LIZARD TAKE A BATH

But who are ye in rags and rotten shoes,
You dirty-bearded, blocking up the way?

James Elroy Flecker

St James's Park, London: I remember kissing a girlfriend for the first time on the bridge across the pond one spring evening. She was achingly clever, a doctor who ran ultra-marathons, sang in a choir and volunteered to rebuild drystone walls in national parks. She was very cool and good and alive. We were walking back from Soho, where we'd seen a show. 'I think we should kiss now,' she'd said. And so we did.

I remember getting stoned with a schoolmate, Jake, in a clump of bushes one afternoon, when we should have been at classes. Other times, I've done countless runs around the park, hill-sprints up the steps by the Duke of York statue. On a bench by the Foreign Office: a young model, more kissing.

I have many very good memories of St James's Park, but this isn't one of them.

I'm not sure any of those other versions of myself would have recognised the junkie who walked through the park that late

Autumn morning. *There goes a good man / there goes a good man having a bad day / there goes a bad man having a good day / there goes a bad man.* Would they have even noticed me? If they had, I hoped they would have looked more kindly on me than the stares I was getting. I was wearing a suit and walking quickly, but I was out of place. The world swayed and wobbled. My suit didn't fit; my pace didn't match; I didn't belong. Not even the pigeons bothered getting out of my way.

Jago had asked to meet for a business breakfast at his gentleman's club. It was precisely the type of thing a fucktard like Jago would say. He ran a small security and intelligence firm somewhere in Mayfair, a dozen flights of stairs above a wine bar, foldout bed for fucking his assistant-du-jour; a very kind wife in the Home Counties and a couple of forgotten children who'd repeat the whole process.

I'd always been told never, ever work for Jago. I'd done one day for him in my twenties, and that evening had got a call from an Old Boy who told me to walk away immediately—'We don't work with people like that.' And so I walked away, and the job went south and someone died very badly. But that was before heroin. You know you hear those stories of junkies reduced to giving hand jobs for loose change so they can score? I wasn't there yet, but this was definitely on the same curve, further down the slope, another small surrender of dignity. 'It's only temporary,' I told myself. But at no point do you ever say, at a fully conscious level: 'This is me. This is who I am.' Denial ain't just a river in Egypt.

It wasn't even a club worth dressing up for, but they had rules, and so I was wearing a suit: a Tweed suit. Never wear Tweed when you're on heroin. I had thought that because it was Scottish it would be ideal. That's not a cheap heroin jab at the Scottish. I genuinely thought that if tweed is good for the heat and cold of the Highlands, it would be suitable for the sweats and chills of clucking. I didn't look cool. It's a thin line between looking dapper, devil-may-care, and looking like a Scottish tramp from the arse end of the Gorbals. Maybe it just looked like a thin line, because it was so very far in my past. I never quite nailed the whole heroin chic thing.

I'd told Jago I'd see him at 11.30. I didn't explain that drug dealers don't get up early. My day—my professional, meet people, engage with reality day—began with scoring. I had two small bags in a clammy hand, stuffed into a pocket. I was worried I would lose them in the old suit, where I'd confuse them with sweat-soaked lint and wads of sweet wrappers. Big Ben struck 10.45. The club was five minutes away, but every moment that drugs are in your hand and not going in your arm is time wasted.

I lurched across St James's Park in the midst of what felt like a mid-October heatwave. My bowels felt loose and my belly cramped and indigested—like the acid had backed up into my glands, my muscles, my joints, and into my brain. My eyes were oily and flat, and let in too much light; atoms danced across my vision in jerky movements. I kept thinking my phone was ringing.

There is a terrible, scraping clairvoyance that comes with withdrawal. I knew stuff. I was attuned to the chatter directly around me, but also aware of hidden antediluvian truths. Office workers had alarmed chicken eyes; there was too much cooing and pecking. It felt like someone had trepanned my third eye with a flint tool. The slime at the bottom of the pond held secrets. The place felt malarial.

The more I tried to measure my pace—get in step with office boys and civil servants—the more stares I drew. People can spot you when you're desperate for a fix. In withdrawal you are savvy to their herd-like condescension, their raspy bleating as you try to move through them. *Just look down.*

The pea grit on the paths was the wrong size, and annoying. There was duck and goose shit everywhere, yet no one seemed to care. The pigeons thrummed with microbes and bacteria. I was conversant with avian flus; I knew the protein coats of the viruses. The tourists were unusually fat that year. And the pelicans could fuck right off.

I could feel the heat of my body radiate through the Harris Tweed, even though I was cold. Heat, damp, mothballs and the smell of ancient Scottish sheep. I thought of the green bones and slimy fleeces I found on the moors in spring. The suit was a mess; the elbows had been darned by a Persian carpet repairer, and I'd sewn the buttons on with whipping-twine from the boat. Duck-egg-blue shirt, too-small Hermès tie, shoes in a sorry state. *There'll be polishing kit at the club*, I thought. *Because clubs are all about polish.* This ditty kept my brain mercifully free of thought for the rest of the walk. The junkie mind adores symbols and mantras.

I arrived at the club, gave Jago's name and asked for a place to freshen up. I ignored the basement loos, a storage room and finally found an old shower room—marked 'Staff'—with a lockable door. Natural light came down from small glass cubes set in the pavement. I could hear people walking above me. The room was painted in school-hall white that had aged the colour of clotted cream; it was sweating and blistered and peeled back on the ceiling. The shower booths were teak; mildewed shower curtains nicotine yellow; rattling pipes frosted at the joints with pissy limescale. The parquet floor was ill-fitted and rattled. In the mirror I saw myself: puffy face, red eyes, greasy, babyish hair—nothing to like. My nose ran. There were institutional smells: industrial bleach, cooked cabbage, the janitor's cheap roll-ups, Brasso. Each smell came upside-down, or like a sentence backwards. All of this telescoped into the periphery as I looked at the little blue bags in my hand.

I unwrapped the cooking kit. It was the standard kit they gave away at needle exchanges and all friendly pharmacies: cooking pot, citric acid, needle, filter, alcohol wipe. Each came in its own little wrapper like some miniature plane meal or a child's toy in a chocolate egg. The cooking pot was the size of my thumb, with a little orange plastic handle to slot on the metal end so I wouldn't burn myself. The citric acid came in a salt'n'pepper-size sachet; the alcohol wipe like a doll's napkin. I put a few drops of water from the tap in the pot and emptied one of the bags into it: light cardboard-brown powder. (Never put the powder in first and then the water, in case the tap is too strong and sends the precious dose down the drain.) Each dose came in a double-bagged wrap no bigger than a pea. It was wrapped twice so you could swallow it if you got busted and they wouldn't burst open as they passed through you. I then put the citric acid in and heated it with a lighter. The acid and heat devoured the powder and left half a thimble full of ginger-ale-coloured liquid. I dropped in a small piece of filter from the kit, unwrapped the needle and drew the liquid up through it to strain out any microscopic debris. I drew it up till the filter went whitish at the edges like an over-pressed teabag. Lastly, I tapped the syringe casing so that all the bubbles went up to the needle, and pushed them out till a small droplet of liquid appeared at the tapering syringe point. *Tap-tap-tap*—that action, in close-up, is so filmic, so *here-comes-the-medicine*, or *trust-me-I'm-a-doctor*, that I've never quite got it out of my head that injecting can be bad for me. Focus on the syringe; forget the cheap suit, forget the dead eyes, forget the mouldering basement. The syringe is shorthand for a cure. It's a magic tool, the wand of science. Maybe it was worse because I had been trained to use a needle, tourniquet, drugs: the blasphemy of a self-medicating medic. But bad medicine? I was about to feel infinitely better. I was about to forget it all. Trust me. *All you're going to feel is a little scratch.*

I then rolled up the sleeve of my left arm and—I am not unexcited to write this—pulled out the tourniquet. It was a standard military Cat-C version, and I slipped it up my arm, over my elbow and pulled tight, locking it off with its own velcro.

Now the tricky bit: finding a vein. When I started the journey, I had veins that stood proud of the muscle—high-pressure hoses, big blue lines like motorways on a map. But in that shower room I was down to minor veins in odd places; maybe I could get a few shots into them before they collapsed and all those countless blood cells diverted to smaller, deeper veins, like traffic around some pile-up on a motorway and forced on diversions down main roads, side roads and single tracks. What vein was I going for that morning? Fuck knows. All the good veins around the inside of the arms were gone. I was still getting veins in the forearms in those days; I wasn't injecting into the backs of my hands, into my wrists, my legs, elsewhere—not yet.

I had a vein on the outside of my left forearm; it was a good vein—it served me well for a while—but it was a bitch to see, at an oblique angle. Come on, let's try it together: make a fist with your left hand, put it to your cheek, point your elbow at the horizon and look down your forearm. Somewhere between elbow and wrist, your basilic vein rides over bone and muscle like a back-country road travelling over hill and dale. Now try drawing a happy face the size of this 'o' with a hyper-fine pen, and then redraw it multiple times in a tight row. When junkies talk about 'track marks', they're talking about the little dots of repeated injections up and down a vein.

I swabbed above the vein with an alcohol wipe—cold flames on my skin, like menthol, as the alcohol evaporated, like tiny angels taking off. Then I lined up the needle.

On the third jab I got it. I could feel the needle go through the vein wall, but sometimes—later—there's so much scar tissue and the veins are so flat it's hard to tell. I pulled back the syringe's plunger and got that tell-tale rose of venal blood. I left the needle in my arm and released the tourniquet. That sound, that

Velcro sound, makes me happy to this day. There is no good, objective, medical word for what I did next: I didn't *depress* the needle or *plunge* it *down*. I banged it in. I jacked up. I shot up.

What was it like? Wrong question. You're still at the other end of the Rabbit Hole. It made your world infinitely better.

A kind light filled the room. The parquet flooring snapped together silently; it fitted perfectly and smelled of church pews. Had it been polished with bees' wax or was that the scent of candles? The walls were warm and dry. My suit fitted; its blemishes were gone. In the mirror there was now a young man ready for adventure. A wild man with polish. Flawed maybe, but noble with it; heroic even. And why not? 'Heroin' was coined as the brand name by the pharmaceutical company Bayer because it made you feel heroic. My tie had a pattern of tiny winged lions clutching a bible, the symbol of St Mark. That seemed to mean something. I cooked up the other bag, split it between two needles and stored them for later in my jacket pocket where more respectable people keep their pens.

Jago was waiting upstairs in a quiet corner of the library, amidst carpets the colours of Neapolitan ice cream, Wisden Almanacs and a couple of taxidermied regulars who all resembled Dennis Thatcher. Jago looked younger than his fifty years— Golden Retriever blonde, keen eyes, overly firm handshake. All I wanted was a job. I knew he had a task for me, but I also knew that I'd have to endure a long bit of banter about how great he was, and I found it exhausting to participate in Jago's self-image.

If you ever want to see the dark Disneyland, the flipped Fantasia of the British male psyche, have a look at the world of private intelligence. It is a carnival of snobbery, secrecy, hypocrisy and impotency, where men who genuinely believe they should have been running the empire are instead errand boys for foreign multinationals. Above all, it is the graveyard of ex-military types and a Valhalla of Walter Mittys.

There is an Argentinian saying: If you want to know a man's fears, listen to his boasts. It works with clothes too. Think of office girls signalling wealth with designer clutches, city drones battery farmed in office cubicles with expensive down exploration jackets or hipsters questing for authenticity. We also mimic those we fear: rich kids dressing 'gangsta' and poor kids dressing preppy. Homosexual men take this to extremes and fetishise the uniforms of those who beat them up and even kill them: Nazis, skinheads, construction workers, cops and bikers. And—no—I can't explain the Indian in the Village People.

Jago mimicked those he deferred to: signet ring, blue blazer with buttons that looked regimental, a striped tie that possibly was something, but wasn't; conversations littered with military TLAs (three-letter acronyms); off-the-peg eccentricity; reports that aped a Vauxhall template. The tie reminded me of non-venomous snakes that perfectly match the colourful banding of their deadly cousins but in a slightly different sequence. *Red on yellow, deadly fellow; red on black, friend of Jack.* Jago was just as cold-blooded, but perfectly harmless.

Despite appearances, Jago had never been an officer, nor was there any record of him passing even basic security vetting. He was a military outrider, a camp follower, a Special Forces groupie. He must have been army-barmy as a child—he bled green—but somewhere in his life he'd had a shot at it and missed. It wasn't his fault, he'd tell you. If it wasn't for some small thing—an army instructor who had it in for him, some bubble in an issue compass, a height restriction on fast jets—he'd be in the breach at Harfleur too.

Morally, he would march to any tune just to be in the parade. Jago had a file on his computer marked 'Fun', and I couldn't tell whether it was Sudoku or Scheisse Liebe. He loved military history, and even believed in it. Chivalry was his big thing, especially the 'Knight in Shining Armour' routine. After I met a few of his Damsels in Distress I realised he was just a sad, old man targeting vulnerable women.

In another century, Jago would have been labelled a Cad or a Bounder. Both terms utterly miss the point, and are instead slights about class: a 'Cad' is an Eton term for a lower-class kid, and a 'Bounder' is one who leaps social boundaries (it used to be interchangeable with 'counter jumper'). It's as if the English are blind to the yellow-toothed, silver-tongued misogyny, and tut at the upset precedence, like queue-barging at a gang-rape.

It's amazing what you can see on heroin. I could look down on Jago, the little wine-bar cavaliero, his third-rate club, the polishing machines and panting passions. He was like a specimen pickled in the formaldehyde of an imagined order. Or spawned from some ancient childhood nursery, the dressing-up box, Commando comics, an angry nanny, some family shame. Secret Squirrels leapt about like Velveteen Rabbits.

I could see it all in miniature far below. Not because I was sitting in judgement or I thought Jago was beneath me. Not at all.

I was simply very, very high.

* * *

The task? Would I waterboard someone? My answer: no. Even on heroin I had some values. But it wasn't just a terrorist—it was far better—it was a tabloid journalist who wanted to be waterboarded and write about it. I would have done it for free, but instead they were going to pay me lots of money.

Here is how it works: a subject is immobilised on their backs with their head pointed slightly downwards. If done on an actual board their hands can be plasticuffed behind their backs and their feet and waist secured as well. A cloth is wrapped over the subject's face, covering their mouth, nose and eyes. The eyes aren't important, but any sensory deprivation adds to the subject's feeling of disorientation and loss of control.

Then water is poured over the cloth, which forms an instant seal over the mouth and nose as good as clingfilm. Actually 'better' than clingfilm, because as the subject struggles to breathe they inhale more water into the breathing passages, triggering a gag reflex and a sensation of drowning. Not enough to induce actual drowning, but enough to create a sensation of drowning. The difference is academic, and 'academic' is the realm of Monkey. Remember how to avoid panic, that breathing is the one action we have control over in a fight-or-flight response, that 'wedge' to avoid chaos and death? This is the opposite.

Waterboarding is about plugging directly into Shrew and Lizard, but way, way deeper. The fear is primordial in every sense. In evolutionary terms you are creating a direct-dial hookup to a pre-reptile, amphibian creature that swaggered around swamps 370 million years ago. Waterboarding subjects don't just desperately need lawyers; they need gills.

When I met the journalist I liked him immediately. Anyone who is willing to subject himself to a fucked-up experiment is clearly a kindred spirit. He was kind, brave and inquisitive. He seemed happy with the arrangements I'd made. I borrowed a friend's barn to give the photos a kidnap/torture feel, and hired an A & E consultant to lend the proceedings some back-up safety and gravitas. More importantly, I wanted the A & E doctor to check and double-check my plans. Buddy-buddy systems are useful for high-adrenaline, high-risk situations, but they're downright essential when high on heroin. Being vaguely professional, I hadn't taken a lot; just enough to get the job done.

The journalist lasted twelve seconds. That might not seem a lot, but it is an eternity in the time-dilating, thrashing darkness of pure panic. According to declassified CIA reports, most al-Qaeda suspects started confessing to everything after interrogators had 'barely washed' their faces. The journalist was tough. He got his story. The experiment had been a success. Or so I thought.

14

WHAT IT FEELS LIKE TO BE EXECUTED
(*STONED*)

I was surprised how much fuss the waterboarding story created. Questions were asked in Parliament. They said I had given an 'irresponsible how-to guide'. So I decided to take the money and head for the Middle East. I picked a hardline country with a death penalty for drug offences and a vigilant secret police. I was looking for a refuge from drugs. In junkie parlance this is known as 'pulling a geographical,' an attempt to break out of the prison of self that addiction creates and restart again in a new place. My plan was to lay low, not sink further. But plans, as I have said, rarely survive contact with the enemy—the enemy, in this case, being myself. Please excuse me if I don't give you the exact details. I still work there, I love the people and am deeply ashamed about my behaviour.

There was a heroin shortage that year caused by the blight on the poppies in Afghanistan. Years ago I had tried to sell a weaponised poppy-blight that the Soviets had developed to the American and British governments to use in Afghanistan, and it seemed doubly unfair that I was now a junkie and that this same blight had magically appeared. Junkies love conspiracy theories, probably because we have detached from our prefrontal cortex and feel intensely that the world is against us but can't rationalise these feelings. We also have an incredible ability to reframe anything towards the negative, put ourselves centre stage and DJ our own pity-party. (This is precisely the opposite of the humour-mechanism we discussed in the Hills chapter.) With 'my' heroin-blight I felt like I had shot myself in the foot, because I couldn't shoot up in my foot, or anywhere else.

This had meant several weeks of very weak and badly cut gear as the stocks dwindled. The flip side of this was a less than acute cold turkey when I landed in the country. I took a long bus ride for the city and caught a taxi into the old town. I stayed with a local family and paid them cash. They gave me a couple of rooms in a separate courtyard and a breakfast of flatbread, honey and yoghurt every morning. In the afternoon one of the houseboys would bring tea. I'd drink the tea with a glug of Kaolin and morphine mixture. I'd brought a couple bottles along from home. It is an old wives' remedy that tastes of clay and peppermint but took the edge off the comedown. That was routine for the first few days, as I sweated out the mild withdrawal.

When I was feeling a bit better I went to one of the main mosques and enrolled in Arabic lessons at the madrassa there. The cleric who ran it was a kindly man who wanted to drink tea and play chess. He liked the bragging rights of having a Western disciple. If he had visitors, I would play along and say that I had travelled all the way from Britain just to study under him. The other students (religious students are called *talebani*) thought it was funny that I was an English Taliban, and that became my nickname.

I was a devout student for an eternity: almost an entire week, if I even lasted that long. One evening, after the sunset call to prayer, while walking back from the centre of town, I took a shortcut through a rougher neighbourhood. During the day it was a flea market, selling clothing from the morgue and cheap Chinese imports of household goods. Down a crooked alley I caught sight of a huddle of men squatting in the dust around an open fire. It was an eternal scene—as old as our mastery of fire itself—and my predicament as an outsider was just as ancient: would they be friendly or not? I felt the flicker of fear, so I followed it and went to have a closer look. Maybe it was just my junkie-senses. The men were mostly middle-aged, though there were two younger men. They were dressed either in jeans and shirts or in the traditional thawb. My eyes tried to adjust to the darkness of the alley and the throw of light from the fire. I said 'Good evening,' then pointed first to an empty spot by the fire, then to myself, and finally gave a questioning thumbs up. They were friendly. They were also smoking crystal meth.

This was new to me. I sat on a low wooden pallet between two guys and held up a $20 bill. A man to my right produced a new glass pipe and held it up, with the other hand he flashed 5 fingers twice: $10. He wore a Casio with a metal strap that reflected the fire. He got out two blue plastic drinking straws that had been crimped at each end: $5 each. These were the drug wraps, sherbet-straws of oblivion. I weighed them in my hand before passing any money over. Squeezing them between fingers and thumb, I could feel the scrunch of crystals inside, a give like wet snow. Ten dollars seemed a little steep for the pipe, but I was still learning numbers in Arabic, so not in a strong position to haggle. Besides, how often do you get a full-blown night out for $20 these days?

I wanted to look like I was hip to the process, but the pipe was a riddle. It was glass with a long thin stem and a sealed bulb, like a test tube with a ball at the end. My neighbour, cognisant of my fuckwittedness, took it from me and produced a powerful lighter from his pocket, a mini-blowtorch with a retracting triangular lid. The flame was blue and roaring, and it reminded me of a blind baby bird with its beak open. He held it to the equator of the bulb and in seconds melted through a small hole creating an air intake; now I had a pipe.

Sensing that I was a newbie, a few others started to help: another guy took my straw, bit off an end, poured several fat, dirty snowflakes into my pipe and then passed it back to me. I made ready to fire up my pipe, but another guy asked me to wait. 'Shway' he said in Arabic—slow down—and pointed to his friend, who gave a quick demonstration: he loaded his pipe with a shard and passed the flame underneath the bowl, which he rotated from 10 to 2. The meth-snowflake collapsed into a liquid and sloshed inside the bowl, then simmered and gave off a vapour, which he inhaled deeply—held for a few seconds—and out again.

Cool. My turn.

It's hard to describe the effects of crystal meth on the central nervous system without resorting to the language of explosives. It was faster than a rush, more than a hit, beyond a blast. I saw cold colours, black lightning and otherworldly shapes like molecules written as cuneiform in a shockwave that was only quenched as their structures were destroyed. I rode it full tilt.

I came back to my senses to laughter and backslaps. I was still sitting upright, but barely in the saddle of reality. I arched back and rocked forwards. My third eye popped back into my head, or maybe I had caught up with it, or maybe I'd finally blown my brains out with the diamond bullet, a crystal 9mm, full-mental jacket. I felt great.

Conversation flowed, mainly Arabic, lots of French and a bit of English, but really it was a speaking-in-tongues that only very powerful drugs can produce. They were all market traders, some locals but a few Afghanis too; this was their post-work ritual on market days. A few of them had permanent shops here. A man brought a gas bottle with a burner and brewed tea, serving it in small glasses laden with sugar. We sat cross-legged in a circle, some of us sprawling on flattened, dusty cardboard boxes, and we fed the fire with discarded packaging from the market stalls and bits of pallet. The flames threw silhouettes against the mud-brick buildings in an alleyway somewhere between an orientalist's wet dream and *Breaking Bad*. In one hand I held a cup of tea that glowed in the firelight, crystals of sugar, a golden sediment. In the other hand I held my pipe, its glass dross-swirled like banded agate, the crystals dirty-glinting with promise. Around me, my new friends told jokes and laughed. I know crystal meth is much maligned, but it makes for a weapons-grade peace pipe.

* * *

One of the men had a DVD shop, and he invited me to have tea there the next day. By 'tea' I mean more crystal meth, but we had tea too. His name was Ammar, but everyone called him Doc because he had a PhD in engineering, which he had studied in Birmingham in the 1970s. Doc was a small man with a big head, and he was always smiling. That's how I saw Doc: his face tilting up and laughing like he was just a floating, happy head. He loved jokes, he loved women and he loved drugs. We became friends and I began to hang out in his DVD shop most afternoons after my classes in the Madrassa.

Doc's shop was a two-room, two-storey concrete building: downstairs a bare room with metal shelves stacked with DVDs and a desk at the back with a long sofa and a few car seats scattered around for his friends. Behind the desk was an ancient ladder, like a siege ladder from the Crusades, that went up through a trapdoor into another room of equal size, where there were lots of foam mattresses and a few gaudy blankets.

For Doc, upstairs was where the magic happened, and not just because that was our drugs den. Doc was the old goat of the neighbourhood, charming and priapic, and he was always off on a romantic quest through the souks of the town. He was very successful: there was a steady stream of female visitors to the shop who he'd take upstairs. All of his girlfriends wore the full Niqab and never spoke to me, so I can tell you nothing of their inner beauty. I am always interested in the seam between the sacred and the profane—and its seamlessness—so I asked Doc why he only slept with very religious women. 'No, Ben,' he said. 'They are all very married, but the niqab lets them move around ... how do you say ... in secret?' And that's how I remember Doc now: always smiling, always chasing—and being chased by— women in niqabs through the maze-like souks like a happy Pac-Man.

The other men who hung out at the shop were Doc's friends and fellow shopkeepers. No one seemed to do much work. We would just drink tea and watch the world go past. Some would play backgammon or chess. I learned how to brew tea to their impossibly high standard on a gas bottle with a cooking ring on top. We didn't even do that much crystal meth. Opium was the main drug of choice. It goes very well with sweet tea.

We'd smoke opium the no-nonsense way: the shop shutters would go down and we'd climb up into the upstairs room. The gas bottle would be passed up the ladder and lit to its hottest, roaring setting, and one of us would heat the tip of a long metal nail on the flames. Meanwhile, Doc would get a ball of opium the size of a plump, golden raisin and impale it on a length of thin wire. All of us would prepare paper straws, one each, to put into our mouths.

Now the fun: we'd sit in a huddled circle with Doc in the middle, and he would 'serve' us one by one. In front of each of us he'd touch the red-hot nail to the ball of opium and create fireworks. 'Chasing the Dragon' is a term nowadays used in the West for smoking heroin off a shitty bit of kitchen foil. The term was originally for opium. When I smoked opium with Doc I understood the difference: the moment hot iron hit the caramel-coloured opium, a dragon was produced: a snapping, globular puff of honeyed smoke that danced and twisted in the air. It had life; it wanted to play. It held its form until I lassoed it with the vacuum from my straw and dragged it into my lungs. It tasted like dried fruit and ancient wisdom, like some prodigal return to a home I'd forgotten in all my wanderings, a groaning feast of fatted dragon and toffee apples from the Tree of Knowledge.

* * *

Over the course of a week we noticed a pair of men hanging around the market, twice at a tea shop on the other side of the square, a few times in a series of different, unmarked cars. Doc and his friends said they were secret police. We'd wave to them and invite them in for tea but they always refused, which only confirmed their role in our eyes, because everyone in the Middle East accepts an invite for tea. After a couple of weeks only one of them remained. He was a large man in his mid-30s with a thick, black rawhide leather jacket and a shock of ginger hair like a copper halo. Eventually Doc got him to join the tea and back-gammon, but—for obvious reasons—we never invited him upstairs to get high.

The man's name was Muthana. He was friendly to the point of bashful, especially when Doc teased him for bravely catching the famous Western spy—me. I liked Muthana, and I think Muthana liked me. He taught me backgammon and told me about his career as a wrestler. He was a famously strong man in his neighbourhood, at his wrestling club and at the gym. He was a Shia, and told me all about Ashura, which was next month. Ashura is a ten-day period of prayer and repentance that com-memorates the Battle of Karbala and the death of Imam Husayn in 680AD. 'Battle' gives the wrong impression. It was a hideous and protracted massacre of a small band of fighters and their families against a vastly larger force. And '680' gives the wrong impression too—because this isn't some distant historical event, but a raw and eternal lament at the heart of Shia faith and identity. During those ten days there are poems, prayers and chanting that culminate in a passion play reenacting the death of Husayn, and although this has happened every year for over a thousand years, the immediacy of the grief is as fresh as if the mourners are hearing the news for the first time. The hard-core purify themselves by scouring their heads and bodies with flails and swords until they are covered in blood. During Ashura, Muthana promised, he would take me to the large mosque for the nighttime rituals.

And that was my day, for most days, for most weeks too: sitting around with friends, drinking tea and getting high, the stream of sights and colours sliding by, the sound of backgammon pieces on the board, laughter, the castanets sound of glass tea cups and saucers, the shouts of the market traders, the distant din of traffic, the call to prayer, more laughter. The days were a dream; the nights less so.

* * *

It's impossible to sleep on crystal meth. On many nights I felt afraid. I would hear sirens outside and the police hammering at the door and know that my time was up. I would go out to meet them and instead face an empty street. Opium can produce aural hallucinations; combined with the paranoia of crystal meth and plenty of residual guilt I was continually persecuted by phantom raids. It got so bad I wanted a real arrest just to get my sanity back. I guess part of me was willing myself to end it.

On nights like those I would walk endlessly through the empty streets and deep into the almost pitch-black souks. I liked it down there. They coiled for miles within the ancient heart of the town. A small amount of starlight or moonlight would come down from evenly spaced portals in the roof, but it was barely enough to see by, even after I had got my night vision. The twisting, chambered corridors, with their shuttered stalls and ancient arches, felt like the windpipe of a dead beast. They were choked with rubbish and deathly still; porters' carts lay abandoned here and there. I couldn't see the rats but I could hear them. Or maybe I couldn't; maybe they were phantom rats too.

I would sit down in a doorway, at floor level, in the heart of the maze and feel safe. Down there, for a few hours, I had my arcs covered. I could see anyone—real or imagined—coming to my right or left in the dark, but most of all I felt safe because no one in the world knew where I was. I wanted to disappear. I wanted an end to all this. It was impossibly quiet and empty. In all my nighttime wanderings I saw a handful of other people down there. Once, two men tried to mug me, but they weren't very good at it, and when they'd got their breath back we went to get some tea and I was glad for their company.

* * *

When it was Ashura I went to the mosque with Muthana in the evening. I made sure I was sober, and that I wore black. We met at a corner of the main square just as the sun was setting, to the honk of traffic and the un-ratcheting sound of shopkeepers sliding their steel shutters closed. The palm trees had been strung with fairy lights to commemorate Ashura, and the minarets were the same celestial blue as the evening sky.

A stream of men were going into the mosque, hundreds of them, all wearing black, and Muthana took my hand in his—which is always disarming for Westerners—and we walked hand in hand into the mosque, into a corridor hung with baize black linen, lit with red diodes, which were draped like the folds of curtains of stalactites, the press of bodies around us flowing and surging forward, the smell of sweat and body odour towards a roaring noise that rose and fell, as booming as an ocean pounding in a deep-sea cave, but as slow as a mighty heartbeat.

In a vast hall, we beat our chests, over a thousand of us, right hand smacking left pectoral, in unison, and chanted 'Ya Husayn'. We beat our breasts—*thump*—60 beats a minute—*thump*—in unison—*thump*—in the dark—*thump*. On a small stage, different men led the prayers and chants. They took turns—we didn't. We kept going.

Time disintegrated, as did my sense of self from my neighbour. We were all beating our hearts so hard we shared the same heartbeat. In that red-lit darkness, the sweat and bodily smells, the booming of the chamber and rhythmic thumping without end, I felt like I was a single pulsing muscle fibre in the heart of a great deity. In that time-dilating and self-dissolving space I glimpsed a life free from drugs.

* * *

The next morning, I was back on the pipe, sucking electric meth fumes to crank me up.

That evening I went back to the darkness and the chanting.

This went on for nine days and nights.

My situation was similar to Niaz's: caught between religion and addiction. Unlike Niaz, I was surrounded by friends and a beautiful and welcoming form of Islam. But at a neurological level it didn't feel much different: the voltage ran through medieval alleyways between the DVD shop and the mosque. It didn't matter which way I rushed.

What I hadn't taken into account when interviewing Niaz—despite all my pontificating about empathy—was the soul-mashing effects of shame. I mean I'd glimpsed it but—fuck—being in the grip of it was wrenching and mashing and horrible. I could see my next fix in the middle of the rituals and I could see salvation when my lungs were full of meth smoke. And, unless I was very deep under the influence of one or the other, I hated myself at all points in-between.

I desperately wanted to stop being a junkie. I yearned for release. I could taste salvation. I would do anything to quit. Except quit.

* * *

The truth is: us smack-heads are almost immune to conversion. Other addictions produce rollercoasters of heavenly highs and infernal lows that cutely segue into religious thinking: Niaz's chronic gambling found a home in the repetitive, numerological corridors of Salafist Islam; alcoholics in the grip of delirium tremens can hallucinate the meteora of brimstone and feel the hellfire on their skins; potheads make a virtue of navel-gazing and take up yoga; while cokeheads quit the Devil's Dandruff and race back to the gods of greed and the markets.

Opiates? We've tasted paradise. Religion might be the opium of the masses, but opiates are also a vaccination for religion. There remains a part of me that regrets not embracing Shia Islam at that moment. It is a beautiful religion, and I make that judgement based on the followers I came to know: some of the kindest, most spiritual and open-hearted people that I have met in my life. It's also a noteworthy bonus that the Shia crescent, from Beirut to Herat, contains some of the most beautiful architecture, gardens, women and food to be found on this earth. I would love to follow that idea to its heart, just to see. I miss it badly.

But it wasn't meant to be. I believed in drugs more. It's an ancient struggle, and men far wiser and more religious than me have struggled with it ...

* * *

If you read the New Testament there is a strange subplot that occurs in Jesus's final hours on the Cross: the bitter wine. He is offered it in three Gospels: he refuses it just before Crucifixion in Mark and Matthew, then Matthew says he takes it while on the Cross, while John writes that he took it just before dying, and then uttered 'It is finished'.

Either way, taking it or not taking it, the choice was written up as an important act. Even as a school-boy I could spot the fuss made over this simple act, and wanted to know why. My religious teacher was a fat and friendly man who was into young boys and old wine—a font of knowledge if you maintained a safe distance. His answer was that the Roman Centurions hated our Good Lord so much that they mocked him with a substandard wine. At that age I was a big fan of pranks, and this didn't strike me as one, not even in the Bible. Nor did it account for the amount of ink devoted to the decision. Our Lord was getting crucified, a cheeky Merlot seemed the least of His problems. I knew there was more to it.

Years later I asked the same question to a Marine Chaplain in Fallujah. The man had fought at the Citadel of Hue and he was more Marine than Chaplain: if they had been Marine-Centurions at the foot of the Cross he probably would have forgiven them. We both agreed that it wasn't really what soldiers did.

It was only after travelling in the Middle East that I understood 'Bitter Wine' is a term for opium-wine, similar to laudanum (from the Latin *laudare* 'to praise'), in many languages. It's not merely bitter, it tastes like shit. Not only is opium 'God's own medicine' in terms of pain relief, it is also a very powerful respiratory inhibitor. As fans of BDSM will know, the dangers of crucifixion—even without the nails—is death by asphyxiation. The Centurions were trying to help end Jesus's suffering, not harm him. Even the Romans had sympathy for their devils.

So the debate about the Bitter Wine is hugely important, because it all boils down to this: could He hack it? Crucifixion is one of the most painful forms of execution ever devised; opiates the most powerful forms of pain relief. That is a hell of a choice. Was he a man, a superman or divine? I'm not saying He did, but I would. These are precisely the type of blasphemous thoughts that deserve a biblical-style stoning.

* * *

It was an error in judgement, and completely mine. The seeds of confusion had been laid a few days beforehand, in the DVD store. I was trying to be helpful and serve customers. I was just getting the hang of the regular stock, and if a customer wanted a specific film then I could get it for them. It was a fun way of trying out my very basic phrases. I'm not good at languages. I find it embarrassing to talk like a baby, it makes me squirm, which is why I did it. One day a customer came in and I jumped up to help him. He was an old man. He looked tribal. He looked regal: flowing robes, long beard and a basilisk stare. He said he wanted something 'black and white', and so I showed him the endless stacks of 1950s Egyptian romantic films we had. Maybe they would remind him of being a young man again, I thought nostalgically (I may have been high).

'No,' he said, he wanted something 'very black and white'. I didn't know very much about pre-war Arab cinema, so I called over Doc. I explained the situation to him.

'Yes,' Doc said in English. 'This man is one of my most loyal customers. He likes really, really black-and-white films.'

I smiled at the old man, who just stared back at me like the filthy Westerner I am.

'That's great,' I said, trying to fill a *really, really* long silence. 'Do we have anything for him?'

'Oh yes,' said Doc. He reached under a metal shelf and pulled out a small pouch that had been attached there with magnets— I'd never spotted it; I admired the cunning—and produced a clutch of DVDs that he fanned out in front of the old man, whose eyes lit up as lust showered his soul.

'This is new!' Doc said in Arabic, and then to me in English, '20 black men and one white girl; they are very naughty'. The Doc had all manner of filth, mainly interracial and lots of anal; I felt the lesbians were under-represented. The only slightly vanilla choice was a compilation of all of Angelina Jolie's nude scenes. Beautiful eyes are noticed much more in the Middle East (not surprising—in many countries in the region, that's all you see) and Miss Jolie's are considered worthy of a goddess.

Now, fast-forward a few days.

I had been left in charge of the store while Doc was off scoring drugs, and Muthana was at the Ashura parade. Doc and I had spent the morning getting fairly baked on opium and crystal meth. They go brilliantly together: opium delivered the bejewelled, exotic pleasure gardens, while the crystal meth slammed on the throttle and took us into hyperspace. Imagine doing all the *caverns measureless to man*, but in the Millennium Falcon.

Now, all I had to do was sit and drink tea and make sure no one shoplifted. Most of the customers were regulars: they would come in, pick a film and drop the right money on the counter. Sometimes they'd need change, and that was good practice for my number-vocab. A large bunch of lads came in, late teens to early 20s. They were all dressed small-town similar: everyone trying to be an individual from the same shop in the souk. They all had whiplash body-odour and an air of being both furtive and hungry, yet wouldn't say what they wanted.

Come on lads, I thought, *we've all been there*. I was a teenager once, I knew that terrible weighted shuffle towards the top-shelf, the spotty, shameful dare of buying your first pornography. I could smell it on them: the horny little fuckers were bug-eyed with wank-lust. I didn't know the Arab word for 'pornography' but made it very clear with a few thrusting motions and the word 'jiggy-jiggy', which was the local slang for shagging and also a fairly universal onomatopoeic for the rusty twang of bedsprings. And even though they knew *exactly* what I was talking about, and they knew that I knew, the cowards still wouldn't budge. 'Fine, fuck off then,' I said in English. And they did.

They came back 15 minutes later with a man in his mid-thirties, all acne and anger, who was the head of the local religious police. They—it turned out—were his cadets. Things got out of hand very quickly. There was yelling, shouting and finger-pointing from them; open hands, denial and bullshit from me. It was no use, and so I pushed past them and tried to lose myself amongst the market stalls outside in the bleached sunlight.

But their leader and his gaggle followed me. He was screaming, mainly at me but occasionally calling on others to witness his righteous cause and join him. I didn't understand his exact words, but language barriers disappear when you are being denounced; it is a feeling older than language. The fear starts as an anxiety like a form of stage fright as the crowd's attention lenses towards you. Then it turns to a darkly primitive fear: not that of an outside predator or enemy, but the nightmare of your own kind turning on you. Shoppers paused and watched; some followed, and the gaggle swelled. I'm not sure why I didn't run. Something in me didn't want to trigger things further. Maybe a small part of me still thought it wasn't happening. A lot of it was just overconfidence from the drugs. But I knew that I needed to get out of this area, to where they wouldn't follow me, to the Shia neighbourhood.

I made it to the edge of the market, where a bank fell away to an abandoned lot about as wide as a football pitch. Normally it would be used as a carpark on market days, but because of the Ashura parades it was difficult to drive into town that day, and so the lot was fairly empty. The edge of the bank was loose sand, detritus and rotting food from the market, and I managed it in three or four bounds. I was almost clear. I aimed for an alleyway on the far side of the lot that was the only way out and led to the Shia neighbourhood. I looked back. A small crowd was spilling down the bank after me like some low-budget biblical film. I watched them for a second too long. When I turned towards the alley, I saw several of the tougher youth run fast around the periphery of the lot to block my exit. I was trapped.

A vague semi-circle surrounded me. The lot was sand and dust, strewn with rubbish and building material; it stank of urine. I could hear the Ashura parade on the main street a block away. The crowd in front of me was a mix of the religious cadets, some of their friends, a few local toughs and curious onlookers. Most of them were listening to the man from the religious police and then staring at me with hatred, back and forth, each time: more hatred, more shouting. I shrugged. Others looked at me and seemed a bit bored. Crowds can be like this, shapeless and unleavened until they reach a critical mass and become a mob. For the first minute it could have gone either way.

There is always a surreal nature to violence, and this was no exception. Maybe my brain was misfiring with the drugs, but it was hard to believe what was happening—too *Life of Brian*, even when they started to pick up stones. Except they weren't stones: the first one I noticed picked up a heavy bit of green glass, the broken butt-end of a bottle; then another picked up a piece of thick tile, another a brick. I understood. The shouting seemed unnecessary. I can't tell you a thing about the people who clutched them, except what they picked up and how they moved; I was alert to anything that telegraphed the first move. And all I could think was 'Oh, this. This is going to be a genuinely shitty, shameful and scary way to die.'

My mind did its usual: printed out snapshots of adrenaline-soaked memories, and I saw many of the things I have told you about in this book. A faded album from a wasted life. Everything since that first execution was merely borrowed time—what isn't? Now I had to pay it back.

The postcards from that particular edge? That broken stub of bottle; the twitchy movements of the man hefting it; the dust from a cinder block in a calloused hand; the fact that no one's skin seemed to fit their skulls as they gurned back and forth between me and their leader; the impossible brightness of the sand that looked like moon dust.

I felt very tired and sorry. I was thirsty too.

The tiredness was a weariness of everything I had become. I didn't care any more. The gravity and mundanity of what was happening made me sick with exhaustion. Or was I just exhausted at being sick? I felt like I was swimming in the event, an inevitability that felt like molasses, and so weary that I would welcome the drowning. Maybe I had it coming. Maybe this was the release I was looking for. A baptism by rocks.

And I was sorry that I had fucked up. I wanted to apologise—not for mercy, but to explain. I wanted them all to understand that I had come to this country to renew myself in a land that I loved deeply, to heal myself and learn—maybe skip the bit about the SAS, heroin and crystal meth—to drink deep, dissolve myself, wash away my sins in the headwaters of the cultures that flowed here.

But try telling that to a screaming mob.

I wanted to escape, but I didn't know how. I thought if I could just remember how I got here I could find my way out.

That was my only thought as more people picked up rocks: *How did I get here?*

From the alleyway came a commotion: Doc and Muthana. Doc was shouting at everyone, but it was only when the crowd saw Muthana that a path cleared: he was covered in blood. His white shirt was ripped and drenched in it. It looked like he had been flayed. He shone red like Mars—like Marsyas—in the glittering, harsh light. In his hands he carried a heavy flail like the weapon it was. It was his own flail, his own blood. He'd come straight from the Ashura procession, where he'd been purifying himself. The message to the crowd was clear: if he was willing to do that to himself, there was no end to what he might do to them. I thought they had come to save me.

Doc walked straight up to me and slapped me across the face. And Doc was small, he had to swing up at a 45 degrees to hit me, but it was harder than I have ever been slapped in my life. I staggered for a couple of steps and then Muthana pushed me over. 'Stay down,' he hissed.

I was on my hands and knees looking at the rocks and dust for a few minutes. Out of the corner of my eye I watched as Doc tore into the religious guy. Then Muthana flashed an ID at him and I saw the man's shoulders drop. Whatever the card said, it trumped anything else on the lot. The crowd began to disperse.

Muthana gave me a hand up and we went back to the shop and pulled down the shutters. Doc brewed up some tea. I sat in one of the low car seats and rocked back and forth, breathing deeply, trying to catch up with myself.

A few friends came over and we all sat around drinking tea and Doc recounted the story. Everyone made fun of me. Doc wasn't angry with me about the porn. He explained to me that you only ever sell it on a one-to-one basis. It's sometimes easy to forget in the Middle East the boundaries between the public and the private worlds that we have lost in the shameless west. (Sure enough, over the next week the majority of the cadets came back individually and bought porn. I didn't bother to serve them, but one gave me a thumbs up: no hard feelings. Other than the one in his pants.)

'What did you shout at the religious guy?' I asked Doc.

'That you were my retarded cousin from Afghanistan.'

After a few cups of tea there was a long silence. Eventually Muthana broke it.

WHAT IT FEELS LIKE TO BE EXECUTED (*STONED*)

'I do know what you do up there,' he said, indicating our drugs den via the trapdoor.

Doc held up his hands, somewhere between surrender and calling a divine witness to our innocence.

'Aren't you going to invite me?' asked Muthana.

And the last thing I remember of that day was the late-afternoon sunlight streaming through the slats of the steel shutters, cutting sworls of blue crystal meth smoke like an electric mist and shining on Muthana, who was still covered in blood. Muthana was an old pro with the pipe; he had done this many times before. He had the slick moves of practice, way better than me. Doc thought this was hilarious.

Muthana was smiling and humming a tune. We were all looking at him and he was loving it. Then he did the damndest thing: he crossed his hands across his chest, his flail in one hand, his glass pipe in the other. With his goatee, the blood glinting in the sunlight, he looked like a golden Pharaoh clutching flail and crook. Muthana jiggled both of them.

'Same, same!' he said, and everyone howled with laughter.

I couldn't tell if this was a new joke or an old joke. Maybe it was a joke we'd been hearing all of our lives and trying to articulate. It was that best type of joke: the cosmic kind. Sometimes you have to be the butt of a joke to really get it.

15

THE LIGHTHOUSE

The lighthouse stood on a small island off the coast of Skye.
'Island' is too grand: it was a semi-tidal spur of rock that ran
east–west, guarding the narrows between Skye and the mainland. The Atlantic crashed against the southern shore of vast
barnacle-clad rocks and deep clefts. The lighthouse tower stood
at its eastern point, sending its bright light down the Sound of
Sleat and across to its sister lighthouse at Sandaig, blinking on
the mainland. The lighthouse keeper's cottage perched on a
narrow ridge of pink-grey granite, salty tufted grass and
heather. Nearby, on the only flat ground, stood a walled
kitchen garden with boggy sedge and an angry old apple tree.
A small tidal causeway joined the islet to Isle Ornsay, which
was separated by a small channel that dried a couple of hours
either side of low-water.

I could give you distances, but nature bends the ruler in the
West Highlands: it was three miles across the Sound, but there
was no straight with the mad tides that rushed between Skye and
the mainland; it was a mile from the lighthouse to the village
jetty on Skye, but twice that in the reverse S around the sinking

sands and bottomless mud; even the hooded crows couldn't fly straight in those winds.

A friend of mine had inherited the islet with its lighthouse and keeper's cottage and didn't know what to do with it. We'd gone up together for a weekend with a girlfriend of his. They left; I stayed. To this day I can't tell you whether it was a refuge or a prison; whether it saved my life or prolonged my addiction. I can try to tell you how beautiful it was, but my words will fall short.

On a fine day, in that straw-gold sun of northern latitudes, the white lighthouse was like a Hopper painting upon the heather and granite, moss and lichen the colour of bronze patina. The surf boomed into the deep channels and foamed bright, woven with dark, olive bands of kelp twisting up from the deep. Across the sun-speckled sea, the distant hills above Sandaig and Knoydart.

When the weather turned, the Sound looked apocalyptic—like John Martin's painting The Deluge—and Loch Hourn yawned like some Celtic or Norse underworld that threatened to swallow us all.

It could be both—and everywhere in between—several times a day. I saw more rainbows on that islet than in the rest of my life elsewhere.

I lived in the lighthouse keeper's cottage with Mia, my Spanish Mastiff. The building had originally been two joined cottages—one for the lighthouse keeper and one for his assistant and their respective families—but in the '60s, after the lighthouse was automated, it had been turned into a single house. Not much had been done to it since then. There were four bedrooms facing south and four rooms facing north: a kitchen with a single-hob cooker, a dining room with a table made of beachcombed wooden fish-boxes, a living room with a fireplace and some bookshelves, and finally a bathroom with an ancient tub and a loo with a huge rock on the seat lid and a sign above it reminding you to put the rock there to keep out the mink who lived near the outflow. Every room looked similar: bare wooden floors, cracked bare plaster walls, heavily shuttered windows and some form of fish-box furniture such as a bedside table or a bookshelf. I'd change rooms whenever I got bored, or if I'd had a bad nightmare.

Slowly, I cut my ties with London and rarely visited family and friends. I sold the sailing barge on the Thames and bought myself a small yacht down in Cornwall that I left to rot. That small island became my entire world; it was enchanted ground.

That far north in summer the days were so long I felt like I might live forever. The air held more light, more colour. The rocks glistened. The foam and the flowers shone. The spectrum was freer up there. The dust seemed very far away.

As above, so below: on perfectly calm days, when the sea was glass, the row-boat flew over spurs of rocks studded with sea anemones like wild flowers, forests of seaweed and long golden beaches far below. The resolution in this undersea world was so sharp it looked close enough to touch. Once, a girl stepped off the rowboat into 20 feet of water thinking it was only welly-deep. She'd gone in with a scream and come out laughing, soaked through. She stripped naked on the shore, only to put her rubber fisherman's boots back on to walk across the purple kelp-pennanted, barnacled rocks. Her wet blonde hair in the sun matched her yellow wellies. Later she wrote me a love-letter accepting my addiction and numerous other faults, and yearning for me either broken or whole. I pretended I never got it.

* * *

Once every few days I'd pick a low tide and walk across the rocks and sand to get my heroin. It arrived courtesy of the Royal Mail to a nearby hotel. If I was in the grip of withdrawal then the head-down trudge was always a terrible walk. I felt like Schrödinger's

Cat, because either the package of redemption, mercy and joy had arrived, or it hadn't, and the utter, impotent, stomach-heaving despair of having to wait another 24hrs was almost too much to bear. On good days I'd lie in the grass and watch the little red mail van pootle down the main road and turn off down to the shore. On rainy days I'd wait under a tree like a troll in the woods. I felt monstrous, what was left of my rational brain atrophied like some Alzheimer Monkey; Shrew was the organ-grinder. It was a full-blown mutiny on the Ark. I'd fucked up the experiment so badly and shamefully that I felt like a broken Pavlov crawling to his chow-bowl as the dogs rang the dinner bell. The mutts trained me so well that even now, years on, seeing a Royal Mail van still gives me a stiffy.

In Spring, flame-bright Bog Iris would bloom in the peaty, seaweed-manured soil at the waterline, and soon after I'd hear the first cuckoo. Then more yellows: broom and marsh marigolds; next pink foxgloves and blue water forget-me-nots and finally heather through to the end of autumn. Always the brine smell, salt and iodine and Atlantic wind. Along the shore, coppices of wet pearl-bright birch, moss-cloaked boulders and damp bracken, peat-bog slipping into tidal mud, iridescent and tannin-stained with rot, mulched seaweed by the high-tide mark and then granite shingle and dirty blond-grey sand scattered with blue mussel shells, bleached limpets, delicate pink crab carapaces with papery barnacles, or worm casts like piped icing.

Once every few weeks I'd walk and row or walk and hitch-hike to a store on Skye a dozen miles away to get tea, tobacco, condensed milk and a few other staples. The island and surrounding seas provided everything else. I'd make endless nettle soup, and experimented with all the types of seaweed I could find. (They're all edible, but kelp was the best.) There was more samphire than I knew what to do with. In the walled garden I dug a raised bed and fertilised it with seaweed and grew lettuce, carrots and potatoes. The apple tree waited until the end of summer to produce the sourest fruit never to ripen, as the sun sunk below the southern walls for winter.

In summer, the waters were rich in mackerel and pollack. I'd bait lobster creels with last year's salted mackerel and haul in stone crabs, velvet and spider crabs; only once did I catch a lobster. There were mussels everywhere, which the locals said were inedible because of the pearls inside, but—if you were careful chewing—they were the best I've ever tasted, and I kept a small jam jar on the dining table full of tiny irregular pearls. My favourite were the razor clams, which I collected at the lowest of Spring tides by pouring salt down their holes. There were regular clams too, cockles and the occasional oyster.

Word of my skills attracted a few phone calls from TV people, who wanted me to present some tough-guy survival show. But I was too far gone lotus-eating to care. If I had been filmed parachuting out of a helicopter into some forbidding wilderness scenario, the first thing I would have done is run off to score drugs—any drugs. That would have made far more interesting viewing than most survival shows. For a start, it would have had a genuine sense of purpose; and been educational and moral too: 'Daddy, why is the presenter sucking off that shaman for those plants,' young viewers might ask. 'Not again, son?'

* * *

Some nights, in wild storms, gannets would aim for the lighthouse, and I'd find them exhausted and stunned amongst the heather in the morning. Gannets are gorgeous birds, a metre long with a two-metre wingspan, white-bodied with dark wingtips and a delicate yellow throat and head. I hated them.

I hated them for their helplessness, and because they always arrived like psychopomps when I was out of heroin. But above all I hated them because I felt utterly duty-bound—even in the midst of bad withdrawal—to help them: one living thing to another on this desolate rock. At first, I experimented with plates of tinned sardines left beside them in the heather. Then with salted mackerel I had for bait for the creels. They all died.

It would send me into a rage: why did they aim for the lighthouse? Where was their will to live? Only writing this now do I suspect that I was really angry at myself: living next to a navigational beacon and yet utterly lost, unable to summon enough strength to return to the world. Once or twice I took them inside—throwing a towel over them and wearing gardening gloves—into the warmth. I'd make a paste of fish and milk from formula, and some of them would take to it for a bit.

If this book were to be a bestseller, this would be the point in our story where broken bird rescues broken man, and together they learn to soar again. But, as before, all my gannets died. Cold turkey staring at cold gannet. I'd lob them into the sea—not easy—like shot-putting a feathered baby, a rigor mortis shuttlecock.

There was no phone or Internet, just a small radio that would only pick up Radio 4 and a local Gaelic music station (two excellent reasons to mainline heroin). Instead, I read books on local history and mythology, field guides on every aspect of birdlife, sealife, plantlife and gardening.

And I shot up, endlessly and religiously. I reused needles until they were so blunt they'd flex as I tried to stick them through my flesh, and then I'd boil them sterile and resharpen their points on a small whetstone made for fishing hooks.

And the otters. The island was theirs; they fished in the bays and played in the rock pools and trampled the grass and heather into miniature paths they snaked along. They got used to me, either because they were habituated to my presence or because I was getting wilder. I'd lie in the bone-yellow grass and watch a mother teach her pups how to fish. Sometimes the pups—the size of a child's glove puppet—would come over to check me out before being scolded in that high-pitched chirrup by their mother. There are few better feelings than fishing on a summer's day at the top of the world with lots of really good heroin fresh in your system and a bunch of great otter buddies.

The lighthouse tower was painted a brilliant white that reflected the fickle weather. On a clear day it was the same colour as a daytime moon. At night on a full moon it glowed the same pure white. In bad weather, when the sea was the colour of an ancient hammered coin, the lighthouse looked like pewter. And in the fiery sunsets of autumn it would glow like iron fresh from the forge against the darkening plum-coloured hills beyond.

People ask me if I went mad up there. I lived wild, away from the constraints of society, but I don't think I ever truly slipped the shackles of reality. Heroin is too good for that. It's not like crystal meth, coke or skunk, any of which can drive you deep into paranoia and lifetime schizophrenia. Nor was there any of the mania and self-hatred of the passionate alcoholic, whose addiction is as medically complicated to shut down as the turning off of a nuclear reactor. Context is everything with heroin. A friend of mine in London swears he never gets withdrawal if he doesn't have any money in his pocket: there is no option to buy, so his brain doesn't even bother playing tricks. I've never managed such levels of mindfulness, but being on the island was close: If I was out of gear and there wasn't a delivery for another day or two, then there were no possible alternatives to torture my mind with.

I was on a rock at the end of the earth. It was not a place to have a thousand thoughts about searching my old suits for a lurking banknote and phoning a dealer, or texting a mate to borrow some money ... and so on, through horrifying eddies of hope.

On bad nights, when the smack was low, I'd hit the whiskey and see things that weren't there, but I was never scared. Some nights the visions were static: hypnagogic hallucinations in that liminal state between this world and sleep, when I'd jerk awake to find a wall missing and the moon-capped waves reflecting on the walls. In these ruinous dreams there was always ivy growing through the cracks in the plaster, or into the rooms, like some childhood wild rumpus. The ivy was the 'tell'; none grew on the island, and so I'd turn over and try to sleep.

There were dynamic visions too: dead friends would sit at the end of my bed, burning with phosphorescence, and I'd acknowledge them, but they never spoke, and there was nothing malign about their visits; they were just what they were: dead but still my friends. Other nights I would hear them walking around the house, step by step, but Mia never cocked her head, so I knew these visions and sounds were just a trick of my mind. If anything, I found them comforting, although I sensed reproachfulness: I had life; they didn't—why had I exiled myself? In the mornings I would feel ashamed that my subconscious had dragged them from death to play a part in my melodramatic puppet show.

Once, the footsteps at night were real: two local kids who thought the place was abandoned and had come out there as a dare. I frightened the shit out of them. I didn't mean to, but monsters in children's adventures are always misunderstood.

Back then, I thought I was very clever in my detective work, as reality crumbled around me: the tell-tale ivy and the dog that didn't bark. Towards the end I wasn't altogether sure whether I was living in a lighthouse and dreaming of a ruin, or the other way around.

On endless nights without heroin to sleep, when it was all too much, I'd sit huddled in the corner of a bare room and hang on to the walls. In these moments I was very aware that I was by myself on a rock off an island off another island at the far north of the world pirouetting around the pole, spinning through the infinite void around our tiny sun. In the mornings I'd wake to find Mia next to me, my sweaty palm-prints drying on the bare plaster walls.

I spent three years there.

16

THE SUCK

OPIATE, n. An unlocked door in the prison of Identity. It leads into the jail yard.

Ambrose Bierce

I want to write about the hell of addiction, screaming wastelands and dungeons of despair, because I feel I owe that to you. But somehow this was worse. It was the suburbs.

The locations aren't important, because being addicted is a form of being lost that I have never experienced before. It's not like being lost in the clag on the Hills, where you can head downhill, follow a stream, hit a road and get your bearings. Nor can you sit it out, wait for the cloud to lift or morning to come. No one is coming for you.

So you keep on going. One foot in front of the other. Because addiction is perseverance too. It is a grey pilgrimage. There is a vague religious quality, a feeling that the suffering somehow makes you worthy, that this is penitence for sins—some sins of commission, but largely those of omission—and that this purgatory might redeem you. But it doesn't.

I spent six months in Norwich, although I see it as a single day—one reproduced every day: a photocopy of a photocopy of a photocopy, each time the resolution imperceptibly lower; the half-life of pixels. Hold yesterday and today side by side and you'd barely notice the difference. But place today and a day from last month next to each other and you'd see one was easier to read, the picture sharper.

The tragedy of my situation—or the comedy—was that heroin had brought me not to the extremes but to the margins. I wasn't in an altered state. I was in the most boring city in England. The Fens are as geographically flat as possible. It was a suburban sprawl without a single redeeming feature within the social landscape. It was the Slough of Despond. It was as utterly inoffensive as any place I had ever seen: everyone dressed the same, everyone was nice. The sheer diabolical genius of something so middling. It was like being in a version of *The Matrix* designed by someone with an '80s home computer.

I avoided my old friends back in London and numbed my senses further with new people. My 'self' was very slowly dissolving, so I spent time with people with less definable selves: less character, fewer interests. Not a single one of them was offensive in any way. They were OK people, but they didn't have much to say that I hadn't heard before: garden-variety opinions, catch-phrase humour, watercooler-level football knowledge, small-town tattoos, sexual hookups after 'Last Orders' like a pact against the loneliness. *Are you dull because I'm shooting up more, or am I shooting up more because you're fucking dull?* At first I drank with military folk I didn't like, then with people who had lame jobs and big dreams, then those with shit jobs and no dreams and finally people with no jobs and not much hope and lots and lots of daytime TV and box sets. And as my act slowly fell apart, I'd shift down a level to another group. Not always a descent—there were good times too—but the downward trend was cumulative: more snakes and fewer ladders.

It wasn't even the economics of it I noticed most—although at the end it was beggars and homeless. So it wasn't the value of the house but the sense that the person there wasn't living a full life or had much pride in their surroundings. Each new house I entered was a slightly less cared-for version of a living space than the last: less of a sense of home, fewer clues as to what type of person lived there, less individual interests to remark upon, more chart music, fewer but wider popular cultural references, lowest-common-denominator decorations, bins unemptied of cans (the cans themselves getting cheaper and the alcohol content stronger as they grew in number), ashtrays overflowing, more unopened mail, the milk in the fridge increasingly further out of date. And, as I passed through the social food chain, the thing I remember most was that each new friend had slightly less on the shelves than the last: some books, fewer books, then just a few paper-backs, then just DVDs, then a few DVDs, then nothing but the TV and then the TV was gone because they'd sold it for smack.

And then people started dying, and that sounds dramatic, but it is the opposite. Not close friends but people I knew from that life. One guy—I can't remember his name—I met with quite a few times when we were waiting for the same dealer in the intersection of alleyways by the redbrick estate by the train station. Nice guy—Ashley?—supported Ipswich Town but shitty dealer: OK drugs but he kept us waiting for ages and his runner was this heartbreakingly beautiful girl in a pink velour tracksuit, who always kept the wraps in her mouth, and she'd try to French kiss me the drugs mouth-to-mouth prison-style for a joke because she knew it pissed me off and I'd tell her to give me the drugs *in my fucking hand* and she'd laugh and play-pout. She was fourteen.

So anyway, me and Ashley (look, it doesn't matter what his name was, he'll be dead by the end of the next page) are standing there waiting in the alley one day in this Norfolk drizzle—you can't even see the top of the cathedral—and I can tell he's in a bad way but assume it's just withdrawal. It is that too, but then he starts telling me about his girlfriend overdosing and he's crying and I'm like, 'She was a great girl mate' (I'd met her twice) and all the while thinking 'Where the fuck are these drugs?', and even in his 24hr-old grief I can see he's thinking exactly the same. So we get the drugs—off the dealer's other runner, this ginger kid with profound learning disabilities, who had a permanent black eye from always getting robbed—and shoot up behind some industrial-sized recycling bins at a supermarket, and now it's a sunny day because that's how back-of-the-net-great scoring smack is.

* * *

I craved drugs. I yearned to be free. In both I was gripped by desire. Trying to give up heroin was like unlocking panic. Or being told 'just relax' in the grip of a seizure. A Gordian knot of twisted and fusing connections. The feedback loop was a short circuit, a spasm. Days strobed in slow-motion epilepsy.

The cycle was exhausting. I had this recurring nightmare of being caught in a vortex. What anaemic sense of spirit I had left felt trapped beneath a waterfall in pitch blackness: the waters driving me under, narcotic depths, fighting for breath and resurfacing, then the powerful eddy drawing me back in. The more I struggled to fight the current, the faster I tired, the more powerfully it gripped. Long shaft, loopback, barb, repeat; the architecture of the hook. Of being hooked.

* * *

Then another few people go see the Great Dealer in the Sky. Two overdose. Another does himself on the train tracks, you know, way out of town before the trains slow. But I wasn't sure he was one of us; junkies are always trying to take credit for fucked-up deaths; there's a certain tribal pride in being the lowest, and you can't let an alky or a mentally ill person outdo you by standing in front of the 14.32 from London in broad daylight. Just *standing* there. Did he face it?

And then Ashley ODs at my friend's house. They were in the same room together when it happened. *Because we've gone down another level after no-jobs-no-hope and we're moving towards no-home; crashing on friends' floors and sofas is the last stage before sleeping in doorways.* My friend tells me 'He was crying all night and then he went quiet; I checked him and he was breathing but the next morning he was dead.' Let me translate that from junkie-speak: he didn't check him.

So people start dying around me and I figured maybe it's the gear or something the dealer is cutting it with, and it doesn't enter my head for a moment that this is simply the end of the line. I remember those months mutely: no sound but a static hush. They remind me of combat in Iraq: the dust, that roaring silence. But this wasn't some neurological condition, or anything to do with fight or flight. Monkey, Shrew and Lizard? Three childhood stuffed toys in an attic in some far-away half-remembered house—embarrassing even.

And I didn't see how bad I was even when a friend took a photo of me on his phone to show me what I looked like. Did he take it in black and white, or is that just how I remember it? I didn't see myself when I had to use mirrors to hit the obscure veins between armpits and pecs. Junkies are narcissists—how else could I look in that reflection and not see the atrophied and bloated waste?

At some level I was aware of how badly I had fucked up the experiment. I'd started with dreams of exploration and investigation, hopes of a Pulitzer. Now I was heading for selling *Big Issue* and scooping a Darwin Award.

The street smack-heads were, as a group, one of the kindest tribes I had ever met. As a whole they were very damaged people, soft on the inside but hard exteriors. They looked out for each other. I saw countless times when people would share their drugs with each other. After a while they began to share their stories, not the pity-for-sale tales they flogged to passers-by for spare change but their genuine life stories. All of them had childhoods of such indescribable levels of pain that made me question whether I was on the same planet as the monsters who had perpetrated it against them. Sometimes I listened diligently, other times, in the grip of a fix, by nodding off and bearing drooling witness. Watching them speak and relive these moments I saw terrified children wearing the skin-suits of battered, track-marked adults.

The street junkies had many of the qualities that are so celebrated in this country: grit, resilience, and dogged persistence. Many of them reminded me of Atlantic rowers or cross-channel swimmers I have known: can-do spirit, never say quit, unbreakable resolve. It was precisely these qualities that were killing us. Resilience is a fine quality of mind with a good habit but it holds you under and unable to change in the grip of a bad habit.

At a walk-in health clinic, I ignored the friendly nurse trying to talk to me as she drained pus from my arm after a jab got infected. I remembered treating junkies with similar problems in the A&E in Wales: the horrified looks the staff gave each other before making me, the FNG (or the Fucking New Guy), do it, and as I treated the junkies with their gurning, silly-me demeanour I thought 'How the fuck can you do this yourself?' If the nurse had asked *me* that question I still wouldn't have had an answer. So I looked away at the brightly coloured health posters on the noticeboard, and I can't remember whether I heard the sound of the pus swilling under my skin or merely felt the contents of the abscess shifting. An observation of an observation of an observation …

But I did notice the books going. I ignored my own reflection and the deaths and instead saw my decay in the things and people around me. And I remember lying on a sofa in a flat and looking across at my good friend as she tried to find a vein in her arm. The stale smell of a too-warm flat, alcoholic body odour, linoleum, the static of the always-on television.

I looked at Mia the mastiff, who looked back up.

'This isn't me.'

Not a big thought or a declaration; perhaps it wasn't even conscious, because I was just so very, very tired of that life. It was like a fleeting upside-down daydream: in my narcotic stupor, just for a moment, I dreamt I was awake and whole.

Did I? Was it real? Having written that, I now don't trust it.

The next day I packed a Bergen with some clothes and my old army sleeping bag and got the train to Cornwall. I stopped in London, where I scored and shot up in the Whitechapel Gallery loos. Then I got the Cornwall train from Paddington. I shot up on the train too, at the back of the 'quiet carriage', in the inside of my thigh. Fuck off quiet people; I dozed all the way down.

I see that day in my mind's eye—those journeys, getting on and off trains—as if I'm watching it through the CCTV of the various stations I passed. It feels like I am trying to piece together a missing person case, or the last hours of a humdrum journey of a man going to commit suicide: the final journey of his life, but utterly like all the other commuters around him. Because that's what quitting is: a form of suicide. Packing my bag felt like loading my pockets with rocks and wading out into still waters—the sensation of drowning, but logic telling you it's air. This is why I had to jab myself senseless: Dutch courage to drink your Kool-Aid and rejoin the world. Getting on the train was as much an act of nihilism as standing in front of it.

I reached the village where I had a boat in the creek and went to the pub, where I had a pint of scrumpy and chips from a van that stopped once a week on the green. Before it got dark, I climbed onto my boat, which I hadn't seen for three years. It was up on the quayside. It smelled of engine oil and mildew. I found a bottle of spiced rum and drank half. I did one more injection by candlelight with Mia next to me. I remember that very happily. It was my last happy memory for a long time.

My 'living' space was a six-foot cabin and a bunk with a mouldy, bare Styrofoam mattress. Daylight came in through a few lichen-mottled portholes. I had stashed lots of water. I pissed in the empty bottles, dark piss, like peat water. Maybe there was a storm, maybe it was just my nerves, but my hearing became fine-tuned, and there was this endless sound of the lanyards and stays of the rigging frapping against the mast that went through the boat and into me. That was my soundtrack; no music, no radio, no Internet.

Medically, this is what to expect from heroin withdrawal: vomiting, diarrhoea, fevers, joint aches, cold flashes, depression. If you're fit and skimming the surface with low dosage then it might not be too bad. But the trouble with withdrawal from a long-term habit is that by the time you desperately need to detox you are the least qualified to stand it. I had been training for this moment for five years, but training to lose. Every single broken promise and defeat was ingrained in me. Mentally and physically I was a puny wreck. But I was about to step into the ring for the fight of my life.

The worst thing about withdrawal is the joint ache and its terrible exponential repercussions. It's called 'kicking the habit' because all your limbs keep moving in this endless involuntary dance.

Which means you can't sleep.

Not much is known about the physical or psychological effects of sleep deprivation beyond 24hrs, because it is medically unethical to push volunteers beyond that. At 24hrs there is a huge drop in cognitive functions such as accurate memory, coherent speech and social awareness. After 24hrs, spatial disorientation and visual misperceptions darkly and rapidly evolve into full-blown hallucinations and a total break with reality. The body, which performs so many vital regenerative tasks while we sleep, begins to wear itself down very fast, towards total system failure and death. Mind and body are locked into a *danse macabre* to insanity and the grave.

Sleep deprivation is torture. It's the go-to choice of the CIA. Top al-Qaeda terrorists who were shackled or put in stress positions in rooms with bright lights and played ultra-loud music (see Barney the Purple Dinosaur theme song) were reduced to howling babies within 48hrs and confessed everything. In fact, sleep deprivation is so successful that most of these people had never been in al-Qaeda, and were making up stories to stop the torture. All I had to do—at any point to stop the torment—was phone a dealer. In the grip of madness, it was mad not to.

I woke up on the first morning early, and by about 10am I was feeling pretty smack sick. It would normally come a bit later, but my animal-junkie jailer was already wise to the escape attempt. So I talked to Mia, and she seemed sympathetic. I had stashed dog food, and the boat ladder was at an oblique-enough angle for her to get on land and shit somewhere. I didn't leave the boat at all, and for a brief moment I thought: I'll ride this.

At dusk a colony of rooks—maybe seventy or eighty strong— would leave their oaks and fly around the valley. Then night came.

Time doesn't exist for a committed heroin junkie. That part of the brain goes offline early on in addiction. In the grip of the drug there is an eternal 'now', an infinity of bliss. Time didn't return simply because the drugs had left my body; the clock remained stopped, and it was an eternity of pain and humiliation.

I kicked and twisted and tried to sleep, but I couldn't. At first it felt like some minor adjustment would see me right—move an arm, adjust a leg—but nothing worked. I felt like a tense but floppy triangle constantly flipping and propping. I stretched every limb and flexed every joint, and when I had finished the last one I would start on the first again, and so on and so on, till I was doing an ever-exhausting waltz of corpse puppetry. Then it felt like I had cerebral palsy: spastic claws and locked jaws, fevers and chills and a static building in my joints. At its worst it was like some medieval break-bone fever. I don't know if there were small snatches of sleep or just black-outs between those mini-seizures, but they were worse than being conscious. In those moments I had glimpses of such nerve-shredding evil that I woke with a start and started to twist once more. They weren't nightmares—they had no form or sense—but in them I knew a singularity where all grief, loneliness, shame and anger came from, and it felt sentient.

This went on for three days.

On the morning of the second day I ate salt out of some mineral craving. That evening I broke down when I saw bits of heroin on the floor. I had done a lot of gear on the boat ages before so it wasn't completely unreasonable. I picked up the bits and put them on some kitchen foil and ran a lighter underneath but it was just acrid smoke from dry mud and dog hair which I tried to relight and inhale in case there was just one molecule of mercy in the fumes. But there was no release, only another deeper level of degradation and despair.

The sweats and the chills were violent and chaotic. My heavy-duty army sleeping bag was soaked in sweat one moment and damp and devoid of warmth the next. I got goose bumps—that's why it's called 'Cold Turkey'—and just as a sick joke (that is quite common in withdrawal), I had lots of spontaneous orgasms. Not even an erection as a warning. Talk about being fucked.

I lost it at about Day 3, or Night 3, and into the morning of Day 4; I gave up, let go.

I let go of ego and felt myself slip under. No more fight. Not myself, not the molecule. Somewhere beneath submission, beyond defeat, towards utter loss. I gave up on giving up. Layers of drowning, or nightmares of waterboarding. I had no one to plead to. But instead of torturing someone for a secret they had, I was torturing myself to find a piece of information I had lost, a truth I had once known, but had forgotten.

Craving and wild desire ran amok. I panicked like I had never panicked before, again and again. Each time I thought 'I can't take this any more,' but there was always more. Deeper and deeper into this chambered pit within myself, like being in a tunnel of collapsing reality, I felt systems within me shut down, down, down. The claustrophobia of my own mind was unbearable: the compression of depths. I couldn't trust my senses. It was impossible to say whether I was going up or burrowing down further into madness. In between seizures of coiling panic, I would listen to my heart thump and wait, in the long pause, for another beat.

At the blackest moment, in the centre of the maze-like terror, I saw a thought flash briefly.

It was when the images in my mind slowed down to a stutter of frames that I realised it was a projection.

This is not real. Addiction is imagined.

It is only a belief—a strongly held belief. It didn't hold me. I held it.

Maybe I should stop holding it?

I came to in the morning with Mia jumping up on the bed, whining and licking my face. She had a habit of eating wild garlic; maybe she'd been into the bins. I'd often caught her eating roadkill and, to be fair to her, I don't know how long we'd been out of dog food. She crept up the mattress—more whining—and then projectile vomited over me. I wasn't even angry. Nor did I have any self-pity, because I didn't have much of a self. In the small cabin we were both drenched, the Styrofoam soaked, my army sleeping bag, my clothes slick with ropey, mucous dog-sick.

I rolled off the bed and fell to the floor. Slowly I tried to wriggle free from my sodden sleeping bag. It didn't feel like a cocoon; it felt like afterbirth. My clothing clung to me like caul. I lay on my back panting.

Some people liken recovery to being reborn, but I think they mean it more in a spiritual sense. Spiritually, I felt aborted. Physically, it was more like being reanimated: I was a zombie, with spastic limbs, clammy chicken flesh, dead-fish pallor, distended stomach, receding gums with stained teeth, cavity-foul breath, bloody eyes—and covered in dog vomit, sweat and spunk.

Lying on the floor of the cabin, I started to see the funny side.

Looking up, I addressed my higher power for the first time in years.

'Is that all you've got?'

I climbed off the boat, stripped down, threw my old clothes away and washed myself with a hose.

Then I took Mia on a walk to the village store to get her some proper food.

17

HOW TO BE COOL (AGAIN)

We are not alone but are cared for by the stars, by women and by our demons.

Sándor Márai

There are worse places to come off heroin than West Cornwall, where the main road forks and forks again, and soon becomes a single-track lane that sinks into the landscape: below deepening hedges and into a nave of bracken, fern and foxglove, vaulted with shady oaks that lead down to wooded rivers where little egrets watch their perfect reflections on quiet waters.

I can write such descriptions now—but back then? Not in those first few days. I was in shock. It was hard to walk without staggering, as if my gyroscope was off-kilter, or the world needed a folded beermat under one corner. There was a madness to things: flowers pointed at me, grass grew in gangs, butterflies were mechanical, there were glitches in the code; the moon hung pale in the clear sky, and it seemed as crazy as any Internet conspiracy that it caused the tides that rolled like blue mercury across the congealed mudflats. I was sane enough to recognise these tremors in reality as my own, but only just.

Physically, I was not in a good place either. I have never felt so weak: not strong enough to tire myself out; not tired enough to sleep properly. At the height of summer I wore a thermal top, still freezing and sweating. My body's thermostat was schizophrenic. My other senses had atrophied too; I had to earn them back again. Summer in Cornwall had all the warmth of a daguerreotype.

I walked because I didn't know what else to do; to at least try to exhaust myself; to try to make sense of what had happened. Walking was something I had been trained to do. Each day Mia and I would push out a bit further than the last. I got a map and covered the oak and beech woods, marking off routes as I went. I walked roads and bridleways, deer-tracks through the woods; I tracked streams up past brackish creeks through moss-choked rocks to springs that tumbled sunlit flecks of shale from fissures deep in the rock below. On long walks I could make it up to the heathland on the Lizard, studded with prehistoric standing stones, Second World War military ruins and ghostly Cold War satellite dishes amid the heather and gorse. The sight of my military boots sloshing through the mulch was both comforting and distressing.

I followed overgrown footpaths and ancient sunken tracks beneath carpets of leaves and mulch. I did press-ups on the forest floor, the beechnut kernels leaving star-shaped marks on my soft, uncalloused hands. On a solitary pine there was a low branch where I could do pull-ups each day as I passed. Slowly my map became a network of trails across the valleys, between the downs and the many tributaries of the flooded valley.

But it wasn't working. I wasn't shooting up, but I wasn't developing either. I feared stalling. And I was haunted by this deep unease that everything I had been through wasn't real. And that wasn't simply the drugs or lack of them.

One day I was lying on my back in a meadow, feeling that kind of lost you feel when you know exactly where you are and it's not good enough. At precisely the moment when I was looking up at the clouds and feeling lonely, my phone rang.

'Alright you twat?'

* * *

The last time Pikey Lee and I had spoken had been a couple of months beforehand; it hadn't gone well. Lee and a few other concerned military colleagues had threatened to haul me off to an obscure training base and handcuff me to a radiator until I sweated it out. I was too gone at the time to be scared, but the episode depressed me. We've all got stoned as kids and a bit paranoid and wondered *how long has that van been there for?* (I also once got hideously stoned inside a surveillance van on a job, a five-hour skunk-driven loop of deep 'Who watches the watchmen?' introspection.) For those who take drugs to extremes, there are secure psychiatric facilities crammed with people convinced there are secret military units out there to get them. It was depressing to think I was finally one of *those people*. It was zero consolation that in my case it was real.

This time Lee was offering something different. I went to see him. We stood on a bright lawn looking over an orchard and down to the sea. He said I should come live with him and his wife Jessica for a bit. In exchange I'd help look after his kid Joshua and do some gardening. So I did.

In the mornings it was Joshua-duties. He was two years old. I am terrible at babysitting, so I just cranked up the cathode-nipple and we watched *Star Wars*. We did this every day without fail, but we did it interactively: each time Darth Vader came on we'd hit the TV with toy lightsabers or shoot at Stormtroopers. And Lego, endless hours of Lego; I'm not sure who benefitted more: the two-year-old kid, or the junkie trying to figure out how to put his life back together.

In the afternoons, I would tend the garden. I planted peas and several varieties of potatoes, lettuce, yellow chard and black kale.

I spent endless hours in the orchard picking apples. On long walks with Joshua we'd pick bags of blackberries, most of which he'd eaten by the time we got home. On one of our walks—with him on my shoulders—he pointed to the scars of track-marks on my arms. 'It's a plant, a poppy,' I told him. 'It grabs you, a lot like a bramble.'

The gardening gave me a practical grip on the world—not simply because I felt kinship with the other vegetables—I relished the simplicity of the tasks without ritual. Above all, it reset my clock to projects that spanned days and weeks—as opposed to the same day, every day: score, inject, sleep. Nature also set a pace to my healing. I would notice scars heal, track marks subside, veins grow and muscle build at the same rate that seeds sprouted, vines grew and fruit ripened.

When Lee got home from work we would go for runs—long jogs through the woods or to a field where we'd do sprint work—and then get the gloves and pads out and do some boxing. It was painful and vomit-inducing at first; I couldn't outrun the shame of what I had done to my body.

Food was our ritual. I helped Lee convert a shed in the garden to use for butchering deer. We travelled across the county to source oak from a Regiment friend's forest to use for the chopping blocks. We found old iron hooks in a bric-a-brac shop for hanging meat. We built a hot-box for curing biltong. In the eaves of the shed Lee put in a small stained-glass window.

Most evenings Jessica would cook. She had been raised by her Italian grandmother and memorised the old lady's recipes: anchovy pasta, tender lamb, hunter's stews of venison, artichokes and roasted vegetables from the garden. We talked about food and we talked about life. Jessica is the kindest and most generous person in this book.

Later, on many evenings, Lee and I would sit out in the orchard by a small bonfire and talk: the heat of the fire and the sparks rising upwards into a duck-egg-blue sky to the west, and the first stars showing to the east. There are three things I can watch to a point of meditation: breaking waves, streams or rivers, and fire. We burned apple logs, which gave off intense heat and a fragrant smoke. I stared deep into the flames and embers as we spoke—I loved that the light of the fire was energy trapped from our own sun decades ago, the cyclical nature of it all.

And that was my day, every day, for months. If this seems quaint, it was. I can't write it another way or stand outside that moment. I was surrounded by good people who gave me their trust, time, food and respect. I had to re-evolve and regenerate: gathering wild food, gardening, building Lego towers, re-seeing the world through the eyes of a two-year-old, explaining the Jedi way to him, to myself; those fireside chats.

I remember watching the flames burn the lichen on the apple logs like fiery fingerprints, and Lee looking like a grinning pumpkin, lit from without. 'It's an outdated concept, but I like it: it's called Maslow's Hierarchy of Needs'. From its base it looked like Pen-y-Fan on that first morning of Selection.

* * *

If I got addicted to heroin, does that mean everyone will? It would be easy to wrap up the book now and flog it as some tough-guy memoir with a strong anti-drugs message—SAS versus heroin!—which would have mass-market appeal. Sadly for my bank balance, the answer is a bit more complicated.

The truth is that 90% of people doing drugs do not become addicted. This is roughly the same for cannabis, alcohol, crystal meth and heroin. These recreational drug users—the infuriating bastards—use drugs privately and quietly and never appear on society's radar.

If you doubt that drugs can be taken without addiction, visit a local hospital's cancer ward, where people are routinely given vast amounts of heroin (as diamorphine) for weeks on end. Cancer patients are given higher doses than street junkies, but very few of them ever become addicted to the drug.

During the Vietnam War, 20% of US troops were addicted to heroin. Back home the top brass were terrified that battle-scarred, smack-head returning soldiers would create a crime wave. Something very different happened: 95% of returning addicts stopped using within a year. Those who did it solo were just as successful at quitting as those who sought treatment. The 5% who continued to use, according to the study in the Archives of General Psychiatry, had been addicts before the war and/or had traumatic childhoods.

So: why me?

Soon after getting off heroin I asked a retired GP in Cornwall how he viewed addicts.

'Nine out of ten suffered deep trauma early in their lives, and one is a cuckoo,' he said.

By 'cuckoo' he meant the wild child and rock'n'roller—that thrill-seeking denizen of excess who set their amplifiers to 11—that accounts for such a small proportion of drug takers but are such a perpetual trope in film and books that they have burned themselves into the public's imagination of what a junkie looks like.

There is a very strong correlation between risk-taking and addiction. More studies have been carried out on males than females but men are more likely to be impulsive sensation seekers. It starts early on, eleven-year-olds who scored highly on high novelty seeking and low harm avoidance were found to be vastly more likely to engage in substance use in later life (twenty times more likely to abuse alcohol by their late 20s).

Did this mean anyone (AKA me) who would be willing to take on the high risks inherent in the heroin experiment were already vastly more likely to become an addict? Combing through the vast piles of academic research I came up with two major conclusions: 1) Yes; 2) I really should have read this stuff beforehand.

But I still didn't like the term 'cuckoo'. Which was odd because I am very fond of the birds. They migrate from sub-Saharan Africa to the far north and hearing the first one in Spring on Skye was a reminder that Winter had ended and Summer was a-coming in. However, Cuckoos are the assholes of the bird family, they mimic the much more dangerous Sparrow-hawk in their plumage and the females lay their eggs in the nests of other species. When the baby Cuckoo hatches it pushes all the other eggs or young out of the nest and then gets fed to bursting by its unwitting foster parents. Maybe, the idea of being a greedy imposter screaming the world down for increasingly large treats felt like a diagnosis that was a little too close to the bone. So, faced with a label I didn't like, I decided to shop around.

So what claim could I make on trauma? Heroin is a pain-killer; no one is pain free. How much pain did I carry? I could tell you that I put a needle in my arm because someone put a gun in my mouth; maybe add some teenage bad behaviour, a few playground scrapes and throw in some early bedwetting, but it all wouldn't add up to much. Or would it? Was I in denial? What constituted trauma?

* * *

So I went to Narcotics Anonymous. There I understood trauma.

At first, signing up to NA was like joining a really shit military unit: low entry requirements (if you're there, you're in), bad tea, rote mantras and over-emphasised comradeship. They even give out medals based on time served.

I sat with groups of addicts in church halls, in community centre rooms, in odd bits of hospitals and health centres. I drank shit tea, I sat my bony junkie ass on foldaway chairs, I hugged strangers, chanted NA verse, and clapped while people got key rings. I heard Dave share his tips for newcomers on his fifteenth sober birthday surrounded by his beaming friends; I watched once-famous actresses play to the biggest audiences they could now draw; I stared at a child's helium birthday balloon in the rafters of the side room of a church as it slowly deflated over a period of weeks.

And slowly I learned to listen. Almost every single person had come to drugs through pain: sexual pain, childhood pain, abandonment, petty cruelty, beatings, horror. I had caught sight of this on the streets of Norwich, but it was only after going to lots of NA meetings that I realised how many people, from every part of society, were simply trying to medicate their trauma.

Part of the problem is in how society views pain. If you have cancer or some other medically recognised pain you get the good stuff from doctors in white coats. If you are damaged and hurting in less acceptable ways you have to score it from criminals on street corners. It's pretty much the same molecule. Who's to say your pain is any different? You have to be sitting very comfortably to sit in judgment.

I've watched people die, seen the horrors of war, and witnessed, in slow-motion, mothers in their first moments of grief for a child; I've worked on ambulances and in ER rooms, I can talk the medical language of different pain scales; I've done SF selection and been an SF instructor watching new recruits go through the most physical pain many of them will ever experience in their lives. The more I know about pain, the less qualified I feel I am to judge it in another soul. Life doesn't give us a choice between getting cancer or getting raped as a kid. Yet we exile junkies to the furthest reaches of our society, into a wasteland of taboo and criminality. No one would suggest a cancer patient score street drugs. Nowadays when I see a junkie begging for change, what I see is someone suffering and trying to medicate some happiness into their lives. I stop and talk to them.

Sometimes I mention my experiences; more often I don't. Most of the times I just shut up and really listen to them. I always give them money.

The point of being in those NA rooms is to find common ground in others' stories. I tried and sometimes I succeeded, but there was something that set us apart, a bridge I couldn't cross without trespassing. I had entered this world as an experiment. Critically, I had told everyone I knew what I was going to do before I did it. When it went wrong, I had exiled myself from friends and family until I sorted myself out. When I reconnected with them, everyone welcomed me back: mates bought me soft drinks, told me what a dickhead I was. They said 'I told you so', and they were right.

In the rooms, I could say 'My name is Ben and I'm an addict' with almost equal conviction as the next junkie, but I'm not sure I've earned the right to put myself alongside most of them; that would be like stolen valour, wouldn't it? In some meetings I sit next to a guy whose story goes like this: raped by his dad, his mom committing suicide, being on smack by twelve, long prison stretches and then he got clean. He was probably swimming in B-process endorphins in his mother's womb as his dad beat her. The majority of the people in those rooms not only came off very hard drugs but came back to very hard lives. And they also had to confront whatever trauma had put them under in the first place. Me? I lived in a lighthouse, strippers brought me drugs and I came back to a truly cool life—and I still found that *incredibly* hard. I was returning to a dream; he had to wake up to a nightmare. We were both junkies, but, in terms of addiction, my mate is Special Forces and I'm a boy-scout.

* * *

Addiction and pain are entwined. The reason why cancer patients or Vietnam vets don't get addicted is because they are treating a specific pain, localised in space and time: once the cancer is cured, or they are removed from the horror of war, they stop using drugs.

But deep-pain—that which is tattooed into some people in childhood—is different. A project in the US called the Adverse Childhood Experiences Study looked at the long-term effects of childhood trauma: sexual or physical abuse, and parental bereavement. For every traumatic event that happened to a child, they were two to four times more likely to become an addict in later life. The renowned addiction expert Gabor Maté has said that in thirty years of treating the junkies of Vancouver he has yet to come across a long-term female addict who was not sexually abused as a child.

It doesn't even have to be horrific abuse. Another long-term study, in the American Psychologist, watched parents and children carry out simple tasks through a one-way mirror. The scientists noted which parents had been loving and involved, or disengaged or actively cruel; years later they revisited the children as adults. Those with indifferent or cruel parents were vastly more likely to be using drugs heavily in later life.

And just as addiction follows pain in individuals, it does the same in communities. Time and time again throughout our history there have been outbreaks of addiction that accompany vast societal changes. Nowadays many former coal-mining towns and fishing ports in Britain are ravaged by heroin. It isn't that the ground is full of coal and the seas are full of fish and these people are too addicted to work; they are addicted because their jobs, livelihoods and communities have been taken away from them. There was a similar phenomenon in the US with the crack epidemic of the 1980s 'destroying' the ghetto. As Chris Rock said, 'Yeah, like the ghetto was so nice before crack.'

In the last few years, poor whites in America are facing an opioid epidemic similar to the crack epidemic of the '80s. It isn't being caused by nefarious drug firms (though their business model has probably exacerbated it); instead it is a fire burning through the already dying blue-collar communities of rust-belt America.

* * *

NA and most rehab clinics use the disease model of addiction. According to the National Institute on Drug Abuse, 'Addiction is defined as a chronic, relapsing brain disease that is characterised by compulsive drug seeking and use, despite harmful consequences'. The drugs cause changes 'In areas of the brain that are critical to judgement, decision-making, learning and memory, and behaviour control'. These changes can be shown on medical imaging of the brain, which is clear proof, they say, that addiction is a disease. The disease model has been hugely powerful in changing the way society sees addicts. It removes the stigma of shame from the addicts themselves, and it opens up huge reserves of medical research funding to seek a cure.

But I never felt like I had a disease. I never felt like drugs poisoned my mind. Sitting in those rooms in NA, I heard the word 'disease' mentioned often. But I also heard many prayers and mantras. How many diseases do you know that can be treated with words? In NA I felt they were trying to cure me with belief. It took me back to my experience on the boat: that addiction is belief.

Those final hours of withdrawal on the boat felt like a dark night of the soul, a crisis of faith, rather than anything chemical. What had actually happened? Had it been real? Or rather, had it really been the battle with heroin I had imagined it to be?

There was something else too that irked me in those long months after I had quit heroin. The fact that I kept returning to was this: the shitty street heroin I was using at the end was under 10% pure. What could account for the rest? What was the nature of this dark placebo?

In one word: learning.

In five words: learning, training, radicalisation, belief, devotion.

Don't let the chemicals fool you—addiction is an inside job.

My fuck-up with the experiment wasn't simply underestimating neuroplasticity—the brain's ability to change over a short period of time—it was failing to see the cause of those changes. I had always thought my battle was against heroin. Even before the experiment I saw it as a fight, and during addiction I pitted myself in a daily struggle with this drug. And every day, as it kicked my ass, I believed in its terrible power even more. I was obsessed with the molecule as the enemy; I had target fixation. Addiction is all about target fixation.

And yet the answer had been staring me in the face all along. It was what allowed the BDSM girls to re-author themselves. It helped send Niaz on his mad journey and added lustre to the objects in Ortiz's collection. It helped shape me as a soldier. It was there when I marched up the Fan as a recruit, and climbed the cliff to jump into the river all those times as a child. It was dopamine. This book has been a pilgrimage down the reward pathway.

I apologise if you saw this plot twist coming—I didn't at the time. I was too busy fighting the molecule to realise I was only fighting myself.

At the heart of addiction is a fiendishly clever confidence trick. It's a bait'n'switch move. This is a con where the buyer is lured into a store with the promise of a desired item at reduced price and then sold a more expensive one with a binding contract of endless instalments. The bait in this case is heroin. For those first six months heroin was bliss but slowly my body developed a tolerance to it—the B-process—and its pleasures began to pale. Upping the dose worked for a while but eventually I settled into a habit of maintenance—scoring simply to feel normal, to function. In parallel, during that period, the reward pathway began to dominate—dopamine was switched for heroin—and a contract written in dopamine is very binding indeed. The currency of dopamine is attention. You pay attention in ever increasing instalments to the drug until you have given yourself over to it completely. As the poet Mary Oliver wrote, 'Attention is the beginning of devotion'.

During those initial 28 days of the experiment, under the cover of a narcotic stupor, while I engaged in my daily heroin ritual and focused on the drug, dopamine had been rewiring my synaptic connections and reshaping how I saw the world, an accelerated and deep form of learning that I took to heart. It was dopamine—rather than a wrathful god or malevolent substance—which had taken every single pixel in my vision and tilted it ever so slightly back towards scoring.

The disease-model scientists are correct to say that addiction changes the brain, but so does any goal-orientated activity that involves lots of repetition until it becomes all-consuming. It could be heroin, but it could also be sex, video gaming or gambling, learning a new language, an instrument or an automatic weapon, falling in love or religious conversion.

This is just the brain doing what it was designed to do: learn. The reward-pathway system is one of the most powerful, transformational learning systems we have.

* * *

The learning within addiction is the same as the training on the weapons ranges and that horrible spiky bush. Amidst the gunfire, in the wash of dopamine and endorphins, I forged new habits—good habits. Remember 'chunking'—the brain's ability to automatise packets of learning? It's the same thing as habit-forming. The difference between a good habit and a bad habit is where it takes you. Dopamine doesn't care either way.

Every shot of heroin during those 28 days trained me to be a junkie, just as every round I fired on the weapons ranges trained me to be a better soldier. In each instance I had automatised my learning, it became second nature. As a soldier I had retained 'manual' control; as a junkie I had lost that control—it was a very dark full-auto satori.

Both forms of training involve vastly accelerated learning powered by feedback loops—some of the most powerful forces in nature. I learned both processes so deeply that it became a way of seeing. Remember that sentence? 'If you know the Way broadly, you will see it in all things.'

This is beautifully expressed at a neurological level by Marc Lewis in *The Biology of Desire*:

> The way we experience things shapes our biological matter, and those biological changes shape the way we experience things subsequently. In other words, changes in brain structure make that way of experiencing things more available, more probable, on future occasions. This can take the form of a self-reinforcing perception, an expectancy, a budding interpretation, a recurring wish, a familiar emotional reaction, a consolidating belief or a conscious memory. They're all different forms of 'permanence' – of the way brain patterns settle into place, so that traces of the past can shape the present. What I'm describing here is a feedback loop: a way of seeing, remembering or acting on the world and a structural change that perpetuates that way of seeing, remembering or acting. Thus the mind and the brain shape each other.

And that was the genius of heroin addiction. It left me with a brain that couldn't comprehend the metamorphosis because it had changed so much itself. A lesson, a way of seeing, that was so broad and profound that I couldn't see the edges of it. How do you know what you are looking at when it is everything you see? It was exactly the same as that moment of revelation in the SAS training: *The moment the training caught was a gentle revelation that was so accelerated and so deep that it had me converted before I noticed it. I got it. Or rather, it got me... It was utterly transformative, on the other side I couldn't understand how I'd never seen it before.* On heroin, I couldn't understand it was everything that I saw. Radicalisation is a lesson so large you cannot see its edges, like a seditious dream that takes over a waking state.

As Marc Lewis also wrote, 'The brain shapes our lives and our lives shape our brain.' Or, as I recently saw written on a lamppost, 'we do not see things as they are, we see things as we are'. At the core of experience and how we perceive our world is a process similar to the algorithms that shape our behaviour online.

Here is a thought experiment: fire up your computer, delete your cookies and try to radicalise yourself online: right-wing, left-wing, porn, celebs, Salafist Islam, model-railways—it doesn't matter. It doesn't take long before your computer develops a 'habit'. In the beginning, the suggested viewing is pretty bland, but it only takes one click before the algorithm comes into play and starts suggesting increasingly extreme viewing; each further click reinforces the likelihood of more extreme content. Ancillary programs take note, and start suggesting other people with similar interests; advertisers pile in to exploit you. The algorithm is not merely shaping how you see the world and where your attention is focused, but moving the reference points that allow you to chart how far you have come, or judge scale. It is tunnel vision, and—in the grip of it—who is to say whether you are peering up a telescope or down a microscope? Within three or four clicks, the narrowing of perspective mutates into a cone of attention, and then the rabbit hole forms.

During those initial 28 days on heroin I had managed to radicalise myself so thoroughly I wasn't even aware of it. I had learned to be a junkie so deeply that I couldn't unlearn it even after that initial cold turkey. The habit had been forged, the program burnt too deeply. I believed in the drugs; I had become a convert.

Belief is a lesson that you feel to be true; it doesn't require proof. A fact is a thing that is known to be true and can be proved. Both are forms of 'truth' that work different parts of the brain: feeling is the realm of Shrew, proof is the realm of Monkey. I felt that heroin had power over me because I craved it. I believed in it intensely, devoutly—but not rationally.

Prior to addiction, all the training in my life had been towards a tough goal—training that followed the pain. It sought the summit. It was aggressive. It aimed for the obstacle. It was that hard path. That training is always rewarding, because doing hard shit in life gives you increased confidence, resolve and focus to do more hard shit, and the more you do, the easier the 'more' gets. It's a virtuous circle, driven by the relentless pursuit of excellence. There are moments when I have trained hard and then—that sweet bit—where I have punched through: mastered a combination, formed a muscle memory or dreamed in another language.

Addiction is also the moment when you punch through: when you 'get' heroin and it 'gets' you. It is a dark training, aberrant learning, the path of least resistance, the downwards spiral, the lust of forgetting, the relentless pursuit of oblivion. It is a journey away from self: I skirted obstacles, dodged hardships and fled from pain. The less I did, the harder that remaining bit became, so I would step down, do even less. I was training towards failure.

The more I failed, the less I believed in myself, and the more I believed in the power of this molecule. It was an all-enveloping way of seeing. We all exist inside a story that the brain tells itself but in addiction that story coils and constricts with each daily retelling. That is what I meant back on the boat, at the crux of withdrawal, that addiction was a projection—it was a loop, spinning with the sheer force of habit: my perceptions shaped how I saw the world, which were then played back to me. I created the world and perceived it simultaneously. The more time I spent in that world, the less able I was to conceive of other, drug-free, realities. The projection was a Mobius strip of devotion. It was a form of fanaticism.

Think back to Niaz. He wasn't snorting roulette balls, yet he was thoroughly addicted to gambling. The brains of chronic gamblers, porn addicts, religious fanatics and heroin junkies all show similar changes; these changes are wrought by dopamine. Remember the analogy of the reward pathway being the laser that illuminates the tank for an airstrike? Addiction is total, all-consuming target fixation. It is only being able to see down the path of the laser beam—a hyper-bright tunnel of attention—because everything else is in the dark, cold, untouched by desire. Addiction is confusing the utter, sheer desire that bathes the target in a celestial glow, for the target itself. Addiction is forgetting you hold the laser; you project the light onto the target, the drug doesn't illuminate you. You hold the belief, the belief doesn't hold you.

That night on the boat, I remembered.

In the same way that I came to understand that pain could be an opinion at the top of the Welsh Hills, so too—at the depths of my despair in withdrawal on the boat—I realised that desire could be an opinion too. The dictionary definition of belief says that it is a 'habit of mind in which trust or confidence is placed in some person or thing'.

* * *

The etymology of 'addiction' contains all the themes we have talked about: learning, training, radicalisation, belief, devotion.

Perhaps the most profound and rapid brain changes that occur in humans happen in females during pregnancy. In those nine months the brain undergoes greater rewiring than during a similar period on heroin. The majority of her thoughts are rerouted to the feeding, care and welfare of that baby, the profound and loving enslavement of motherhood. We say that a mother is devoted to her baby. We would never say that a mother is addicted to her baby. Yet the word 'addiction' means 'devotion' in Latin. That's a good way of thinking about addiction: pregnant with a bad idea. And—not to be too flippant—like many unwanted pregnancies, it starts with a bad romance that looked very attractive at the time.

Me? I'm a slag, and thought it would be fun. The risk aroused me. Dopamine is the bridge between high-risk taking and addiction. People with highly developed dopamine systems are more thrill-seeking—they get more of a kick out of it than other people—but that same turbo-charged dopamine system is a dangerous thing paired with narcotics.

However, for the vast majority of addicts, the idea of addiction is seductive because everything else in their lives looks so very bleak. It appears exponentially rewarding against the dark background of trauma. For them, the first jab—their first glimpse of a pain-free life—has the power of revelation.

Addiction comes from the Latin words *ad* (to, towards) and *dico* (say, state, affirm). The verb *addico* means to pledge yourself to something, to surrender to, to devote yourself or even enslave yourself. In the medieval period, people spoke of being addicted to god or to study or to love. It was a laudable term; it implied perseverance in the face of adversity for a greater cause.

Addiction felt like an idea that was murmured to me under a narcotic stupor; an infectious packet of information somewhere between a meme and a virus and a religion. It grew within me and came to define everything about me.

Addiction is an idea that most people will never 'get', yet for the very few, it could be one of the most profound experiences of their lives. It can enter an individual like a lover's whisper or an epiphany on the Road to Damascus. It can run amok in broken communities like a religious cause or a popular delusion.

In the grip of addiction I felt devoted, convulsed with the cause. The reward pathway was a relentless and respite-less pilgrimage down a tunnel of attention that was as sacred as the nave of a church. It was pure belief. I projected all my intense desire onto a molecule like it was a holy relic; injection was a ritual for me, loaded with potency and meaning. What is belief but a lot of meaning wrapped around a grain of truth? The 'fact' of heroin—the physical dependency and sickness of withdrawal—was only a small fraction of addiction. The rest of it—the dark placebo or nocebo—was all me, my biology. The nature of addiction is nature.

Emotionally—and belief is powered by emotion—my break with heroin felt not like a spiritual awakening but like being rejected, betrayed, abandoned. This is why addicts are so prone to conversion. Hard drugs and hard religion are interchangeable. They are forms of belief. Both sufferers are brainwashed by dopamine.

Niaz had al-Qaeda waiting for him. It was a seamless switch between the casino and that radical mosque. At a dopamine level, I doubt his brain even spotted the difference.

Many addicts wind up in rehab, and most clinics use the disease model. But again, if addiction really is a disease, then where is the medicine? Even the most advanced rehab facilities only offer a few pills to ease the physical withdrawal, and then they switch to a twelve-step belief-based programme to treat the addiction itself. Just as the pills are a substitute for the drugs, the belief mimics the addiction. It's another bait'n'switch.

Go online and watch a US-style 'My Drugs Hell' reality show. Turn the volume down and watch the men in white coats, the clawing, screaming junkie and the innocent/guilty family members; behold the roles they all play. How much medicine do you see? How much actual science? Are you watching an intervention or a medieval exorcism? Sometimes I wonder whether addiction isn't just a form of possession in our godless age.

Paradoxically, one of the main problems with rehab may be that it is too soft, and the pills that ease the withdrawal actually deny the junkie valuable pain and a metamorphic rite of passage.

There is a hoary bit of addict wisdom that suggests the tougher the withdrawal—and the more it is earned in the face of adversity—the less likely the relapse. Why give someone an epidural during their own rebirth?

Maybe there is some truth in that, but at what cost? The withdrawal on the boat was tough because it was done solo, and involved almost total sensory deprivation for three whole days. To this day I can't work out whether it was a waterboarding or a baptism, the death of my opiate cult-of-one or the rebirth of self-belief. Maybe my rational half and animal-craving struggled in the depths till one of them drowned; Monkey and Shrew in some final cartoon chemical apostasis. It felt like being thrown into a washing machine on spin cycle with some self-help books and lots of bricks.

Three days tends to be the goldilocks zone in torture and transformation; it sends you just mad enough to slay the old you but not the new you too. It's a narrow margin, somewhere between talking to dogs and gods. After three days it's time to roll the stone back from the cave mouth or tickle the tonsils of the whale and be vomited up onto dry land. That last sentence implies that I had total agency; a hell of a lot of it was luck too. Sometimes, on mad adventures, we wash up on the shores of reason through no particular fault of our own.

Most addicts have the softer, higher powers of NA waiting for them. Statistically, NA is just as successful as a trip to the rehab clinic, and is far, far cheaper. There are 12-step belief-based programmes for all manner of addictions: Alcoholics Anonymous, Gamblers Anonymous, Overeaters Anonymous, Debtors Anonymous, Sex Addicts Anonymous and Workaholics Anonymous. Don't let the tribalism fool you; underneath all of these are precisely the same belief-based programme. If heroin addiction is a disease caused by the drugs, how come its antidote is the same as the cure for all these other woes?

HOW TO BE COOL (AGAIN)

If you are reading this and think you might have a drug problem, then please visit NA. If you are reading this and have a problem with people taking drugs, you should visit NA as well. I went because I couldn't think of a better reason not to. I still do occasionally. I might not agree with some of the terminology, or believe in the disease model, or higher powers, but that's missing the point. The reason NA really reminded me of the military is because neither are about big concepts or shiny medals: it's about fighting for yourself and the person next to you.

I didn't have al-Qaeda or rehab waiting for me. For those first few months I didn't even have NA. I had Pikey Lee.

Lee saw beating addiction as another form of Selection, an ordeal that would leave me better off than I was before. Bad experiences, moral lapses, disease models? That was all 'pathetic fallacy' shit to Lee. That was emotion. That was conspiring in your own failure.

Over the weeks and months I spent with Lee and his family I got a little faster, ran a little longer, hit the pads a little harder. I remember the happiness I felt again running along a trail through sun-drenched woods, I pushed myself further and broke through into a flow-state, my first for years: that nectar, sap of life; that juice that is worth the squeeze. It was like an old friend dropping by unexpectedly and rekindling a relationship. I had crossed the return threshold. I was back in touch with myself. Or maybe I had just broken back into my personal stash of anandamide, dopamine and endorphins that I had been hooked on all my life.

Slowly, Lee's training replaced my previous training of addiction; self-belief conquered chemical belief. As Erasmus said: *A nail is driven out by another nail; habit is overcome by habit.*

But most importantly, Lee didn't even believe in recovery. To him, that was mere resilience. Getting back what I once had wasn't good enough in his eyes. It was a way-mark to be passed, not the peak to aim for. What Lee really believed in was post-traumatic growth.

The neuroscience seems to back this up. All those brain changes we saw in addiction—the long slide down the totem pole, the atrophying within the Prefrontal Cortex, the defriending of Monkey and Shrew—they're not permanent. Unless you have lobotomised yourself with a catastrophic overdose, all those synaptic connections grow back within several months of abstinence to a normal baseline. That's resilience. But then the brain keeps sprouting new growths. A recent medical study showed that synaptic density within the Prefrontal Cortex continued to evolve and increase beyond the baseline of people *who had never taken drugs*. How fucking cool is that? The trauma of addiction and the adversity of the struggle to overcome it stimulated the brain to new levels of vitality, complexity and sophistication.

There is still plenty of room for belief—especially self-belief—in that kind of transformative healing. Back on the boat that summer—with Ernesto, Rob and others—I had seen how mindset helped determine which people might suffer from PTSD, who will recover, and who will go on to new heights with post-traumatic growth. Belief shapes our perception of what is possible. I tend to think of PTSD and addiction as cousins: one is a spasm within the fear circuit, the other is a fusing within the reward pathway. I can't help but think that if you believe in recovery then that's the limit of what you will feel, but if you believe in post-traumatic growth you are more likely to reap its rewards. All the energy of that reward pathway has to go somewhere: 'aiming high' sounds a lot like 'shooting up,' doesn't it?

What did that feel like? Slow. It was fucking slow. The heroin experiment had kicked my ass like I'd never been beaten before. After six months I was myself again, and then I started to feel better than I'd ever felt before: a strange combination of being both more vulnerable and stronger at the same time; a bit wiser, a lot more humble. I felt my lust for life return, but then something else: a deeper appreciation of this world than I'd ever thought possible. Maybe I'm the same asshole I always have been, and I'm just making up my better qualities. But that's what belief is, isn't it: making stuff up? And if you believe that belief can rewire the mind then you might as well dream big.

18

EPILOGUE

We may say vices wait on us in the course of our life as the landlords with whom we successively lodge, and if we travelled the road twice over I doubt if our experience would make us avoid them.

Duc de Rochefoucauld

Being sober, I began to pick up the phone more.

Ernesto was the first to call. He'd bought a whorehouse in the Canary Islands—just the property, not the business. He invited me out there to go surfing. The whorehouse had recently been decommissioned or deconsecrated or whatever you do with a whorehouse—deactivated? I wrote the withdrawal chapter of this book there, in a curtained booth with a wipe-clean bed, a happy ending amongst so many happy endings.

Of all the extremists and strange tribes I knew during that period the strippers found the most contentment: one is an artist, one is a musician and another is a partner in an investment firm in New York. One has a kid with an academic who's also a jiujitsu hero, two married SAS men and have families too. One actually joined the military and became an officer in a psychological warfare unit in a Middle Eastern country—head-fuck or what? Only one lady fell further into a life of prostitution, exploitation and shame when she left the strip club to work in PR.

As for Rob Paulson, he left the SAS and spent three years working in Iraq as a mercenary. He spent his R & R in Pattaya, Thailand which had a big ex-military scene. Rob drank himself senseless and got deep into crystal meth and crack. It was a life that chewed up a lot of very good men: some died in Iraq, others overdosed or took their own lives in Thailand. So Rob, being Rob, married his crack dealer, adopted her infant son and moved to a remote part of Australia, where he spends his time shark fishing (catch and release) and coaching the town's football team. 'No one said it could be done,' he told me over a drink. 'No one said I could settle down and lead a prosperous life. No one believed I could do that. I was tired of everything, mate: having to be on the ball and battle-fit all the time in Iraq, tired of the drug abuse in Thailand. I had nothing else left to prove. Normality was the last frontier.'

Me? I got a job doing security work in war zones. I love it: taking journalists and diplomats into the high-risk areas and—so far—getting them back safely. I'm freelance and get to pick the best projects: I only take people who are doing good things out there, leaving the world slightly better than they found it. I've found a balance of sorts: a few big trips a year, enough danger to keep me sharp, to get my fix.

Do I have regrets? Yes and no. I regret the pain and anxiety I caused family, friends and others close to me.

I don't regret what I did to myself. It was a leap of faith. I know I would have regretted not doing it far more. I am shocked and delighted to still be here. It feels like a bonus round.

I've found the right dosage of risk: enough to keep me going, not too little to make me bored. Do I fear a relapse? The heroin doesn't worry me too much. I hope not, as it would be very boring to go back to all that. I'm more worried that some other idea of utter stupidity will seize me with such cat-killing curiosity that I will just have to do it.

A few years ago, on a recce in Kashmir, I saw reports of heroin addicts using cobra venom. The addicts paid nomadic snake charmers to let the cobras bite them on the tongue. After an initial one-hour blackout period, one patient said he had a high that was better than heroin, and it lasted three to four weeks. Some venom users say it has cured them of their heroin addiction and others report 'happiness, grandiosity and excessive sleepiness' for almost a month. There are even 'snake dens' where different species of poisonous snakes are available to customers.

You have to admit, that is interesting. It's cobra venom for fuck sake: there must be a B-process like a moon-shot; it's the type of dose that could turn you into a superhero. Please tell me you're just a tiny bit curious? Tempted?

* * *

My work has taken me to Iraq and Syria in recent years. It feels good to be back there even though the job involved much down-time in northern Iraq, waiting for a Black Hawk. I had an understanding boss who told me to 'take it easy, eat lots of kebabs and finish the book'. So I did. And then I began to explore the area.

The Zagros mountains on the Iraq-Iran border are a fractured paradise. The scale of them stretches the mind, the deep banding of geology and human history, layered with myth, secrets and hidden meaning. It is a feeling I have only ever seen elsewhere in the Caucasus: mountains that seem to exist as the headwaters of all the hope and all the woe in the world.

It is a liminal space where I am caught between the lust of the exotic and a love of home. I am at my most alive and young, and the world feels fresh and impossibly old at the same time. Clouds lose their grandeur against the flanks of the mountains. Up in abandoned high valleys, there are crumbling walled gardens hanging with fruit and laden with such déjà vu that you would think you've returned to Eden, to a state of grace like a summer in childhood.

Ancient rivers carve great canyons through which spurs of the Silk Road run. In caves above one valley they have found human remains, 60,000 years old, of a man who shouldn't have lived beyond childhood but was cared for and fed by his clan, and it is the first record we have of human kindness. Beside him, another burial, showing a low-kinetic weapon injury, is the first example of inter-human violence. In those dark caverns is a half-remembered dream I've had before. In another valley, in the droughts last summer, they discovered a lost city founded by Alexander. It is a place where we can know ourselves anew in ruins or come to terms with what we are in conversations with the *other*.

It is a land of blazing sun and snow-capped peaks, of walnut and mulberry trees, and towns where people come to trade objects and ideas, insults and jokes. The souks are full of laughter, counterfeit goods, dark honeycomb from the forests, glistening goat carcasses and shockingly bitter pomegranate juice.

In the evening I like to watch the sun set—there, more than anywhere, I feel closer to the heart of the mechanism—as it bathes the peaks in flame and sends the sky peacock colours into indigo, and as the light goes, so go the centuries, rewound through the call to prayer, until it is night and stars and campfires.

Tomorrow, if the helicopter doesn't arrive, I will explore the caves.

NOTES

INTRODUCTION

9. *a Bison-Man or Minotaur.* For further reading on Palaeolithic art please see: *The Mind in the Cave*, David Lewis-Williams (Thames & Hudson, 2004); *What is Paleolithic Art?* Jean Clottes (University of Chicago Press, 2016). For planning your own visits: *Cave Art*, Paul Bahn (Frances Lincoln, 2012).

2. HOW TO BE COOL

25. gunshot—*in the amygdala.* The Emotional Brain, Fear, and the Amygdala, Joseph Ledoux (*Cellular and Molecular Neurobiology*, 2003). For more general reading see *Anxious: The Modern Mind in the Age of Anxiety*, Joseph LeDoux (Oneworld Publishing, 2015).

26. *was probably higher.* *Left of Bang* Patrick Van Horne & Jason A. Riley (Black Irish Books, 2014).

29. *time slows or even stops.* 'The Neural Substrates of Subjective Time Dilation' (*Frontiers in Human Neuroscience*, 2010).

29. *giving you a sense that you are.* 'Does Time Really Slow Down during a Frightening Event?' (*PLOS One*, 2007).

31. *and can help people bond.* 'Tend and Befriend: Biobehavioural Bases of Affiliation Under Stress' (*Current Directions in Psychological Science*, 2006).

31. *suspicion as it can create bonds.* https://www.psychologicalscience.org/news/releases/the-dark-side-of-oxytocin.html

32. *selves to be masters of our fate.* The neural architecture of the fight-or-flight mechanism may be tattooed even deeper into our religions and

societies than we care to admit. Barbara Ehrenreich, in her jaw-dropping book *Blood Rites* argues that much of human nature was laid down during the earliest days of our species when we weren't flint-chipping heroes but tiny bands of very scared prey. It is a scenario deeply imprinted in our neural substrates which we ritualise to this day. The old gods demand sacrifice because they are our predators. Somewhere in the Early Bronze Age animal sacrifice was substituted for human sacrifice. It is recorded in our myths: the swapping of Iphigenia for a deer; the Golden Ram in the story of Phrixus and Helle; God demanding Abraham sacrifice his son Isaac and then suggesting a sheep will do. Many ancient religions are littered with tales of offering up the best and the brightest to dragons from the deep or to Minotaurs in their mazes. Chaining a youth to the rocks, tying them to a tree, binding them on a mountaintop or nailing them to a cross deeply impresses our Shrew brains.

34. *'Relax, look around, make a call'*. For a very good book about decision making in hostile environments see *The Men, the Mission, and Me: Lessons from a Former Delta Force Commander* (Dutton Caliber, 2010).

34. *communication among brain systems*. Scream: *Chilling Adventures in the Science of Fear*, Margee Kerr (Public Affairs, 2017).

3. SELECTION

58. *not only itself, but even living itself*. Motivation and Personality, Abraham Maslow (Pearson, 1997).

58. *what contributed to a life that was worth living*. https://www.ted.com/talks/mihaly_csikszentmihalyi_flow_the_secret_to_happiness?language=en#t-63499

59. *feedback and the challenge/skill balance*. Flow, Mihaly Csikszentmiyalyi (Rider, 2002).

63. *did just that, but with dead fish*. https://news.stanford.edu/news/2011/august/humor-coping-horror-080111.html

4. FULL-AUTO SATORI

73. *his theory of Transient Hypofrontality*. 'Functional neuroanatomy of altered states of consciousness: The transient hypofrontality theory' (*Consciousness and Cognition*, 2003).

82. *were criminals, homosexuals—and even French.* *SAS: Rogue Heroes*, Ben MacIntyre (Viking, 2016) is the best account of the early days of the Regiment.

5. IRAQ–BATTLE FOR RAMADI

96. *collective mindset and moved as one.* Flow states in military operations are explored in depth in *Stealing Fire*, Steven Kotler and Jamie Wheal (Dey Street Books, 2018).

108. *berserker warrior in the Lewis Chessmen.* For more on the Berserkers and a brilliant history of drugs in war see *Shooting Up*, Łukasz Kamieński (Hurst, 2016).

109. *In 2006, an Italian neuroscientist.* https://www.cnr.it/en/focus/081-10/electrocortical-effects-of-mdma-are-potentiated-by-acoustic-stimulation-in-rats

6. THE GIFT OF GAME

122. *fight stronger than a love of life'.* *A Fighter's Heart*, Sam Sheridan (Atlantic Books, 2009).

123. *Theory also explains most of addiction.* For more on Opponent Process Theory see *Never Enough: The Neuroscience and Experience of Addiction*, Judith Grisel (Doubleday, 2019).

124. *more reward out of it than regular folk.* 'Midbrain Dopamine Receptor Availability Is Inversely Associated with Novelty-Seeking Traits in Humans', David H Zald, Ronald L Cowan, Patricia Riccardi, Ronald M Baldwin, M Sib Ansari, Rui Li, Evan S Shelby, Clarence E Smith, Maureen McHugo, and Robert M Kessler (*Journal of Neuroscience* 28, no. 53 2008).

124. *pain increases our ability to tolerate it.* *Endure: Mind, Body and the Curiously Elastic Limits of Human Performance*, Alex Hutchinson (HarperCollins, 2019).

125. *empathetic decisions in their lives.* For a closer look at flow states, peak experiences and positive personality traits see *The Rise of Superman*, Steven Kotler (Quercus, 2015).

126. *her book 'Prone to Violence'.* *Prone to Violence*, Erin Pizzey and Jeff Shapiro (Hamlyn, 1982).

128. *overused term for a little understood condition. Odysseus in America,* Jonathan Shay (James Bennett Pty, 2003).

129. *where trauma could be discussed openly.* For a profound and beautifully written book on returning to 'civilisation' please read Sebastian Junger's *Tribe* (Twelve, 2016).

131. *They could self-author who they were.* MDMA is currently being tri-alled as a treatment for PTSD in the United States. Because it is a Schedule I controlled substance, that research must be privately funded, which is being done by the Multidisciplinary Association for Psychedelic Studies, or MAPS. Initial results are very good, and in 2017 the Food and Drug Administration granted MDMA-assisted psychotherapy 'Breakthrough Therapy' status. Dr Rick Doblin, founder and executive director of MAPS, believes that MDMA will receive full approval by 2021. https://www.psychiatryadvisor.com/home/conference-highlights/us-psych-congress-2019/psychedelic-assisted-therapy-how-mdma-is-changing-treatment-for-ptsd/

132. *than resulting psychiatric disorders.* 'Posttraumatic Growth: Conceptual Foundation and Empirical Evidence', Richard G. Tedeschi and Lawrence G. Calhoun (*Psychological Inquiry*, 2004).

132. *show some element of PTG.* https://www.michaelahaas.com/what-is-posttraumatic-growth/

133. *and love adventure, risk, and uncertainty. Antifragile: Things That Gain from Disorder,* Nassim Nicholas Taleb (Penguin Books, 2013).

134. *very bad things is not going under. On Mental Toughness,* interview with Martin Seligman, HBR's 10 Must Reads (Harvard Business Review, 2018).

134. *with hypothetical reasons for this.* 'Positive change following trauma and adversity: a review', Linley PA, Joseph S (*Journal of Traumatic Stress.* 17 (1): 11–21, February 2004).

7. TWO COLLECTORS

143. *account of his size and legendary energy.* There has been plenty of spec-ulation that Ortiz was the inspiration for Utz, the eponymous hero of Chatwin's novel. In fact, the real life Utz was Rudolf Just, a com-pulsive Meissen collector. However there are parts of Utz's dialogue

in the book—especially with regard to private collections vs public museums—that are pure Ortiz.

8. HE'S NOT THE CALIPH; HE'S A VERY NAUGHTY BOY

156. *unwanted self and begin a new life.* The True Believer, Eric Hoffer (Harper Perennial Modern Classics, 2010).

164. *psychologists studying gambling addictions.* 'Dark Flow, Depression and Multiline Slot Machine Play' (*Journal of Gambling Studies*, 2018).

165. *that are used in religious experiences.* https://www.wired.co.uk/article/mormons-experience-religion-like-drug-takers-feel-highs-neuroscientists-say

165. *getting us to pursue goals repeatedly.* From *The Biology of Desire* by Marc Lewis, copyright © 2015. Reprinted by permission of PublicAffairs, an imprint of Hachette Book Group, Inc., and by permission of Scribe Publications, copyright © 2016.

9. TIE ME UP, DON'T TIE ME DOWN

180. (*thirty lashes for an alky, sixty for a junkie*). http://siberiantimes.com/other/others/features/beating-addiction-out-of-you-literally/

180. *groundbreaking book* Playing on the Edge. *Playing on the Edge: Sadomasochism, Risk, and Intimacy.* Staci Newmahr (Indiana University Press, 2011).

181. *this type of people 'emotional ninjas'.* Scream: Chilling Adventures in the Science of Fear, Margee Kerr (Public Affairs, 2017).

182. *spiritual experience is known as 'sacred kink'.* 'Sacred kink: finding psychological meaning at the intersection of BDSM and spiritual experience' (*Sexual and Relationship Therapy*, 2018).

182. *or the Native American Sundance ordeal.* 'Altered States of Consciousness during an Extreme Ritual' (*PLOS One*, 2016).

183. *merely witnessed the prayer and song.* https://www.newyorker.com/science/maria-konnikova/pain-really-make-us-gain

183. *similar their heart rate activity was.* http://www.spsp.org/news-center/blog/ritualized-suffering

183. They ran missions into altered states. 'Consensual BDSM Facilitates Role-Specific Altered States of Consciousness: A Preliminary Study' (*Psychology of Consciousness: Theory, Research and Practice*, 2017).

10. THE GREAT HEROIN EXPERIMENT

200. *sick people and therefore ... it is valid.* See https://www.youtube.com/watch?v=Hd4rgyZzseY for footage and interview.

201. *called it* hul-gil, *or 'plant of joy'.* For a general history of drugs see *The Pursuit of Oblivion*, Richard Davenport-Hines (Weidenfeld & Nicholson, 2012).

202. *mucous membranes and into the bloodstream.* For other ingredients of Witches' Flying Ointment see https://www.theatlantic.com/technology/archive/2013/10/why-do-witches-ride-brooms-nsfw/281037/

17. HOW TO BE COOL (AGAIN)

282. *likely to engage in substance use in later life.* 'Behaviour of boys in kindergarten and the onset of substance use during adolescence' (*Archives of General Psychiatry*, 1997).

282. *likely to abuse alcohol by their late 20s*). https://www.nclap.org/risk-taking-behavior-and-addiction/ and also: 'Novelty seeking, risk taking, and related constructs as predictors of adolescent substance use: an application of Cloninger's theory' (*Journal of Substance Abuse*, 1994).

286. *who was not sexually abused as a child.* Gabor Maté's *In the Realm of the Hungry Ghosts* is one of the best books I have read about addiction (Vermillon, 2018).

286. *1980s 'destroying' the ghetto.* For a great history of the war on drugs see Johann Hari's *Chasing the Scream* (Bloomsbury, 2015).

290. *Thus the mind and the brain shape each other.'* From *The Biology of Desire* by Marc Lewis, copyright © 2015. Reprinted by permission of PublicAffairs, an imprint of Hachette Book Group, Inc., and by permission of Scribe Publications, copyright © 2016.

294. *a kick out of it than other people.* 'Midbrain Dopamine Receptor Availability Is Inversely Associated with Novelty-Seeking Traits in Humans' David H Zald, Ronald L Cowan, Patricia Riccardi, Ronald M Baldwin, M Sib Ansari, Rui Li, Evan S Shelby, Clarence E Smith, Maureen McHugo, and Robert M Kessler (*Journal of Neuroscience* 28, no 53 2008).

297. *The neuroscience seems to back this up.* 'Dissociated Grey Matter Changes with Prolonged Addiction and Extended Abstinence in Cocaine Users'

(*PLOS One*, 2013). See *Biology of Desire* for interpretation of this study and also a fascinating look at neuroplasticity in patients with webbed-fingers.